NATURALIZING EPISTEMIC

MW00813667

An epistemic virtue is a personal quality conducive to the discovery of truth, the avoidance of error, or some other intellectually valuable goal. Current work in epistemology is increasingly value-driven, but this volume presents the first collection of essays to explore whether virtue epistemology can also be naturalistic, in the philosophical definition meaning "methodologically continuous with science." The essays examine the empirical research in psychology on cognitive abilities and personal dispositions, meta-epistemic semantic accounts of virtue-theoretic norms, the role of emotion in knowledge, "ought-implies-can" constraints, empirically and metaphysically grounded accounts of "proper functioning," and even applied virtue epistemology in relation to education. *Naturalizing Epistemic Virtue* addresses many core issues in contemporary epistemology, presents new opportunities for work on epistemic abilities, epistemic virtues and cognitive character, and will be of great interest to those studying virtue ethics and epistemology.

ABROL FAIRWEATHER is Lecturer in Philosophy at San Francisco State University. He is the co-editor (with Linda Zagzebski) of *Virtue Epistemology: Essays on Epistemic Virtue and Responsibility* (2001).

OWEN FLANAGAN is James B. Duke Professor of Philosophy at Duke University. His books include *Varieties of Moral Personality* (1991), *Consciousness Reconsidered* (1992), *The Really Hard Problem: Meaning in a Material World* (2007), and *The Bodhisattva's Brain: Buddhism Naturalized* (2011).

NATURALIZING
EPISTEMIC VIRTUE

EDITED BY

ABROL FAIRWEATHER

San Francisco State University

and

OWEN FLANAGAN

Duke University

CAMBRIDGE
UNIVERSITY PRESS

CAMBRIDGE
UNIVERSITY PRESS

University Printing House, Cambridge CB2 8BS, United Kingdom

One Liberty Plaza, 20th Floor, New York, NY 10006, USA

477 Williamstown Road, Port Melbourne, VIC 3207, Australia

4843/24, 2nd Floor, Ansari Road, Daryaganj, Delhi - 110002, India

79 Anson Road, #06-04/06, Singapore 079906

Cambridge University Press is part of the University of Cambridge.

It furthers the University's mission by disseminating knowledge in the pursuit of education, learning and research at the highest international levels of excellence.

www.cambridge.org
Information on this title: www.cambridge.org/9781316642832

First published 2014
First paperback edition 2017

A catalogue record for this publication is available from the British Library

Library of Congress Cataloging in Publication data
Naturalizing epistemic virtue / edited by Abrol Fairweather and Owen Flanagan.
pages   cm
Includes bibliographical references and index.
ISBN 978-1-107-02857-9 (hardback)
1. Virtue epistemology.   2. Naturalism.   I. Fairweather, Abrol, editor of compilation.
BD176.N38 2014
121–dc23
2013039682

ISBN 978-1-107-02857-9 Hardback
ISBN 978-1-316-64283-2 Paperback

Contents

Contents

Contributors

MARK ALFANO is Assistant Professor of Philosophy at the University of Oregon.

HEATHER BATTALY is Professor of Philosophy at California State University, Fullerton.

DAVID COPP is Distinguished Professor and Chair of Philosophy at the University of California, Davis.

ABROL FAIRWEATHER is Lecturer in Philosophy at San Francisco State University.

OWEN FLANAGAN is James B. Duke Professor of Philosophy at Duke University.

PETER J. GRAHAM is Professor of Philosophy at the University of California, Riverside.

ALLAN HAZLETT is Reader in Philosophy at the University of Edinburgh.

DAVID HENDERSON is Robert R. Chambers Distinguished Professor of Philosophy at the University of Nebraska-Lincoln.

TERENCE HORGAN is Professor of Philosophy at the University of Arizona.

CARRIE ICHIKAWA JENKINS is Associate Professor of Philosophy and Canada Research Chair at the University of British Columbia, and Professor of Theoretical Philosophy in the Northern Institute of Philosophy at the University of Aberdeen.

CHRISTIAN MILLER is Professor of Philosophy at Wake Forest University.

CARLOS MONTEMAYOR is Professor of Philosophy at San Francisco State University.

RAM NETA is Professor of Philosophy at the University of North Carolina, Chapel Hill.

DUNCAN PRITCHARD is Professor and Chair of Epistemology at the University of Edinburgh.

CHAPTER I

Introduction
Naturalized virtue epistemology
Abrol Fairweather and Owen Flanagan

I Virtue epistemology: metaphysical and normative

This volume aims to launch a powerful and largely unexplored position in epistemology: naturalized virtue epistemology. Most debates in virtue epistemology have been decidedly axiological and aim to clarify the goals, values, and ends constitutive of epistemic evaluation. Value-driven inquiry has now become quite complex in the large literature on the value problem (and the related Meno problem), which examines whether the value of knowledge can be reduced to the value of any proper subset of its parts (Zagzebski 1996; Kvanvig 2003; Pritchard 2007). Normative epistemic inquiry has also been useful in meeting more traditional problems in epistemology, such as Gettier problems (Turri 2011) and problems of epistemic luck more generally, as well as the structure of knowledge (as etiological rather than foundational or coherentist), and Chisholm's "problem of the criterion" (Riggs 2007). Virtue epistemology has opened many new areas of inquiry in contemporary epistemology including: epistemic agency (Greco 1999; Zagzebski 2001; Sosa 2007), the role of motivations and emotions in epistemology (Fairweather 2001; Hookway 2003), the nature of abilities (Millar 2008; Greco 2010; Pritchard 2012), skills (Greco 1993; Bloomfield 2000), and competences (Sosa 2007), the value of understanding (Kvanvig 2003; Grimm 2006; Riggs 2009), wisdom (Ryan 1999; Zagzebski 2013), curiosity (Whitcomb 2010; Inan 2012) and even education policy and practice (Baehr 2011). The virtue turn in epistemology that started with the early work of Sosa (1991) and Zagzebski (1996) has now produced a large and mature literature in normative epistemology.

While the growth and impact of virtue epistemology has been impressive and important, it has come with insufficient attention to the empirical grounding of these normative theories, and thus runs the risk of endorsing free-floating epistemic norms cut loose from the real-world phenomenon they must evaluate. To this end, virtue epistemologists should heed the exhortation given by Anscombe in "Modern Moral Philosophy" (1958) to constrain normative theorizing in ethics with an empirically adequate moral psychology, and might even do so optimistically since Anscombe (and Foot, later Geach, and still later MacIntyre) was led to endorse virtue theory precisely because it appeared more psychologically plausible than deontology or consequentialism. The same cautionary (and perhaps optimistic) point holds for epistemic psychology and normative epistemology.

Greater concern for empirical adequacy can be seen in a few empirically focused works on virtue ethics (Russell 2009; Snow 2010; Slingerland 2011; Miller 2013), but these laudable efforts have come largely in response to 'situationist challenges' which question the existence and/or explanatory salience of character traits on the basis of research in social psychology. Flanagan (1991) was the first to raise worries about situationism for virtue theory, recommending a certain caution with reference to overconfidence about character traits. But swiftly an extremist position arose and philosophers were asked to take seriously a debate that was already long dead in psychology about whether there were any such things as character traits (Flanagan 2009). Nonetheless, the long tradition of empirical challenges to character-based psychology has been largely ignored by virtue epistemologists until very recently (see Axtell 2010; Alfano 2012). Moreover, it cannot be assumed that any satisfactory empirical ground for virtue ethics will offer the same grounding for virtue epistemology. For example, the successful CAPS (Cognitive-Affective Personality System) research program used by Snow and Russell to ground virtue ethics shifts the focus of evaluation from "objective stimulus" to "construed stimulus," but arguably skips over the main epistemic question in the process, which is precisely whether the subjective stimulus tracks or accurately represents the objective stimulus. Virtue epistemology will have to earn its own response to situationism. If the demonstrated success on the normative side can be paired with equal success on the empirical side, an extremely powerful perspective in epistemology is well in hand, arguably one of most promising general epistemologies on offer today. The current volume is the first collection of essays on naturalized virtue epistemology.

The most important motivation for naturalized virtue epistemology does not come from naturalism per se, but rather from the insight that virtue theory is heavily metaphysical and empirical, as well as normative. Any attribution of a virtue to an agent will assume some taxonomy of agent-level dispositions that are both explanatory and praiseworthy. The truth-makers for virtue attributions will thus be of a highly nuanced metaphysical kind, and this must be some form of disposition in any theory considered truly virtue theoretic. Any truly virtue-theoretic account of a phenomenon will need some form of these metaphysical commitments, otherwise it becomes unclear how virtue-theoretic normativity is distinct from a range of other sources of normativity (e.g. responsibility, rule-consequentialism, deontology). Virtue-theoretic normativity is distinct in part because of this dispositional commitment.

Many of the chapters in this volume examine empirical findings on the nature of cognitive dispositions and personality traits (Alfano, Battaly, Miller, Pritchard), and this is clearly one direction for naturalized virtue epistemology to take. However, some naturalistically minded virtue theorists will prefer traditional accounts from Aristotle, Plato, the Stoics, Aquinas, and others that appeal to some form of teleology, function, or essence rather than the most recent results in psychology. For Aristotle, virtue is not any admirable or praiseworthy quality, it is a quality that makes you good at performing your function, and thus must draw on a substantive account of human nature (see Korsgaard 2008). We say that naturalized virtue epistemology can be pursued metaphysically or empirically, and possibly both at the same time. Contemporary empirical work in psychology on person-level dispositions like 'generosity', 'conscientiousness', and 'narrow-mindedness', rationality and inference is thus one fertile source for naturalized virtue epistemology, as is metaphysical work on the essences, natures, and kinds relevant to sustaining the human form of life. One metaphysical debate long underway within virtue epistemology is whether epistemic virtues are best seen as faculties (see Sosa and Greco), skills (Greco, Bloomfield) or character traits (Baehr, Zagzebski). But these issues have largely been decided on normative grounds, with different philosophers arguing that different disposition types support the set of normative standings necessary to make the full range of evaluations that matter in epistemology. Naturalized virtue epistemology (scientific or metaphysical) shifts to an empirical basis for understanding the nature and explanatory power of faculties, skills, and character traits, and thus continues to ask the same questions about which disposition types to countenance and how to account for the causal-explanatory properties of the virtues. As we will see below, this empirical turn will have important (and largely positive) normative implications for virtue epistemology.

Virtue attributions also engender predictive commitments such that to attribute a virtue (V) to an agent (S) is to assert that (S) will satisfy a set of conditionals linking situations (C) and virtue-relevant behaviors (B) in roughly the following way: if an agent S is V, then most of the relevant following conditionals will be true of S: $(C_1 \rightarrow B_1), (C_2 \rightarrow B_2), (C_3 \rightarrow$

B_3) ... ($C_n \rightarrow B_n$). Given these behavioral-predictive commitments, virtue attributions make a real claim about the world and the truth value of such attributions should be empirically testable. Whether an agent does or does not possess virtue-constituting dispositions will be an empirically testable proposition. If we know the actual cognitive dispositions that constitute a given virtue, empirical research should inform us of the causal mechanisms that underlie their manifestations across a range of relevant circumstances. We argue below that this is very important information for the normative aspect of virtue epistemology. The most plausible and promising way of handling these empirical commitments is to do it naturalistically. In the remainder of this Introduction, we examine two significant worries for a would-be naturalized virtue epistemology and then summarize the essays here collected.

One problem a naturalistic turn might create for virtue epistemology is the persistent worry about normativity in naturalistic theories. Any difficulties on this score will be particularly worrying for a value-driven epistemology. A second worry is that the relevant results from the sciences will signal bad news for virtue epistemology. It may turn out that, according to our best psychological theories, people either do not possess or rarely manifest the kinds of dispositions countenanced by virtue epistemology.

2   Worries about normativity: Quine and Moore

Any call to naturalize an epistemic theory immediately brings us to W. V. O. Quine and his famous paper "Epistemology Naturalized" (1969). Quine is often seen as defending the extreme position that a purely descriptive empirical psychology should outright replace traditional epistemology. Since the latter is inherently normative (see Kim 1988), Quine has been accused of being unable to account for the normativity of epistemology and "changing the subject," and this makes naturalized epistemology and normative epistemology appear to be very strange bedfellows. How can the approach to knowledge that aims to remove normativity from epistemology (naturalized epistemology) be united with the most overtly normative approach to epistemology (virtue epistemology)? One reply is that naturalization does not eliminate the normative so much as it tames and explains it (Flanagan 2006). Another way of thinking about naturalism and normativity that goes back to G. E. Moore (1993), rather than Quine. The Moorean approach to naturalism and normativity will be just as important in the present context because virtue epistemology has always borrowed heavily from virtue ethics, and Moore had moral properties in mind when he raised the Open Question Argument against naturalistic accounts of goodness. Let us begin with Moore, and then work our way back to Quine.

Moore's challenge to naturalism in ethics is that we can easily see that no predicate expressing a natural property can have the same meaning as the predicate 'is good'. For any candidate natural property (e.g. pleasantness), a competent speaker can, without contradiction, make the following remark: "I see that x is pleasant, but is it good?" The goodness of x, even given that it is pleasant, is an 'open question', unlike the goodness of x in "I see that x is good, but is it good?", which is clearly a closed question. Moore argued that any natural property proposed to analyze a moral property will be subject to open question arguments, and thus commits the naturalistic fallacy. Two points interest us here. First, it is now very clear that Moore is making the wrong kind of semantic demand, namely that any adequate analysandum must entail or have the same (conceptual) meaning as the analysans. Second, epistemic normative properties might fare much better than normative properties in ethics in meeting the Moorean demand. On the first point, we now know that sameness of conceptual meaning is the wrong thing to demand between a concept and its proper analysis. With advances in semantics from Putnam, Kripke, and others, we now say that statements like 'water is H_2O' involve terms that differ in (conceptual) meaning, but pick out the same property. This is a very successful naturalistic analysis of water, even though it would fail to meet Moore's demand for sameness of meaning. While the specific demand is wrong, Moore is certainly right to think that some constraint must be imposed on naturalistic accounts of normative properties. But if not sameness of meaning as Moore demands, then what? A modified Moorean demand might require that some statements couched in naturalistic terms will constrain prescriptions (perhaps through an 'ought implies can' principle), provide a supervenience base for normative facts, or provide truth conditions for normative claims.

Epistemology may have an easier time meeting these modified Moorean demands than ethics. Alvin Goldman (1994) argues that normative epistemic facts about when an agent is justified or has knowledge supervene on natural facts about the reliability of the processes used in forming the relevant beliefs. This might be plausible as a general thesis in epistemology, but most virtue epistemologists insist that reliabilism cannot adequately explain the value of knowledge. But if reliabilism cannot account for the additional value of knowledge over true belief, it cannot give the right supervenience basis for normative epistemic properties. One additional normative standing that facts about reliability will need to support involve 'credit' for holding a true belief, which is often identified by virtue epistemologists as the value that knowledge has but a mere true belief might lack. Moreover, the presumably natural facts about when a given true belief is 'due to', 'caused by', or 'from' an ability in the agent are very plausibly taken to be the supervenience base of normative facts about epistemic credit. While this points to a seemingly clear way in which virtue-reliabilism meets modified Moorean demands on normative epistemology, the 'because of' relation has proved notoriously difficult to properly formulate, and some virtue epistemologists have given up any such attempt. This should not be taken to show that virtue epistemology fails to meet Moorean demands after all, but rather that we need a more naturalized virtue epistemology that furthers our understanding of the relevant causal-etiological relations to show the way.

We now return to Quine. Jagewon Kim (1988) raised the classic normativity challenge to Quinean naturalized epistemology, but his objection has now received many responses which mute the perceived force of his original objection. Naturalized virtue epistemology may nonetheless face a special normativity worry because virtue epistemology has consistently been championed as the most overtly normative way to do epistemology. It is one thing to show that an epistemic theory (e.g. process reliabilism) can eke out some normative content once naturalized, but quite another to bill your epistemic theory as robustly and overtly normative and then attempt a naturalization project.

Fortunately, the situation vis-à-vis normativity is not all that bad. Naturalized virtue theory has a number of sources for maintaining the normatively focused inquiry that has distinguished it from other perspectives in epistemology. Research in evolutionary theory, meta-cognition, and bounded rationality all strongly support the existence of robust cognitive dispositions. Remembering that the metaphysical side of virtue epistemology requires a taxonomy of cognitive dispositions and an account of their causal explanatory role in producing epistemically assessable agent-outcomes, empirical facts about these dispositions and their manifestations will provide normative content for virtue epistemology. Normative facts about what an agent with virtue (V) in situation (C) ought to do are identical to facts about how the relevant disposition will actually manifest when in (C). If we are talking about a real psychological disposition, the way it ought to manifest in various situations is an empirical issue and is best understood by consulting work in cognitive psychology, social psychology, evolutionary biology, and other relevant sciences. Given that disposition (D) is a virtue and that (D) is attributable to an agent (S), we can now say that S normatively-ought to do whatever S dispositionally-ought to do. A dispositional-ought just is a normative-ought here, and the former is an empirical issue. It will be true of all meaningful dispositions (and certainly of natural dispositions) that the bearer of the disposition ought to manifest certain behaviors in certain conditions: the fragile glass ought to break, the sugar ought to dissolve. Call this a merely dispositional-ought. Considered just as such, dispositional-oughts have no prescriptive force. But with just the premise that D is a virtue, we can now collapse what S normatively-ought to do into what S dispositionally-ought to do. Since what S dispositionally-ought to do is an empirical issue, so too is what S normatively-ought to do. A number of additional important normative statements for virtue epistemology will be inferred using principles of disposition theory relating to masking, mimicking, and finking, but this takes us beyond the scope of the present inquiry.

It may rightly be objected that, as stated, we have simply assumed that a given disposition (D) is a virtue to make the point above, and the main normative work of virtue theory is precisely to determine exactly that. It may be that naturalized virtue epistemology leaves this particular question to an autonomous virtue theory to work out, but it is clear that merely identifying which dispositions qualify as virtues does nothing to provide prescriptive content for specific situations; that depends on how the virtue constituting dispositions will actually manifest across the relevant range of circumstances. So empirical work on dispositions is still doing important normative work here. A more robust naturalized virtue epistemology will aim to settle the question of which dispositions will be virtues on empirical grounds as well. It is not our intent here to distinguish either of these projects from the other, but just to note that naturalized virtue epistemology can take either modest or robust forms, and that the metaphysics of dispositions might perform essential work for generating the prescriptive content of virtue theory.

3 Metaphysical worries: situationism and virtue epistemology

If a naturalized virtue epistemology can provide empirically informed and falsifiable disposition attributions that also ground prescriptive epistemic norms, this would be an attractive general epistemology. However, some philosophers claim that work in social psychology supports skepticism about the existence of the right kind of person-level dispositions, virtues and the like, as well as their causal powers. This is the situationist challenge. Owen Flanagan (1991) first formulated the situationist challenge in his brief for psychological realism in ethics, and suggested a measured response to the research, a response which was already available in Aristotle, and that had been sensitively explored in contemporary literature by Martha Nussbaum (1986), among others. There are persons, characters, traits, virtues and vices, but persons, traits, virtues, and the like, are fragile, of variable consistency, resiliency, and robustness. Quickly, an extreme, occasionally eliminativist, response to the situationist challenge emerged in ethics. There are no such things as character traits or virtues, or if there are such things they are effervescent, ephemeral, short-lived, merely linguistic vapors (Harman 1999, Doris 2002). The current consensus favors the moderate view, one that was absorbed inside psychology thirty-five years before philosophers got all fussed-up, to the effect that there are genuine morally relevant dispositions that occur in complex, dynamic causal fields and that need to be carefully individuated; for example, honesty-at-work versus *honesty tout court* (Flanagan 1991, 2009; Merritt 2000, Sreenivasan 2002, Miller 2003, Kamtekar 2004, Russell 2009, Snow 2010, Slingerland 2011). Dispositional traits of variable scope, range, depth, texture, and kind (virtues, vices, thinking styles, emotional patterns, temperamental traits, skills, habits, etc.) are real, and they partake in complex causal relations with all the other inner and outer features of the complex ecologies that make for human life as we know it. The causal powers and actual role of any particular disposition depend on it, its kind, how superficial or deep it is, and on how it interacts with the rest of a person and her world at any given time.

Still, some philosophers continue to ring the bell for the extremist view arguing that situations out-predict and out-explain character traits or other dispositional features (Alfano 2012, 2013). There are two mistakes here: first, even if we restrict ourselves to only situations, roughly, current stimuli, and the traits we antecedently ascribe to some person (she is honest), it is false empirically that situations out-predict and out-explain character traits (Flanagan 2009). But second, conceiving prediction and explanation in terms of only two variables, situations and traits, is impoverished, a sophist's trick. We commonly use knowledge of history, culture, politics, and economics in explanation and prediction in addition to knowledge about some individual and the situation she is in. Zip code, sadly, is more predictive of educational achievement than almost any other variable. Zip code does not name a situation, nor does it name a character trait. It designates a world. The key point is that the predictive power of situations fades to relative insignificance the more we know about history, culture, economics, race, gender, personality, and traits.

Whereas ethics generally, and virtue ethics in particular, has had twenty-five years to work out its response to the hyperbole about situationism, virtue epistemology needs to make its own peace with this research.

A number of contributions in this volume (Alfano, Battaly, Miller, Pritchard) examine situationist-style arguments applied to virtue episte-mology rather than virtue ethics. Mark Alfano (2012, 2013) has tried to fill this dialectical niche by applying situationism to both responsibilist and reliabilist virtue epistemology, arguing that both fall prey to an incon-sistent triad along the following lines: (1) Non-Skepticism: most peo-ple know quite a bit; (2) Virtue Epistemology: knowledge is virtuously formed true belief; (3) Epistemic Situationism: most behavior is explained by often trivial features of situations, rather than by personal characteris-tics or traits. This issue will be examined in a number of chapters in this book. The consensus appears to be similar to the one in moral psychology: namely, that (3) Epistemic Situationism is false.

If virtue epistemology is held accountable to empirical results, it will have to be to the best and most diverse range of results, but research in meta-cognition, the big-five personality factors, and bounded rational-ity presents much better prospects for naturalized virtue epistemology. As these research programs mature, it is highly likely that the basic commit-ments of virtue epistemology will be vindicated.

Below we introduce the chapters that appear in this volume. They address a wide range of issues relevant to the project of developing a natu-ralized virtue epistemology.

"Warrant, functions, history" by Peter J. Graham

Peter Graham defends a proper functionalist form of virtue-reliabilism which takes proper functioning as its central norm. Epistemic warrant consists in the normal functioning of belief-forming and -sustaining psy-chological processes. When the process has forming and sustaining true beliefs reliably as a function, especially an etiological function, a token belief that results from a properly functioning system quite plausibly has a form of warrant. While Graham shapes his understanding of proper func-tioning around evolutionary theory and philosophy of biology, he extends his account of etiological functions to include artifacts and social facts. Graham provides a compelling epistemic teleology with significant con-nections to evolutionary theory and the social sciences.

"The epistemic 'ought'" by Ram Neta

Many naturalistic epistemologists take empirical evidence concerning our cognitive powers to cast doubt on the claim that our beliefs ought to be consistent, or that our degrees of belief ought to be probabilistically coherent. Neta argues that, in doing so, they are implicitly confusing cognitive competences with epistemic virtues. In this chapter, Neta distinguishes competences from virtues, explains why epistemic "oughts" imply that we have the relevant cognitive competences, but not the related epistemic virtues, and finally describes the constitutive relationship between epistemic virtues and epistemic "oughts." Neta defends a virtue-theoretic account of epistemic oughts in terms of normal epistemic functioning.

"Naturalism and norms of inference" by Carrie Ichikawa Jenkins

Jenkins defends a normative and naturalistic account of basic inference. While reliabilist virtue epistemology has focused on abilities like perception and memory, and responsibility, virtue epistemology has focused on traits like open-mindedness and conscientiousness, much less attention has been given specifically to virtues of the act of inferring. Suppose that a subject S makes a token inference from [P & P→Q] to Q. To focus ideas, let's take this to be a matter of her transitioning from a belief in the premise to the adoption of a new belief in the conclusion which she now holds on the basis of her belief in the premise (which is retained throughout). This inference (as distinct from S's belief in the premise and/or conclusion) is available for distinctively epistemic normative assessment. The inference itself might be described as epistemically good or bad, warranted or unwarranted, justified or unjustified, appropriate or inappropriate, correct or incorrect, permissible or impermissible, and so on.

"Indirect epistemic teleology explained and defended" by David Copp

David Copp examines connections between meta-ethics and "meta-epistemics" and defends a pluralist epistemic teleology that provides a new motivation for epistemic instrumentalism. J. L. Mackie proposed that morality as a "device" needed to solve a "problem" faced by humans because of "certain contingent features of the human condition." Copp proposes that the standards of normative epistemology are similarly geared to the epistemic problem, which is also faced by humans because of "certain contingent features of the human condition." To achieve what we value and meet our needs, we need information, so we need to be able to assess evidence and form beliefs that are reliably at least approximately accurate. But our untutored processes of belief-formation are not in general reliable in all the circumstances where we need them to be, given the kind of things we value and aim to achieve. So we need our processes of belief-formation to be regulated by appropriate epistemic standards.

"Moral virtues, epistemic virtues, and the Big Five" by Christian Miller

Virtue epistemology should be informed by an important development in personality psychology called the 'Big Five' personality traits or 'Five-Factor Model' of traits (John *et al.* 2008). On standard lists, these traits are extraversion, agreeableness, conscientiousness, neuroticism, and openness, and their narrower facets often include traits such as modesty, altruism, kindness, cruelty, generosity, and forgiveness. Yet this work in psychology has been barely mentioned in the philosophy literature, even by virtue ethicists who are eager to defend their view from the situationist challenge. The chapter focuses on the Big Five approach, specifically on the question of whether it provides empirical support for the widespread possession of the moral and epistemic virtues. Miller argues that it does not. He reviews some of the recent discussions in philosophy concerning the empirical adequacy of the virtues, provides an overview of the Big Five approach in personality psychology, and then offers three reasons for why this approach does not offer any support for thinking that most of us are indeed virtuous people.

"Epistemic dexterity: a Ramseyian account of agent-based knowledge" by Abrol Fairweather and Carlos Montemayor

Abrol Fairweather and Carlos Montemayor argue that a modification of F. P. Ramsey's success-semantics (re-conceived as an account of justification rather than truth or content) provides a foundation for an action-centered normative naturalism with appealing features for both reliabilist and responsibilist virtue epistemology. In conjunction with recent empirical work on motor control and divided agency, they argue that plausible accounts of both the ability condition and the etiological condition commonly required for knowledge in virtue epistemology are supported by the action-centered epistemic norms. A rival contextualist causal salience account from John Greco is discussed in detail and it is argued that Ramsey's principle supports a unified framework for explaining the epistemically important features of agents, interests and contexts.

"Re-evaluating the situationist challenge to virtue epistemology" by Duncan Pritchard

Duncan Pritchard argues that virtue epistemology, when properly understood, has nothing to fear from the empirical data offered by situationists. Pritchard argues that the situationist critique of virtue epistemology as applied to responsibilist and reliabilist virtue epistemology is unsuccessful. In particular, he argues that the crucial distinction is not between responsibilist and reliabilist renderings of virtue epistemology, but rather between modest and robust construals of this position. The situationist challenge to virtue epistemology at best only impacts on robust virtue epistemology, but since robust virtue epistemology can be shown on independent grounds to be an untenable thesis, this is not in itself a cause for concern. The empirical data appealed to in the situationist critique of virtue epistemology are compatible with the modest rendering of virtue epistemology; in fact, they actually lend additional support to the view over its robust counterpart.

"Stereotype threat and intellectual virtue" by Mark Alfano

Research in social psychology and educational psychology suggests an important distinction for virtue epistemology. It turns out that telling schoolchildren that they're smart leads to better performance until they encounter a hard problem that they can't readily solve. At that point, those who've been told they are smart actually perform worse than those in the control condition. By contrast, telling schoolchildren that they're hardworking leads to better performance, and that enhanced performance continues even after they run into a difficult problem. These results suggest an important distinction between primarily motivational epistemic virtues (sedulousness and curiosity) and primarily cognitive ones (intelligence). Research in moral virtues has long emphasized their motivational role; it turns out that the epistemic virtues should be thought of in this way as well. Another interesting bit of evidence related to this topic is the recent work by Angela Duckworth and her colleagues on the virtue of grit. Duckworth has found that grit correlates with such diverse achievements as national spelling bee success, retention at West Point, and grade point average in high school. In fact, grittiness is more predictive of academic success than IQ.

"Acquiring epistemic virtue: emotions, situations, and education" by Heather Battaly

This chapter uses empirical work in cognitive and social psychology to argue that acquiring knowledge is not always sufficient for acquiring epistemic virtue. Battaly addresses two recent empirical challenges to the acquisition of moral virtue – non-cognitive emotion; and situationism – and applies them to epistemic virtue. She argues that to possess epistemic virtues, one must perform epistemically virtuous acts. For instance, to be open-minded, one must consider alternative perspectives appropriately. But knowing which acts are epistemically virtuous does not always cause one to perform those acts. A public speaker can know that it is virtuous to consider reasonable objections to her views, and yet fail to consider them. The factors that prevent knowledge from causing action can be internal to one's psychology, or externally located in the environment or 'situation'. Accordingly, our public speaker can fail to do what she knows she should because her emotions influence her actions, e.g. she may be too angry to consider the objections. Alternatively, she can fail to do what she knows she should because features of her situation influence her actions, e.g. she may be in an environment in which others unanimously dismiss the objections. Philosophers and psychologists have argued that emotions and features of situations can prevent us from performing acts that we know to be morally virtuous. This chapter argues that emotions and features of situations can also prevent us from performing acts that we know to be epistemically virtuous.

"Virtue and the fitting culturing of the human critter" by David Henderson and Terence Horgan

Two classic themes from virtue epistemology are important for any epistemologist serious about the real business of understanding how best to develop systems of true beliefs. They also fit easily within naturalized epistemology. (1) What is proper and fitting in the way of forming beliefs is relative to a kind of natural cognitive and sensory creature. Human epistemology is different from and more ambitious than corvid epistemology because humans, in myriad ways, have more powerful cognitive endowments than crows or ravens. (2) What is fitting and proper to cognitive systems such as those of humans is a matter of a repertoire of cognitive processes, many of which must be developed or learned – fostered or cultured. Notably, humans are social creatures, and this is significant in their epistemic lives. The consequence may be taken as a less familiar element of virtue theory: humans, as deeply cultural creatures, must and should develop and practice their epistemic arts in a social-cultural setting. All this is consequential for the relation between virtue theory and naturalized epistemology. Henderson and Horgan explore and defend a further implication of such a naturalized virtue epistemology: Rules or programs that purport to describe normatively appropriate modes of belief-formation really can only provide, at best, approximate characterizations; they are somehow not fitting to the best that humans can manage. What is developed or cultured can be a kind of capacity, and this culturing will need to draw on information about the kinds of creature being cultured.

"Expressivism and convention-relativism about epistemic discourse" by Allan Hazlett

Consider the claim that open-mindedness is an epistemic virtue, the claim that true belief is epistemically valuable, and the claim that one epistemically ought to cleave to one's evidence. These are examples of what Hazlett calls "epistemic discourse." In his contribution, Hazlett proposes and defends a view called "conventionalism about epistemic discourse." He argues that conventionalism is superior to its main rival, expressivism about epistemic discourse. Conventionalism says that epistemic discourse describes how things stands relative to a conventional set of "epistemic" values; such discourse is akin to normative discourse relative to the conventional rules of a club. Hazlett defends conventionalism by appeal to a "reverse open question argument," which says, pace expressivism, that epistemic discourse leaves the relevant normative questions open.

CHAPTER 2

Warrant, functions, history
Peter J. Graham

1 Virtue epistemology and proper function

According to John Greco and John Turri, virtue epistemology has two basic commitments.[1] The first is that epistemology is a normative discipline and not merely a branch of natural or social science, pace Quine. This implies, among other things, that epistemology should focus on epistemic norms, epistemic value, and epistemic evaluation.

The second is that epistemology should follow a direction of analysis found in virtue ethics. Broadly speaking, in virtue ethics the moral rightness of an action is determined by the properties of the agent; the action is right only if based on the ethical virtues of the agent. Similarly, in virtue epistemology the epistemic rightness of a belief is determined by properties of the agent that caused the belief; the belief is warranted or knowledge (or otherwise epistemically valuable) only if based on the epistemic virtues of the agent.

Virtue epistemology standardly divides into two camps: virtue-reliabilism and virtue-responsibilism. The two camps talk about different things when they talk about epistemic virtues. Virtue-reliabilists talk about reliable belief-forming faculties such as perception, memory, and reasoning. Virtue-responsibilists talk about character traits such as open-mindedness and conscientiousness.

I am a virtue-reliabilist about epistemic warrant, for I seek to understand epistemic warrant in terms of features of reliable belief-forming faculties.

I presented an earlier version of this chapter to an audience at Soochow University in Taiwan. I am grateful to feedback on that occasion, and especially from Ernest Sosa. I am grateful for useful comments from Colleen Macnamara and Zach Bachman. This work was supported by a research grant from the UC Riverside Academic Senate and by a Visiting Professor Fellowship at the Northern Institute of Philosophy, University of Aberdeen.

[1] Greco and Turri 2011.

Some philosophers use 'warrant' for that property that converts true belief into knowledge. I do not use 'warrant' this strongly. Instead I use 'warrant' the way most epistemologists use 'justification' or 'justifiedness'. Warrant is then not sufficient for converting true belief into knowledge for warrant so understood does not metaphysically entail truth. I prefer 'warrant' because 'justification' connotes the ability to justify, and so tends to over-intellectualize knowledge, especially perceptual knowledge and the knowledge of small children and higher non-human animals.[2]

I believe the best way to develop virtue-reliabilism about warrant is along proper functionalist lines, for virtue is a teleological notion. An epistemically virtuous process is a normally functioning belief-forming process that has forming true beliefs reliably as a function; virtue-reliabilists should be proper functionalists.

I have argued elsewhere that epistemic warrant consists in the normal functioning of the belief-forming process when the process has forming true beliefs reliably as a function.[3] A belief is warranted when the process has functioned normally, when normal functioning is constitutively associated with reliably inducing true beliefs and avoiding error.

The adequacy of a proper function virtue-reliabilism, however, obviously turns on the nature of functions. I endorse the *etiological* theory of functions associated with Larry Wright, Ruth Millikan, Peter Godfrey-Smith, Karen Neander, and many others. On the theory, functions turn on histories that explain why the item exists or operates the way it does. If warrant requires functions, and functions require history, then warrant requires history.

At least within epistemology, it is commonly thought that if warrant requires functions, then warrant requires natural selection. And so many within epistemology are inclined to see my view as requiring a history of natural selection over generations for warrant.[4] Indeed, according to the philosophical zeitgeist, if you hold a "proper function" view of warrant, you think only God or Mother Nature can assign functions.[5] So if

---

[2] For more on my use of 'warrant', see Graham 2011a. See also Burge 2003.

[3] Graham 2010, 2011a, 2011b, 2011c, 2012a.

[4] Sandy Goldberg writes "Most recently Peter Graham [has] endorsed the view that only 'naturally evolved' processes count [towards doxastic justification] … [where a process confers justification iff reliable] in those environments in which the process evolved" (2012: 109, 117). David Copp says that proper functionalism "rests on the claim that the human cognitive system was selected for in the evolutionary development of the species" (this volume). See also the friendly presentation of my view in Evans and Smith 2012: 194 and the implicitly critical one in Lyons 2011. I am partly responsible for this reading of my work, having emphasized natural selection as a source of function for perception and our capacity to comprehend and filter assertive communication.

[5] Witness Richard Feldman and Andrew Cullison: "According to the proper functionalist view about justification, justification is a matter of forming beliefs in accordance with a design plan that is

you think God did not design us, then you must think Mother Nature did all the work. So if warrant requires functions, then warrant requires generations.

But isn't that asking too much? What about learning? Can't learned perceptions and acquired belief-forming competencies warrant their corresponding beliefs? Why *nature* and not also *nurture*? And what about Swampman? Can't he have warranted beliefs, even if he has no history at all?[6]

I shall argue that proper functionalism without God does not require natural selection per se for functions, and so does not require natural selection per se for warrant, for natural selection is not the only source of etiological functions. I discuss sources of functions that take considerably less time than natural selection. If warrant turns on functions, and functions turn on history, then warrant turns on history. How much? In some cases, not much.

By treating epistemic virtue in terms of functions, and functions in terms of history, have I set out to *naturalize* epistemic virtues, and so to naturalize epistemic warrant? No. Rather I have set out to *understand* functions, virtues, and warrant. If it turns out, however, that the account of functions I advance is naturalist in the intended sense, then my account will satisfy those with a naturalist agenda.[7]

aimed at acquiring true beliefs. While the view mentions a *design plan*, the view is supposed to be theologically neutral. That design plan may come from God (if there is one) or via natural selection and evolution (if there is no God)" (2012: 98). In Sosa's discussion of Plantinga, he too suggests that a design plan (and so a function or purpose) can arise only from God or Mother Nature. "The problem for proper functionalism is [that it takes] it to be impossible that there be someone with warranted belief who has no design plan imposed by any agency or process that designed him ... [for proper functionalism requires design by God or evolution for warrant]" (1993: 55, 57).

[6] Goldberg, Copp, and Lyons reject proper functionalism for this reason. Goldberg and Lyons think Swampman would have justified beliefs, without saying why Swampman would have beliefs, let alone warranted beliefs. Copp says epistemology should ignore our evolutionary roots. "Perhaps human beings popped suddenly into existence, out of thin air ... Nothing in epistemology turns on whether our cognitive system is the way it is due to its having been selected for" (this volume). Sosa (1993) imagines a Swampbaby that is discovered by a hunter and then grows to adulthood, having learned all sorts of things. He proposes this as a counter-example to proper functionalism.

[7] According to Neta 2007, the account I offer here counts as naturalist, or nearly naturalist. Kornblith 2002 would probably agree. For a structurally similar view of warrant that ties warrant to functions and functions to norms, see Burge 2003. Burge ties warrant to representational functions. Burge believes it is a priori necessary that the function of the perceptual system is to perceive, and to perceive is to represent accurately. Hence the representational function of the perceptual system is to represent accurately. He argues similarly for any belief-forming competence or capacity. He also argues that representational functions do not reduce to biological (or other obviously "naturalistic") functions. I discuss Burge in Graham in press a and in press b.

The rest of the chapter is organized as follows. In sections 2 and 3 I explicate etiological functions. You'll see why etiological functions require history. In sections 4 and 5 I review my proper functionalist view of warrant. Then in sections 6 to 10 I discuss sources of functions.

2   Etiological functions

Like many words, 'function' has many overlapping and related senses. In the sense I intend, the *function* of a thing denotes what it's for, its purpose. The heart is supposed to pump blood; that's its function; that's what it's for.[8] Functions in this sense are (typically) effects. By beating the heart causes the circulation of blood. But not every effect (even highly regular effects) is a function in this sense. Your heart regularly and reliably makes a rhythmic noise, but making noise is not a function of your heart; that is not what it is for. Your nose regularly and reliably holds up glasses, but you do not have a nose in order to hold up glasses. There are functional effects that explain why something exists, and then there are non-functional, "accidental" side-effects that do not.

Larry Wright (1973) argued that this distinction strongly supports an *etiological* condition on functions, where functions are consequences that *explain* why the item exists. Here is Wright's analysis:

A function of X is Z if and only if:

(1)   X does Z (Z is a consequence [result] of Xs being there, i.e. Xs are disposed, do, or can do Z).
(2)   X is there because it does Z (that Xs are disposed, do, or can do Z explains why X is there).

Wright's condition (2) then says that for any function, there must be some *feedback mechanism* that takes the satisfaction of (1) as input and generates existence or continued existence as output. Functions thus arise from *consequence etiologies*, etiologies that *explain* why something exists or continues to exist in terms of its consequences, because of a feedback mechanism that takes consequences as input and causes or sustains the item as output. Functions are then *explanatory* features or effects.

Non-functional features or effects are *non-explanatory* features or effects, and so in that sense "accidental," even if non-accidentally regular. By

---

[8] There are some so-called philosophical naturalists who deny that the heart has a function in this sense, for they deny *functions* in this sense, and certainly deny functional *norms* in this sense. I shall discuss such views in future work.

beating regularly, hearts pump blood, and we have hearts because they pump blood. Though by beating regularly hearts make noise, we do not have hearts because they make noise. Noses keep air warm and dry, and we have noses because they keep air warm and dry. And though they hold up glasses or nose rings, we do not have noses because they hold up glasses or nose rings.

Malformation raises an obvious difficulty. Consider a heart that's heavily malformed. Malformed, it can't pump blood, and *it* certainly does not exist because *it* can pump blood. But then *this heart* fails both of Wright's conditions. Even so it still has the function of pumping blood; that's what it is supposed to do.

This difficulty is easily avoided by incorporating a type–token distinction. True, certain malformed token hearts cannot pump blood. But the *type* can have the function of pumping blood provided a feedback mechanism takes past *token* hearts as input and produces or maintains hearts *because* past token hearts pumped blood. Then the heart (type) exists because it (tokens of the type) pumps blood.

Distinguishing types from tokens has other benefits. For instance, you may have wondered how future consequences can explain present existence. We can dispel the worry, for *current* tokens of functional items acquire their functions from *past* tokens going through a feedback mechanism. The past thus explains the present.

There's another problem not so easily avoided. Mark Bedau (1991) noticed that Wright's definition applies to some cases of non-living, inorganic materials. He describes a case from Richard Dawkins involving clay crystals that build dams in streams. The dams result from layers of sediment stacking up on top of one another according to the pattern laid down by the crystal. As a result the crystals replicate themselves; the dam is a tower of new crystals. Once the dams are built, the stream cannot wash the clay downstream; the dam thus stays in place. These crystals build dams, and they exist because they build dams; the crystals meet Wright's two conditions. But intuitively building dams is just something these crystals *do*, not something they are *supposed* to do. Intuitively there's *nothing* they are for; they have no purpose or function.

Following Hempel (1959), Ruse (1971), and Bedau (1991), Peter McLaughlin (2001) argues that we should include a *benefit* or *welfare* condition. Functions are not just explanatory features or effects. Functions are means to some *good* or *benefit* of the containing system. In order for Z to be a function of X, doing Z must do the system of which it is a part some good, and this good must be relevant to the feedback mechanism that explains why X exists in the system. Functions arise through a feed-back mechanism that involves explanatorily *beneficial* effects. Pumping blood helps *you* survive; pumping blood is a means to many of your ends; it clearly does *you* a lot of good. That's why, according to Hempel, Ruse, Bedau, and McLaughlin, it's a function of your heart to pump blood. The clay dam, on the other hand, doesn't have a good. Replicating isn't a means to any end, for the crystals or the dams have no ends, either as individuals or as members of a kind.

Putting Wright, Hempel, Ruse, Bedau, and McLaughlin (2001: 83) together, we arrive at the following abbreviated analysis of natural functions:

A function of X in S is Z iff:

(1)   X does Z in S.
(2)   Z benefits S.
(3)   X exists in S because Z benefits S (X is the product of a feedback mechanism involving the beneficial character of Z to S).

In this account, condition (3) says that for any function, there must be some feedback mechanism that takes the satisfaction of (1) and (2) as input and generates existence or continued existence as output. In recent work Larry Wright agrees: consequence etiologies that ground functions are *virtue* etiologies (Wright 2012).[9]

There are two points deserving emphasis. The first is that the whole purpose of turning to history is to mark the difference between explanatorily beneficial effects and other, non-explanatory, accidental effects, whether beneficial or not. The turn to history is driven by the need to distinguish explanatory functional from non-explanatory accidental effects. Without any history, there's no basis to draw the distinction.

The second is that the etiological account of function, as stated, is entirely neutral on possible feedback mechanisms. The account does not entail any particular feedback mechanism; it allows any possible feedback mechanism to generate functions, as long as it is a feedback mechanism taking beneficial characters or effects as input and produces existence or persistence as output. Etiological functions metaphysically entail feedback; they do not metaphysically entail any particular kind. This is what allows for a plurality of actual sources of etiological functions.

---

[9] Adding the beneficial effects condition marks a change in my view, for I did not include it in earlier work. It also makes naturalizing functions, and so naturalizing warrant, more challenging, for now the notion of benefit must be explicated. I will not try to do so here.

3 Normal functioning

The etiological account of functions entails an account of normal functioning and normal conditions. On the etiological account, functions arise when an item produces a beneficial effect that in turn enters into a feedback mechanism, where the mechanism explains why the item persists or reoccurs because of the beneficial effect. The full explanation for why and how all of this happened will cite how the item *worked* or *operated* so as to produce that effect and the *circumstances* – both internal or "inside" and external or "outside" the individual or organism.

What counts as normal functioning and normal conditions falls out of the historical explanation. *Normal* function*ing* is the way the item *worked* or *operated* when it underwent feedback for its beneficial effect; *normal* working *just is* working that way. Normal conditions are those circumstances (and circumstances of relevantly similar kind) where all of this happened. Look at the item's history, at the beneficial effects that help explain why it persists and recurs, at how it worked to produce these effects, and where it all happened. *Voilà*, normal functioning and normal conditions (Millikan 1984).

For example, a muscle in an organism's chest pumps blood by beating regularly. In turn it is connected in a systematic way with other parts of the organism, embedded in a certain type or kind of environment. If pumping blood explains, in part, why the muscle recurs through benefiting the kind or the individual, then it comes to have pumping blood as a function. The way the muscle worked when it entered the feedback mechanism for pumping blood equals normal functioning. Normal conditions are then those circumstances (and circumstances of similar type) where all of this occurred.

Given the way normal functioning and normal conditions are determined, normal functioning and normal conditions are then constitutively, explanatorily interrelated with function fulfillment. Normal functioning, normal conditions, and function fulfillment are all holistically interrelated. In particular, normal function*ing* is individuated and explanatorily understood in terms of the function of the item, for *normal* function*ing* just is *operating* or *working* the way the item operated in normal conditions so as to produce the functional effect. *Normal* function*ing* is then constitutively associated with function fulfillment.

Normal functioning constitutively "aims" at, contributes to, and conduces function fulfillment. For normal functioning is non-accidentally and explanatorily understood in terms of the function (and so the "aim") of the item. By functioning normally, the item non-accidentally and constitutively fulfills its function (and so achieves its "aim"). By functioning normally, it non-accidentally and constitutively contributes to function fulfillment; normal circumstances contribute the rest. And by functioning normally in normal conditions, it non-accidentally and constitutively conduces function fulfillment.[10]

Though holistically interrelated, it's important to see that normal functioning and function fulfillment are token-distinguishable; on particular occasions you can have one without the other. Consider a world-famous surgeon who needs to remove your heart during a very complicated surgery to cure a disease in the middle of your chest. She may place your heart in a sterile dish and stimulate it with electrical wires so that it beats normally – it operates exactly the way it should – but no blood is passing through. Your heart then functions normally (it's in perfect shape), though it doesn't fulfill its function. And so on occasions a normally functioning heart may fail to fulfill its function for it's not in normal conditions.

4   Three functional norms

Before turning to known feedback mechanisms on beneficial effects, I will review my view of warrant as turning on functions. After all, without seeing why warrant should turn on etiological functions, one might wonder what the fuss is all about. But first I shall spell out the category of functional norms, for I see the normativity constitutive of warrant as a species of functional normativity.

When philosophers discuss norms, they typically discuss norms that prescribe or guide behavior or thinking, such as prudential, moral, or social norms. Prescriptive or guiding norms are norms that we can represent, discuss, consider, internalize, subscribe to, consciously follow, flout, debate, challenge, and so on. Social norms, for example, are regularities in behavior in a group prescribed by members of the group. If the norm were not represented by a sufficient number of the group, the group would not prescribe the behavior, and so the norm would not exist.

There are norms that do not require the capacity to represent, think, internalize, or subscribe to a norm. There are norms that are neither prescriptions nor guides. Functional norms are norms in this broader sense.

---

[10] This marks an interesting difference with functions from conscious, intentional design. An item can have a function from conscious, intentional design without ever fulfilling its function. Just think of the dustbin of failed inventions. Thus whatever fixes normal functioning and normal conditions isn't holistically interrelated with function fulfillment for consciously assigned functions.

When there are functions, there are norms. Functional norms are standards or levels of "possible performance that is in some way adequate for fulfillment of a function or purpose."[11] The heart's function, then, determines standards or levels of performance in fulfilling its function. Given the heart's function, we can ask how well it performs. When it fulfills its function and operates normally, it meets levels of adequacy for performance in fulfilling its function and thereby fulfills norms. Such norms need not prescribe or guide. No norm tells the heart what to do. The heart does not look up or represent any norm to guide its activity. Functional norms are a broader kind than prescriptive or guiding norms. They do not depend on the aims or intentions of individuals, on being represented or being endorsed.

I identify three functional norms for any item with an etiological function: function fulfillment, normal functioning, and function fulfillment *because* functioning normally. Function fulfillment is trivially a level of performance adequate for fulfillment of a function. When your heart pumps blood, it meets a norm trivially associated with its function. Normal functioning is also a level of performance in some way adequate for fulfillment of the item's function, for it is the explanatorily relevant way the item non-accidentally fulfills its function in normal conditions; it is the way the item is *supposed* to *work* or *operate* so as to fulfill its function. When your heart functions normally, as it should, then it meets a second norm associated with its function. Function fulfillment *because* functioning normally is likewise meeting a norm in this sense; it is the explanatorily relevant way the item fulfills its function in normal conditions through meeting norms adequate for the fulfillment of its function or purpose.

Notice the structural parallel with Ernest Sosa's three-part normative structure for the exercise of a competence, a structure also elaborated by Wayne Riggs, Duncan Pritchard, and John Greco, among others. For Sosa, a competence is a reliable capacity to achieve some *aim*. Aim stands to function. If the competence fulfills or achieves its aim, the exercise of the competence is *accurate*. Accuracy stands to function fulfillment. If the competence is reliable in normal conditions, and the exercise is non-defective, then the exercise of the competence is *adroit*. Adroitness stands to normal functioning. If the exercise is also accurate because adroit, then the exercise is *apt*. Aptness stands to function fulfillment because functioning normally.

---

[11] Burge 2010: 311. I have taken the contrast between functional norms and prescriptive and guiding norms from Burge. Burge calls functional norms *natural* norms. Though natural, he does not intend to convey that they are naturalistic in some strong, reductionist sense of the term.

If aims require the individual who possesses the competence to represent the aim, then the category of functional norms and functional achievements is broader than Sosa's three-part structure, for functional norms do not require, as such, any representational capacities. Functional norms arise prior to mind. But since aims can determine functions, given a feedback mechanism, Sosa's three-part structure could be a species of functional normativity. Functional normativity does not exclude represented aims, goals, and so on.

For norms for items with etiological functions, normal functioning *encodes*, for partly constituted by, function fulfillment. We then understand the second norm of normal functioning in terms of the first norm of function fulfillment – the second norm is constitutively associated with the first – for normal functioning is constitutively associated and explanatory understood in terms of function fulfillment for items with etiological functions.

5   Epistemic warrant as normal functioning

I now turn to my account of warrant. Assume a belief-forming process has forming true beliefs reliably as an etiological function. There are then three functional norms it can meet: function fulfillment, normal functioning, and function fulfillment because normal functioning, where the second (and so the third) is constitutively associated with the first. Since these norms are understood in terms of promoting true belief and avoiding error, they are epistemic norms. Some epistemic norms are then functional norms. Meeting these norms are then epistemic achievements, goods, or successes.[12]

Epistemic warrant consists in fulfilling epistemic norms, for warrant is a normative status or achievement. Epistemic norms are norms understood in terms of promoting true belief and avoiding error. But this premise does not itself establish that warrant consists in functional normativity, for there are many kinds normativity, and so possibly many kinds of epistemic normativity.

There are, for instance, epistemic norms that prescribe and guide. Some tell us when we should inquire and for how long. Some prescribe techniques of critical reflection; they tell us how to assess and evaluate reasons

---

[12] This argument is independent of my view of warrant. You can deny that warrant requires functions and still accept that functions entail norms, that there are epistemic functions and so epistemic norms associated with those functions, and so accept that there are epistemic achievements, goods, or successes that consist in fulfilling functional norms.

for and against. Some prescribe thresholds for decision, conviction, or judgment. Some epistemic norms also guide. They guide when we inquire and for how long. They guide our reflection. They guide our judgments and levels of conviction. When they guide, we represent, endorse, and follow these prescriptions. We consult the norms in order to guide our inquiry, reflection, and assent.[13]

But I do not believe warrant requires following norms that prescribe or guide. This is partly because I believe warrant applies broadly through-out the animal kingdom. Higher non-human animals, small children, and even ordinary adults either cannot, or need not, represent or think epi-stemic prescriptions or epistemic guides for their beliefs to enjoy warrant. A chimp or ape can have a warranted perceptual belief without even hav-ing the capacity to think about functions, norms, truth, accuracy, war-rant, evidence, thresholds, and so on. Since warrant consists in fulfilling epistemic norms, but warrant applies broadly, the relevant norms cannot be prescribing or guiding norms. The normativity constitutive of warrant is neither prudential, moral, nor social.

I believe warrant consists in fulfilling functional norms associated with the epistemic function of the belief-forming process. Of the three func-tional norms, I believe warrant consists in fulfilling the second, the norm of normal functioning.

I believe this because I believe warrant may persist outside of normal conditions, and a system may still function normally outside of normal conditions, though it normally cannot explanatorily and non-accidentally fulfill its function outside of normal conditions. If warrant required func-tion fulfillment, then warrant would be restricted to normal conditions.

An individual may stumble outside of normal conditions without any awareness that this is so. The animal's functional capacities may still func-tion normally, even though the individual is no longer in normal condi-tions. The animal's capacities then fulfill a norm constitutively associated with function fulfillment. This is then a functional good or success. Organs too may operate normally outside of normal conditions. Recall the heart removed from the chest during a complicated surgery; it may operate (beat) normally, even though it is not pumping any blood, for it is no longer in normal conditions.

[13] I have discussed epistemic norms that prescribe and guide in Graham in press c. In a similar vein, Copp (this volume) isolates epistemic norms that are social norms that approximate ideal norms, where ideal norms are those that, when followed, solve our needs to acquire relevant information to help meet other needs. Kornblith (2002) identifies epistemic normativity with instrumental nor-mativity. Though these are all genuine kinds of epistemic normativity, I do believe warrant involves a different kind of epistemic normativity.

If the function of a belief-forming process is an epistemic function, then functioning normally is an epistemic good or success, even if the individual or the process is no longer in normal conditions. So there are epistemic goods that persist outside of normal conditions. The massively deceived, disembodied brain-in-a-vat vividly illustrates such a possibility. Outside of normal conditions, without any awareness that this is so, an individual's belief-forming processes may function normally. The massively deceived brain-in-a-vat may still function normally, despite failing to fulfill its epistemic functions.

This view of epistemic warrant as normal functioning is reliabilist in spirit, for it sees warrant as constitutively associated with promoting true belief and avoiding error, for normal functioning is constitutively associated with reliably getting things right when that is the etiological function of the belief-forming process. Warrant entails reliability in normal conditions, for warrant is grounded in reliability in normal conditions. Warrant, however, is not restricted to normal conditions.

This view explains why warrant aims at, contributes to, and conduces truth, three traditional marks of epistemic warrant. Normal functioning "aims" at reliably getting things right, and so "aims" at truth. Normal functioning non-accidentally and explanatorily contributes to reliably getting things right. And in normal conditions, normal functioning non-accidentally and explanatorily conduces towards true belief.

If warrant is constitutively, explanatorily, and non-accidentally associated with promoting true belief and avoiding error, if warrant consists in meeting epistemic norms, if animals and small children can meet those norms, and if warrant persists outside of normal conditions, then warrant consists in normal functioning when the belief-forming process has forming true beliefs reliably as an etiological function.

Since functions require history, warrant requires history. But if warrant requires history, how much history does warrant require? It all depends on how much history etiological functions require. In the remainder of the chapter I review sources of functions that don't require an awful lot. I'll start, however, with natural selection, which seems to require an awful lot.

6   Directional and maintenance selection

Natural selection requires three elements: variation, copying (inheritance), and beneficial consequences (fitness). Imagine birds that use their color vision to prey on a population of beetles. Imagine these beetles vary in color: half are brown and half are green. Imagine further that the beetles feed and live on a leafy green plant. The green ones are hard to see and so more likely to live long enough to reproduce. The brown ones, on the other hand, are easy prey. Now assume that their coloration is inherited, so that green beetles are more likely to produce green offspring than brown, and brown are more likely to produce brown offspring. Over time green coloration will come to predominate in the population. And now we have change in the population of beetles over time: once fifty–fifty, nearly all are now green. Within the beetle population coloration *varies*; their coloration is *inherited*; and coloration has obvious *consequences*: green beetles are camouflaged in their natural habitat; brown beetles don't stand a chance. Here's a case of modification with descent – evolution – through natural selection.

Natural selection takes time; it works over generations. As a feedback mechanism it takes frequencies of beneficial traits in earlier generations as input and produces frequencies in later generations as output. Even so, evolution by natural selection can happen very fast for organisms that reproduce rapidly (think of fruit flies and bacteria). But for organisms like us, evolution by natural selection often moves very slowly.

Or at least this is obviously true for *directional* selection, selection that leads to a change in the frequency of certain traits. *Maintenance* selection, on the other hand, maintains the frequency of traits in a population. Most mutations, for example, are harmful. They produce malformations that often lead to death well before the opportunity to reproduce, or diminish opportunities for reproduction. Because harmful they are selected out, in favor of the normal variant of the trait. The non-malformed trait then continues to exist and predominate in the population because of its relative superiority. Because of the prevalence of such harmful mutations, nearly every trait in a population is currently undergoing some form of maintenance selection.

Maintenance selection is full-blooded natural selection. It involves variation, inheritance, and beneficial consequences. It explains why a type of trait is preserved, upheld, or maintained in a population. And so it assigns functions for the very same reason that directional natural selection does. Maintenance selection, like directional selection, is a feedback mechanism on beneficial consequences.

It is a contingent, empirical question how many generations are required for directional selection to assign functions, or a change of functions. If the human heart last underwent directional selection 10,000, 30,000, or 100,000 years ago for its current form and function, then functions from directional natural selection would require considerable history indeed. But since the human heart undergoes maintenance selection in every generation, functions from maintenance selection require considerably less. If humans were, *per impossible*, created out of nothing a generation ago, maintenance selection would be at work, assigning functions.

7 Self-replication and repair

I now discuss another source of etiological functions. In *What Functions Explain*, McLaughlin argues for a non-hereditary feedback mechanism alongside natural selection (2001: 162–90). He thinks the ordinary metabolic activity of an organism that sustains the organism's own self-replication and repair fits the bill.

The ordinary operation of your metabolism keeps you alive. And this is partly because the ordinary metabolic activity of your systems and subsystems involves repairing and replacing the cells of your body, and so continually repairing and replacing the various systems and subsystems that make up your body. Your heart, by pumping blood, contributes to its own reassembly and repair, and thereby keeps you alive. Your heart thus persists in your body because of a feedback mechanism – normal metabolic activity – that takes earlier cycles comprising one group of cells as input and produces later cycles comprising another group of cells as output. An earlier *cycle* of your heart, by pumping blood, contributes to the existence of a later *cycle*, partly in virtue of its beneficial effects to you. Any trait that is advantageously integrated into the normal metabolism of your body contributes to *its* own reassembly and repair, and thereby to your continued life.

How does your metabolism generate functions? Once again, take your heart. The normal operation of your metabolism generates pumping blood as function provided (1) your heart pumps blood; (2) pumping blood (and so blood circulating through your body) benefits you; and (3) your heart exists or persists in your body because pumping blood benefits you. Both natural selection and your metabolism generate the same function for your heart. It's then over-determined that a function of your heart is to pump blood. A belief-forming psychological capacity will then have the function of reliably inducing true beliefs via the creature's metabolism provided (1) it reliably induces true beliefs; (2) reliably inducing true beliefs benefits the creature; and (3) the creature possesses such a capacity because reliably inducing true beliefs benefits the creature.

The normal operation of the metabolism of an organism is a feedback mechanism alongside natural selection taking earlier beneficial effects as input that produces functions as output. Where natural selection takes earlier generations (and so distinct tokens of the type) as input, the normal operation of the metabolism of an organism takes earlier cycles as input (and so maintains a token of the trait through time); it explains the continued existence of traits within individuals over *cycles* in virtue of their beneficial effects.[14] A first-generation trait within an individual organism could then acquire a function provided it is advantageously integrated into the metabolism of the organism.

This difference suggests a difference between the *species* or *population* as system and the *individual* as system. By pumping blood, hearts contribute to the survival of individual organisms long enough to reproduce and propagate the species or population. That's clearly a benefit to the species or the population. And by pumping blood, hearts contribute to the survival and wellbeing of the individual organisms themselves, which is clearly a benefit to the very individual in question, never mind the species or population.

These two mechanisms interact. Natural selection benefits the individual by preserving traits beneficial to individuals; you have your beneficial traits because of a long ancestral history involving natural selection. And normal self-replication and repair benefits the species or population, for if you don't self-replicate and stay alive, you can't propagate your kind. But they do not always overlap, which shows why we should distinguish the two. For many creatures engage in activity that benefits only the species. Salmon swim upstream to fertilize eggs only to die. Some male spiders, right after mating, get immediately killed and eaten by the female. Some creatures hatch their eggs internally. The hatchlings then eat their way out, obviously killing their mother in the process. Mules provide an example of the opposite kind of case, where their organs clearly benefit the individual mule, but nothing they do contributes to reproduction, for mules are sterile.

8   Interlude on Swampman

This distinction between *cycles* and *generations* – between metabolism and natural selection as mechanisms – helps dispel Swampman, for

---

[14] And so we need to qualify our earlier point about the importance of the type–token distinction in our account of functions: functions require either earlier *tokens* of the item for the type to acquire a function, or earlier *cycles* of the token for the token to acquire a function. But even then we'll still need the type–token distinction to accommodate malfunctioning, for a malfunctioning token may never fulfill its function; earlier cycles then don't contribute to later cycles of that very token.

metabolism takes very little history to generate functions. Swampman is a creature of philosophical science fiction. Imagine a bolt of lightning hitting a log in a swamp and creating a molecule-for-molecule duplicate of Barack Obama, a duplicate that bears absolutely no causal or explanatory connection to the real Barack Obama or to any other real human being, living or deceased. The physical duplicate – Swampman – is then a cosmic accident of vast proportions. Assuming for the sake of argument such a possibility, some philosophers find it natural to say that Swampman's "heart" has a function just like Obama's heart, even though Swampman bears no causal or explanatory relation to Obama, or to any other real human being or biological entity, living or deceased.

Swampman is a full-body example of what biologists call hopeful monsters. In nature, new organs or traits often arise very slowly through a series of micro-mutations; small changes through a gradual process of variation, selection, and replication. But once in a blue moon a macro-mutation arises: an almost entirely new trait or organ, very different in kind from its ancestral trait. In actual cases nearly all of these are deleterious to the recipient; the recipient soon dies or is unable to reproduce and the trait is selected out through maintenance selection. Think of extreme birth defects. But sometimes one of these macro-mutations actually benefits the recipient. These traits are called "hopeful monsters." A hopeful monster is a beneficial macro-mutation. Since they are mutations, they don't have an evolutionary history; they are "first-generation" traits. Thus they don't exist because of natural selection; natural selection works only on traits that already occur (though it can increase the probability that various traits will emerge). Swampman is just this sort of case taken to the extreme.

If Swampman's organs have functions, must we reject the etiological account? Hopeful monsters are a problem only on the assumption that natural selection is the only feedback mechanism generating functions. But since it's not, hopeful monsters are not a problem. True, the first cycle of a hopeful monster has no function, even if it has a beneficial effect. But without a feedback mechanism in play there's no distinguishing between functional effects and merely accidental, albeit beneficial, effects; only persistent and recurrent traits have functions (Hempel 1959; McLaughlin 2001: 67–68, 168); that's the whole point of the function–accident distinction. Once the hopeful monster starts to benefit the organism and thereby contribute to its own self-replication and repair, it enters a feedback loop that partly explains its own continued existence. Its effects are then functional, not merely accidental, for its effects play an explanatory role. The same holds for all of Swampman's beneficial organs and traits. Swampman at the moment of his creation has no functions; over time Swampman's organs and traits acquire functions. But then we have an explanation for why someone might think his organs do indeed have functions, for over time they do. The existence of hopeful monsters – even Swampman – is not a problem for an etiological theory of functions that takes a broader view on feedback mechanisms. Some history is required for functions, just not an awful lot.

Of course the recalcitrant philosopher may insist that Swampman has functions at creation. If they do, all I can do at this point is pass the baton, and invite them to develop a better account of functions, an account that treats the function–accident distinction just as well without any appeal to any history whatsoever, consistent with their recalcitrance. Good luck.[15]

9 Trial-and-error learning

I now turn to a third feedback mechanism: trial-and-error learning. Psychologists call trial-and-error learning *operant conditioning* or *instrumental learning*. Imagine a four-year-old learning to tie his shoes. As any parent knows, this isn't a trivial task. My parents moved my fingers for me. I got one part of the process partially right, but the rest was a mess. Somehow, over time and with enough effort, I learned to tie my shoes. Now it's effortless.

It's a trite observation in textbooks on learning and memory that trial-and-error learning parallels natural selection. Natural selection requires variation, consequences, and copying: the variation is genetic, the consequences driving selection involve relative fitness, and copying involves transfer of DNA from parent to child. Trial-and-error learning involves three similar factors: variation in behavior, consequences involving positive and negative rewards, and lasting change in neural structures (modified structures in the individual "descend" from earlier structures).

Variation in behavior occurs for a number of reasons. Many variations are induced by the situation; they may arise from the situation due to innate modules, the current motivational state of the individual, prior

---

[15] I do not accept the metaphysical possibility that Swampman, at creation, has a mind or that its organs have any functions. Mind presupposes explanatory, non-accidental relations between the individual and a subject matter. Swampman by definition is a cosmic accident. Swampman at creation has no thoughts, beliefs, perceptions, memories, and so on. Similarly functions presuppose explanatory, non-accidental beneficial effects. Swampman by definition bears no explanatory relations to anything at all. At creation there is nothing his heart is supposed to do.

Pavlovian conditioning, or even prior operant conditioning. Another source of variation is the variability inherent in all human behavior. Jerome Frieman reports in his textbook: "Individuals do not perform the same action exactly the same way each time they do it. Even when the individual is well practiced and the stimulus situation is identical on each occasion, there will still be some behavioral variability in how a behavior is performed" (2002: 260). The first source of variability is called *induced* variability. The second is called *behavioral* variability.

Trial-and-error learning involves "trials" – variations in behavior – "errors" – negative reinforcers – and "successes" – positive reinforcers. Trial-and-error learning requires the individual to find behaviors that reduce negative reinforcers and increase positive reinforcers. If the individual can learn, then over time – sometimes very quickly – the individual will find the correct behavior that avoids negative reinforcers and obtains positive reinforcers. Induced variation produces the "trials" that eventually lead to a solution. Behavioral variability then makes more efficient behavior possible through hill-climbing; once the solution is found, behavioral variability produces a more efficient solution. Negative and positive reinforcers select among variants. Successful behaviors are selected by their beneficial consequences; successful behaviors, in virtue of their consequences, are more likely to occur again in similar situations (Frieman 2002: 263–64).

What feedback mechanism makes this possible? What feedback mechanism "integrates information about the behavior" with its consequences? Whatever the details, it involves sensation or perception and memory. The individual must sense or perceive both the behavior and its consequences, and the individual must record and process that information and translate it into future behavior (Frieman 2002: 270). When we learn through trial-and-error learning, we rely on perception and memory to select the right behavior among its variants in virtue of its consequences. Sometimes it is automatic, and sometimes very slow. Sometimes it is entirely conscious, sometimes entirely unconscious, hidden from view. Even single-celled organisms "sense" and "remember" and so learn by trial-and-error.

How does trial-and-error learning generate functions? Take the neural structure underlying my ability to tie my shoelaces, or the behavior (the motion of my fingers) that it causes when I want to tie my laces. (1) It ties my shoes; (2) tying my shoes benefits me (I get what I want, I avoid frustration, I earn the praise of my parents and others, my shoes stay on, I don't trip, etc.); and (3) I have the structure or can perform the behavior because tying my shoes benefits me. It's then the function of the structure or the behavior to tie my shoes.

Take any skill you've acquired through learning: passing a soccer ball with your feet or catching a baseball with a glove; pronouncing English verbs and Chinese tones; speaking in public or writing elegant prose; hitting a distant target with bow and arrow; the list is endless. On the present account, nearly every one of these behaviors or the underlying structures will have functions, where the function is often named by the name of the skill: the function of structure underlying my ability to pass a soccer ball is to pass soccer balls. Many of these skills are acquired without consciously and deliberately setting out to acquire them – think of first-language learning, or the learning of various habits that benefit you in one way or another, habits acquired from positive and negative reinforcers that drove selection of the behavior, without your awareness that you were headed in that direction. Other skills are acquired consciously and deliberately. You may very much want to be a good soccer player, an excellent first-baseman, or a world-class archer. Either way, the underlying structure has a function, for the structure results from a feedback mechanism on beneficial effects. Performance normativity is then a species of functional normativity.

Trial-and-error learning, like the normal operation of your metabolism, is a non-hereditary feedback mechanism generating functions; you can acquire all sorts of skills your parents never dreamed of. And now we have another mechanism that doesn't require much history, and so we have another way Swampman can acquire functions; if he has sensory and perceptual capacities, memory, and the mechanism underlying operant conditioning, then he can learn through trial-and-error learning.

Learning also takes us beyond the scope of the "narrowly" biological, where the narrowly biological covers anatomy and physiology, to the "broadly" biological, where biology includes psychology, anthropology, and sociology, especially the learned behavioral traits of individuals. "Nature" has given way to "nurture" as a source of functions.

10   Learning and derived functions

Trial-and-error learning, of course, isn't the only form of learning. Psychologists tend to define learning very broadly. As a result they think there are many forms indeed. In general they see learning as a relatively permanent change in the organism that isn't due to normal development.

You may be wondering about so-called one-off learning, where I learn how to do something without the process of trial-and-error. Is one-off learning a source of functions? Yes it is. Let me explain. The ability to

learn – and to learn in various ways – is itself functional. Though classical empiricists and psychological behaviorists tend to emphasize learning
at the expense of the innate, they agree that the ability to learn is built
in. But then, we might ask, why is it built in? Mother Nature builds it
when the organism needs it to survive. Some organisms really need to
learn various things, while others do not. Birds that nest on ledges on
cliffs, for example, do not need to learn to recognize their chicks, for the
only chicks they'll ever significantly interact with are their own. Birds that
nest on crowded beaches, on the other hand, do need to learn to recognize their chicks, for they will see and interact with plenty of chicks that
are not their own. "Learning is an option, like camouflage or horns, that
nature gives to organisms as needed – when some aspect of the organism's
environmental niche is so unpredictable that anticipation of its contin-
gencies cannot be wired in" (Pinker 1997: 242).

But if that is so, then our various abilities to learn will have learning –
and so adapting to our environment in beneficial ways – as a function.
The general ability to learn, when it leads to learning new abilities, results
in those abilities having "derived" functions named, in part, by their beneficial effects. What is learned has a function derived from the general ability. In Millikan's (1984) jargon, learning has adapting to the environment
as its *direct* function. The structure or behavior that results has a *derived*,
indirect function.

This means "one-off" skills and abilities – even perceptual categories and
belief-forming capacities, if there are any – have *derived* functions. It also
means that functions from trial-and-error learning will have their functions twice determined. For since trial-and-error learning itself involves
consequence selection as a means of adapting to the environment (and so
generates direct functions), and since the capacity to learn from trial and
error results from consequence selection (and so generates indirect functions), items that result from trial-and-error learning will have their functions over-determined as both direct and indirect functions.

11   Conclusion

Teleological views of mind and psychological capacity pervade the history of philosophy. It's thus not unusual to find broadly functional views
on the nature of warrant and other epistemological properties embraced
in the history of philosophy. Proper function, virtue epistemology has
a long history. My view of warrant falls within this teleological frame
of mind.

Discussions about the role of functions within epistemology focus on two sources: God and Nature. And when it comes to Nature, natural selection is the paradigm case. And then for the naturalist there is often only the paradigm, natural selection.

But once we review the sources of etiological functions beyond directional natural selection, we see that belief-forming processes may have forming true beliefs reliably as an etiological function from any number of functions. There are many ways belief-forming processes may acquire an etiological function, and so many ways they may acquire the etiological function of forming true beliefs reliably, and so many ways warrant may arise. Warrant requires functions, and functions require history, and so my account of warrant requires history. How much history is required, however, turns on the details of the particular case. I have not examined those details, but I have shown that, at least in principle, the history required may be considerably less than one might have otherwise thought.

CHAPTER 3

The epistemic "ought"

Ram Neta

Given how you are currently situated, there are some propositions that you ought to accept, other propositions that you ought to deny, and still other propositions concerning which you ought to suspend judgment. Furthermore, you ought to be more confident of the truth of some propositions than of others, and you ought to be just as confident of the truth of some propositions as of others. In short, in your judgments, suspensions of judgment, and degrees of confidence, you are subject to *epistemic oughts*. But does your subjection to these epistemic oughts imply that you *can comply* with these oughts? In epistemology, does "ought" imply "can"?

Many epistemologists have recently argued that the answer to this question is negative, and they have done so not simply by describing putative cases of "ought" without "can," but rather by defending views concerning the epistemic "ought" that explain why we should expect this "ought" *not* to imply "can." For example, Nicholas Wolterstorff, Richard Feldman, and Hilary Kornblith have all articulated views about the epistemic "ought" that explain why this "ought" does not imply "can," i.e. why it is sometimes beyond our abilities to have the credal state that, in a particular case, we ought to have. In this chapter, I want to combine the insights of the views that these authors have defended, and build on them. In building on them, I will end up developing a view of the epistemic "ought" on which it does imply a certain kind of "can." But I also want to argue that the kind of "can" that is implied by the epistemic "ought" is also a kind of "can" that *implies* the epistemic "ought." In other words, I will argue that, in epistemology, not only does "ought" imply "can," but that very same "can" also implies "ought." This account of 'oughts' and 'cans' will be

Thanks to Selim Berker, Matthew Chrisman, David Copp, Abrol Fairweather, Doug Lavin, Eric Marcus, John Roberts, Nate Sharadin, and especially Geoff Sayre-McCord for helpful discussion of an earlier draft of this chapter.

virtue theoretic in that epistemic norms are cashed out in terms of proper functioning and essential kinds.[1]

I realize that this will be a hard sell. But I think that my conclusion will be easier to accept once I make it clear precisely what sort of "can" it is that is implied by the epistemic "ought." To state my conclusion immediately but telegraphically, the "can" that is implied by the epistemic "ought" is the "can" of *competence*, not the "can" of *opportunity*. Of course, this distinction needs to be spelled out much more fully.

One caveat before I begin: the considerations that have been adduced in the literature concerning whether "ought" implies "can" are, by and large, metaphysical considerations – not semantic, let alone formal. This indicates that the kind of implication at issue in the debate – and so the only kind of implication with which I concern myself here – is metaphysical. I am interested in the issue of whether it is possible (in some suitably broad, and so "metaphysical," sense of "possible") for it to be the case that a creature ought to comply with some epistemic norm, even though it cannot do so. I will not at all be concerned with the semantic or syntactic properties of "ought" or "can" constructions; I take these properties to be neutral with respect to the metaphysical issue in which I am interested.

In order to isolate the kind of "can" that is implied by the epistemic "ought," I'll begin by considering three recently proposed views of the epistemic "ought." It will turn out that, while each of these views is insightful, and to some extent true, none of them is explanatorily adequate. In developing our own account of the epistemic ought, we will therefore need to supplement the views that we consider.

1 Wolterstorff on the proper function ought

Nicholas Wolterstorff distinguishes two kinds of "oughts." (His distinction is not intended to be exhaustive. While it is intended to be exclusive, it is not clear that it need be in order to serve our present purposes.) First, there are "oughts" of obligation, failures to comply with which are *blameworthy*. And second, there are "oughts" of proper functioning, failures to comply with which are, in some way, improper, even if not blameworthy.[2] Wolterstorff does not offer an account of proper functioning, but

---

[1] A kindred approach to ethical (rather than epistemic) norms can be found in Korsgaard's (2008) metaphysical reading of Aristotle's function argument.
[2] Wolterstorff 2010.

he attempts to clarify the notion of proper functioning at issue here by appeal to other, typically non-epistemic, examples:

> [L]et me offer some other examples of the use of "should" and "ought" that have nothing to do with accountability, and so, nothing to do with praise and blame.
>
> (i)   "You ought to be walking on it in two weeks" – said by a physician as he finishes binding up a person's sprained ankle.
>
> (ii)   "It should have black spots all over its shell, not just around the rim" – said by one person, ladybug in hand, explaining to another person what ladybugs look like.
>
> (iii)   "That's strange; you ought to be seeing double" – said by a psychologist to his subject while conducting an experiment in perception.
>
> (iv)   "Here your poem ought to have some breathing room; it's too dense" – said by a teacher of creative writing to a fledgling poet.
>
> (v)   "That's puzzling; you should have believed it was in the other dish" – said by a psychologist to his subject in the course of conducting an experiment on the formation of inductive beliefs.

In none of these cases would there be any inclination whatsoever, on the part of the person speaking, to blame the person or object being spoken about. The patient is not to be blamed if, after two weeks, his foot is still too painful to walk on; the ladybug is not to be blamed for lacking some spots; and so on. And, of course, in none of these cases is there a relevant intention in view. The language of "should" and "ought" is used in such cases to point to what a properly formed specimen of the type in question would be like, or to how a properly functioning specimen would operate – conversely, to point to a feature of the specimen in hand that marks it out, or marks out its functioning, as malformed. Clearly this is a standard use of such language.[3]

This "standard use" is precisely the use of "ought" that Wolterstorff thinks is involved in the epistemic "ought."

Wolterstorff is right that the epistemic "ought" is not the "ought" of obligation: while we might have some obligations when it comes to our credal states, such obligations (if indeed there are any) are at least typically not what we're talking about when we say that someone ought to

---

[3] Wolterstorff 2010: 79. Some readers have been tempted to think of some of Wolterstorff's cases (especially cases (i) and (iii)) as expressing probability claims. This temptation should be resisted. Case (i) might involve a physician speaking to a soldier who – as the physician well knows – is about to face a very high risk of death on the battlefield. The physician says (i) not because she thinks that the soldier is likely to be walking on his leg in two weeks, but rather because she thinks that, if the healing process goes normally and is not impeded in any way, then the soldier will be walking on his leg in two weeks. And while the psychologist who says (iii) is doubtless surprised by the patient's failure to see double, her expectation that the patient sees double is an expectation based on her assumption that nothing is interfering with the proper operation of the patient's visual system.

believe something. For instance, given the evidence that I currently possess, I ought to be more confident than not that the value of my stock portfolio will increase more than 1 percent over the next year. But I would not be violating any obligations if I were not more confident than not that the value of my stock portfolio will increase more than 1 percent over the next year. Of course, I might be violating an obligation I have, say, to my family if I pulled all my money out of my stock portfolio right now and invested it in gold, stupidly thinking that it would be a better investment. And it might be rational for me to do just this if I were rationally extremely confident that the value of my stock portfolio was not going to be going up nearly as much as the value of gold. But, given my evidence, I could not be rationally extremely confident of this. Still, merely to be confident of this proposition, so strongly at odds with my evidence, is not, by itself, to violate any obligations.

So the epistemic "ought" is not the "ought" of obligation. Is it, as Wolterstorff claims, the "ought" of proper functioning? Let's suppose that it is, and see where that supposition takes us. Of course there are many proper functions: which of these could we plausibly take to fix the epistemic "ought"s? We can narrow down the answer to this question by pointing out that epistemic "ought"s concern our credal states. So clearly, the "ought"s mentioned in Wolterstorff's examples (i), (ii), (iii), and (iv) are not epistemic. But what about Wolterstorff's example (v)? Recall:

(v)   "That's puzzling; you should have believed it was in the other dish" – said by a psychologist to his subject in the course of conducting an experiment on the formation of inductive beliefs.

Depending on how this example is fleshed out, the "should" here could be epistemic or non-epistemic. Consider each of the following two elaborations:

(v_a)   The psychologist shows a subject a series of pairs of covered dishes, and tells the subject that a small object is located in one of the dishes. The psychologist then removes the covers to reveal that the small object is in the left dish, and nothing is in the right dish. After this happens 10 times, the psychologist then repeats the trials but this time asks the subject to identify which dish the small object is in, and the subject does. On each of the next 90 trials, the small object is in the left dish. Finally, the psychologist presents the subject with the pair of covered dishes a 101st time, and asks the subject in which dish the small object is located. The subject says that it's in the right dish, and the psychologist says "that's puzzling; you should have believed it was in the other dish."

(v_b) The psychologist shows a subject a pair of covered dishes, and tells the subject that there is a small object located in one of the two dishes. Then the psychologist tells the subject (whose name, let us suppose, is "Alice," and who, let us also suppose, has never taken any courses in formal logic) that if the small object is located in the left dish, then her name is Alice. Finally, the psychologist asks Alice which dish contains the small object, and Alice says, sincerely, that she has no idea which dish it is in, but she is going to guess the right dish. Now the psychologist says "That's puzzling; you should have believed it was in the other dish."

While the psychologist's "should" in case (v_a) is plausibly epistemic, the psychologist's "should" in case (v_b) is not: the psychologist in case (v_b) is expressing puzzlement that Alice does not seem to process material conditionals in the way that almost all logically uneducated people (and even most logically educated people) do when they are confronted with the Wason Selection Task.[4] The results of the Wason Selection Task show that, in most domains, people reason as if, when a material conditional is true, and its consequent is also true, then its antecedent must be true. While such reasoning is not epistemically rational, it may nonetheless be normal for humans to reason in this way, at least in most domains.[5] Perhaps it is not merely normal, but natural – indeed, perhaps there is even some hard-wired feature of our reasoning competence that determines that we reason in this way, at least in the absence of any correctives.

So there is a perfectly good way to flesh out case (v) on which the psychologist's "should," though it is the "should" of proper functioning, and though it applies to the subject's credal states, is nonetheless not an epistemic ought. If we want to identify the epistemic "ought" as a proper function "ought" we must say more than Wolterstorff says about the proper function that determines the epistemic "ought."

2   Feldman on oughts of good credal performance

In an essay critical of Wolterstorff's discussion of epistemic oughts, Richard Feldman anticipates the point that we made above regarding Wolterstorff's

---

[4] Wason 1966.
[5] There is evidence that people do not generally make the same mistake when the task domain involves policing of behavior for compliance with social norms. See Cosmides and Tooby 1992.

example (v).[6] Perhaps then Feldman's own discussion of epistemic oughts will help us to specify the distinctive kind of "ought" that is epistemic.

Feldman takes the epistemic "ought" to fall into a general category of "ought" that he calls "role oughts." Here is what he says:

> There are oughts that result from one's playing a certain role or having a certain position. Teachers ought to explain things clearly. Parents ought to take care of their kids. Cyclists ought to move in various ways. Incompetent teachers, incapable parents, and untrained cyclists may be unable to do what they ought to do. Similarly, I'd say, forming beliefs is something people do. That is, we form beliefs in response to our experiences in the world. Anyone engaged in this activity ought to do it right … I suggest that epistemic oughts are of this sort – they describe the right way to play a certain role … these oughts are not based on what's normal or expected. They are based on what's good performance.
>
> Furthermore, it is plausible to say that the role of a believer is not one that we have any real choice about taking on. It differs in this way from the other roles mentioned. It is our plight to be believers. We ought to do it right. It doesn't matter that in some cases we are unable to do so.[7]

Just as Wolterstorff was right to claim that epistemic "ought"s concern proper functions, and not obligations, so too Feldman is right to claim that epistemic "ought"s concern "good performance" in the role of a believer. Furthermore, Feldman's claim helps to fill an explanatory gap in Wolterstorff's account: while it might have been natural for the experimental subject in case (v_b) to believe that the small object was in the left dish – while such a belief might have been the result of the proper operation of her native cognitive capacities – such a belief would not have constituted "good performance" in her role as a believer. Good performance is not simply the performance that results from any proper functioning of any of our capacities, since those capacities are designed to solve evolutionary problems effectively. At least some of those capacities might not be designed to solve reasoning problems correctly.

But while Feldman's account helps us better to understand the epistemic "ought," it leaves us with a question. There are plenty of roles that we have no choice about occupying, and there are standards of good performance for many of those roles, but nothing follows about whether or not we ought to comply with those standards of good performance. If you are born into slavery, then (typically at least) you have no choice about being a slave. And presumably there are standards of good performance

---

[6] Feldman 2001.
[7] Feldman 2001: 87–88.

for slaves: a good slave is one who does not try their master's patience, who does what she is told without complaint, who works whenever her work is needed, and so on. But from the fact that you have no choice about being a slave, and that there are standards of good performance for slaves, it does not follow that you ought to satisfy those standards. So why would it follow, from the fact that you have no choice about being a believer, and that there are standards of good performance for believers, that you ought to satisfy those standards? Without an answer to this question, Feldman's account of the epistemic "ought" as a role "ought" fails to provide an explanatorily adequate account of the epistemic "ought." Feldman is right to claim that we have no choice about being believers, and he is also right to claim that the epistemic "ought" depends on standards of good performance for believers, and he is also right to claim that the epistemic "ought" applies to us by virtue of our being believers. Indeed, I will concede even more than this: Feldman is also right to claim that the first two of these facts are *in some way* (which I will not specify until section 4 below) involved in grounding the third. But Feldman fails to explain how this grounding obtains – he does not help us to understand what it is about our being believers, and about the standards of good performance for believers, that makes it the case that we (believers) ought to comply with those standards. Why is it that people born to be believers ought to satisfy standards of goodness for believing, even though it's not the case that people born into slavery ought to satisfy standards of goodness for a slave?

3   Kornblith on regulative ideals of credence

Our criticism of Feldman's account of the epistemic "ought" was anticipated by Hilary Kornblith, in an article critical of Feldman's account of the epistemic "ought."[8] Perhaps, then, we can develop an adequate account of the epistemic "ought" – an account that explains why we ought to satisfy the standards of good performance for believers – by supplementing the true claims that Wolterstorff and Feldman make with some additional insights from Kornblith. Here is what Kornblith says:

> [M]uch of what [Feldman] says about role oughts offers important illumination on the subject of epistemic oughts. Thus, when Feldman argues that standards of good performance in a role must in some ways take account of human capacities, and yet, at the same time, "it is not the case that

[8] Kornblith 2001.

the existence of those standards implies that individuals must have basic or non-voluntary control of that behavior that is judged by those standards," I believe that what Feldman says applies not only to standards of good performance in roles, but to ideals in general. An appropriate human ideal must in some ways be responsive to human capacities. Ideals are meant to play some role in guiding action, and an ideal that took no account of human limitations would thereby lose its capacity to play a constructive action-guiding role. At the same time, our ideals cannot be so closely tied to what particular individuals are capable of that we fail to recognize that some individuals at some times are incapable of performing in ideal ways.[9]

I think Kornblith is right to think of epistemic oughts as ideals of cognitive performance that play some role in guiding that performance. Because they are *ideals* of cognitive performance, it cannot be trivial to satisfy them. But because they *guide* cognitive performance, it also cannot be impossible to satisfy them. Epistemic oughts are ideals of cognitive performance that are, to put it crudely, neither too easy nor too hard.

Unfortunately, if we leave it at that, we face a problem. Consider the following three normative propositions:

(a) Your confidence in a proposition ought to be proportioned to the degree to which your evidence supports that proposition.

(b) Your confidence in a proposition ought to be proportioned to the degree to which you reasonably take your evidence to support that proposition.

(c) On weekdays, your confidence in a proposition ought to be proportioned to the degree to which your evidence supports that proposition; on weekends, your confidence in a proposition ought to be proportioned to the degree to which you reasonably take your evidence to support that proposition.

All three of (a), (b), and (c) describe ideals of cognitive performance that are neither trivial nor impossible to satisfy. Some philosophers believe, quite plausibly, that (a) is a norm of cognitive performance for us. Other philosophers believe, also quite plausibly, that (b) is a norm of cognitive performance for us. But nobody believes, and it would be utterly implausible to believe, that (c) is a norm of cognitive performance for us: (c) is not what Kornblith would regard as a "human" ideal. But why is this? If (a) could plausibly be regarded as a norm of human cognitive performance, and (b) could plausibly be regarded as a norm of human cognitive

---

[9] Kornblith 2001: 237–38.

performance, then why not (c) as well, which simply combines (a) for some days of the week with (b) for other days of the week?

The answer to this question seems obvious: it is just because norms of cognitive performance cannot advert to factors irrelevant to the evaluation of such performance, e.g. what day of the week it is. But this answer simply raises another question: what makes the issue of what day of the week it is any more irrelevant to the evaluation of cognitive performance than any other factor? What determines which factors are relevant to the evaluation of cognitive performance, and which factors are irrelevant? I am not here asking an epistemic question about how we figure out which factors are relevant (though that is an interesting epistemic question). Rather, I am asking a metaphysical question, a question about what fixes it that certain factors are relevant to the evaluation of human cognitive performance. In the paper that I've discussed, Kornblith does not answer this question. But a satisfactory account of the epistemic ought needs to answer this question.

You might think that the answer to this question is clear enough. The epistemic norms governing cognitive performance, you might think, are norms our compliance with which promotes the attainment of some distinctively epistemic goal (e.g. the maximization of accuracy in our belief-system, and the minimization of inaccuracy). Tailoring your cognitive performance differently to different days of the week cannot help you to satisfy any such goal, and so cannot be epistemically mandatory. But while it is true that tailoring your cognitive performance differently to different days of the week cannot help you to satisfy any such goal, and while it is also true that tailoring your cognitive performance differently to different days of the week cannot be epistemically mandatory, it is not clear how the former fact can explain the latter. The former fact could explain the latter only if epistemic mandates are determined by what helps us to achieve some distinctively epistemic goal. But if that metaphysical thesis were true, then what would make it mandatory for us to comply with either norm (a) or (b) above? Would compliance with (a) or (b) promote the level of accuracy, or diminish the level of inaccuracy, in our belief-system? Is there any empirical evidence that indicates that proportioning your confidence to the evidence leads you to the truth more often than not doing so? I don't know of any such evidence, and indeed I have seen some evidence to the contrary.[10] But, even if this were not the case and

---

[10] Bishop and Trout (2005) discuss evidence to the effect that, in a number of domains, human experts trying to proportion their beliefs to their evidence ended up getting far fewer true answers and far more false answers to questions in their domain of expertise than did software that weighted the

there were evidence to the effect that proportioning your confidence to the evidence leads you to the truth more often than not doing so, why ought we to follow that very evidence in proportioning our confidence in the proposition that proportioning your confidence to the evidence leads you to the truth more often than not doing so? There is no way of answering this question without begging the question. Consequently, we have no non-question-begging reason to believe that following (a) or (b) would promote the epistemic goal (whatever precisely that goal may be) better than following (c) would.[11]

In short, while Kornblith is right to regard epistemic oughts as guiding ideals of cognitive performance, he tells us too little about what factors determine the content of these ideals.

4 A more complete account of the epistemic ought

So let's review what we've learned so far about epistemic oughts. As the authors we've discussed have claimed, and as we are prepared to accept, the epistemic ought is a particular kind of proper function ought; a kind of ought that is determined by standards of good performance for believers, and so one that applies to us by virtue of our being believers; and a particular kind of guiding ideal of cognitive performance. But we have not yet succeeded in explaining more specifically what kind of proper function ought they are, how our being believers makes it the case that we ought to satisfy standards of good performance for believers, and what fixes which factors are relevant to determining how we ought to conduct ourselves cognitively. In the present section, I offer an account of the epistemic ought that fills these explanatory gaps. The basic idea of the account is to explain the epistemic "ought" – the "ought" that we employ when we say what someone "ought to believe" or "ought not believe" or "ought to be less confident of," etc. – as a relation that obtains between individual credal agents, on the one hand, and a natural kind of which they are all individuals, on the other. In order to spell out this account, I need to begin with a few remarks about biological species, and the individual organisms that belong to those species.

relevant variables *randomly* in generating answers to those same questions. So, even if someone is not in possession of this evidence concerning relative accuracy, she would get to the truth much more often simply by accepting unquestioningly whatever answers the software generates, rather than by considering the evidence herself.

[11] Incidentally, I am very skeptical that epistemic norms are determined consequentialistically at all. My skepticism can be summarily expressed by Selim Berker's slogan that consequentialism in epistemology "does not respect the separateness of propositions." See Berker 2013.

A biological species is a particular kind of homeostatic system – i.e. a system that operates to maintain itself in a particular kind of state. A particular individual belongs to that species just in case the following biconditional is true of that individual: it possesses (at least in some form, be it immature, disordered, decayed, or otherwise) the capacities that are engaged in the operations of the species if and only if it ought to exercise those capacities to maintain itself in the particular kind of state characteristic of the species. Let's call this latter the "goal state" of the species, and, derivatively, of individuals of that species. Goal states will differ, of course, for different kinds of homeostatic systems – both biological and non-biological. The goal states for antelopes differ from the goal states for lobsters, which differ from the goal states for elm trees, which differ from the goal states for corporations. Different individuals of the same species of homeostatic system share the same goal state (that is at least part of what makes them individuals of the same type), but they will typically differ in the extent to which they possess the capacities necessary to realize that goal state. If a particular kind K has a goal state G, then there is a proper function sense of "ought" on which it is true that each individual K "ought" to achieve G if and only if it can, and so it "ought" to perform in various ways and occupy various states that are involved in achieving G if and only if it can. If operation O is one of the operations necessarily involved in achieving G, then each individual K ought to O in order to achieve G if and only if it can.

Here are some examples of this kind of proper function "ought":

> The tiger nurses its young for about three to six months, to give the cubs time to develop their teeth; this particular (normal maternal) tiger ought to nurse its young for at least another month.
>
> The caterpillar eats host plants like anise, parsley, and carrot; this particular (normal mature) caterpillar ought to be eating anise, parsley, carrot, or other host plants – don't keep feeding it cactus.
>
> Bermudagrass grows under high pine-tree shade; this particular patch of (normal) Bermudagrass ought to have more exposure to sunlight than is available when you pitch the tent over it.

Each of the proper function oughts mentioned above applies to *capable individuals* of a kind K by virtue of the goal state of individuals of that kind; a goal state G that they have by virtue of being individuals of a kind that operates so as to maintain itself in state G. The individual member of the species ought to realize that goal state if and only if it has the capacity to do so.

Wolterstorff is right to claim that epistemic oughts are proper function oughts. I now want to add that the creatures to which epistemic oughts apply are members of a homeostatic kind that has as its goal state the state of *operating rationally*. Different individuals of this kind – let's call them "rational subjects" – will differ in the extent to which they possess the capacities necessary to achieve this goal state.[12] At least some will not have those capacities, and so will not be able to achieve this goal state. Despite this variation, though, it is nonetheless true that the rational subject operates rationally, and so individual rational subjects *ought* to operate rationally if and only if they can. For instance:

> The rational subject does not simultaneously believe that *p* is true and believe that *not-p* is true; a particular capable rational subject ought not to believe that *p* is true and also believe that *not-p* is true.
>
> The rational subject's confidence in the truth of *p* is proportional to the degree of support that her total evidence provides *p*; a particular capable rational subject's confidence in the truth of *p* ought to be proportional to the degree of support that her total evidence provides *p*.

As I noted above, individual homeostatic systems can operate to maintain themselves in a particular state by means of various mechanisms. But the mechanisms by means of which they operate can themselves have proper functions, and in some environments the proper function of the mechanism can conflict with the proper function of the individual system that operates by means of that mechanism. Consider, for instance, the *Sphex* wasp that Daniel Dennett has made famous (for the sake of making an orthogonal point about agency).[13] Here is the behavioral description quoted from Wooldridge:

> When the time comes for egg laying, the wasp *Sphex* builds a burrow for the purpose and seeks out a cricket which she stings in such a way as to paralyze but not kill it. She drags the cricket into the burrow, lays her eggs alongside, closes the burrow, then flies away, never to return. In due course, the eggs hatch and the wasp grubs feed off the paralyzed cricket, which has not decayed, having been kept in the wasp equivalent of deep freeze … the wasp's routine is to bring the paralyzed cricket to the burrow, leave it on the threshold, go inside to see that all is well, emerge, and then drag the cricket in. If the cricket is moved a few inches away while the wasp is inside

---

[12] Readers familiar with Aristotle's account of 'ergon' will notice a similarity of structure in the account defended here and Aristotle's function argument. See Korsgaard 2008.
[13] Dennett 1984: 11.

making her preliminary inspection, the wasp, on emerging from the burrow, will bring the cricket back to the threshold, but not inside, and will
then repeat the preparatory procedure of entering the burrow to see that
everything is all right. If again the cricket is removed a few inches while
the wasp is inside, once again she will move the cricket up to the threshold
and re-enter the burrow for a final check. The wasp never thinks of pulling
the cricket straight in. On one occasion, this procedure was repeated forty
times, always with the same result.[14]

The *Sphex* wasp feeds its young by dragging a paralyzed cricket into a suitable burrow; so an individual capable *Sphex* wasp *ought* to feed its young
by dragging a paralyzed cricket into a suitable burrow. But the mechanism by means of which the *Sphex* performs this operation is a mechanism
that is designed to ensure that the wasp checks that the burrow is suitable
before dragging the paralyzed cricket from threshold to burrow; and so,
on a particular occasion, the mechanism that operates within a particular wasp *ought* to insure that the wasp checks that the burrow is suitable
before dragging the paralyzed cricket from threshold to burrow. In some
situations, however, the two aforementioned oughts come into conflict:
in particular, when the paralyzed cricket is moved away from the threshold while the wasp is checking the burrow, the proper function ought
to which the mechanism is subject will conflict with the proper function
ought to which the wasp itself is subject. Thankfully for the *Sphex* wasp,
such situations do not arise frequently in its habitat.

Just as the proper function ought governing a mechanism can, in some
situations, conflict with the proper function ought governing the homeostatic system that operates by means of that mechanism, so too the proper
function ought governing a cognitive mechanism can, in some situations,
conflict with the proper function ought governing the rational subject. For
instance, if the machinery by means of which we process conditionals naturally leads us to reason incorrectly about conditionals when performing
the Wason Selection Task, then this would be a case in which the rational
ought would conflict with the proper function ought that governs that con-
ditional-processing machinery. Rational subjects that operate by means of
such machinery are in luck, then, if their wellbeing does not often depend
upon their ability to reason well about material conditionals.

I have described a particular kind of homeostatic system – the rational
subject – as a system that operates rationally, and so as a kind the individuals of which ought to operate rationally if and only if they can. Of course,

---

[14] Wooldridge 1963: 82.

I have said nothing so far about whether there are any individuals of that kind, and, if there are, who they are. But, if there really is a homeostatic system of the kind that I've described and if it is a biological kind, then the individuals that are members of that kind will be essentially members of that kind. That much is true of the individuals of any biological kind of homeostatic system: rabbits are essentially rabbits, lobsters are essentially lobsters, and crabgrass is essentially crabgrass. So, if there is such a kind of homeostatic system as the rational subject, and it is a biological kind, then individual rational subjects will be essentially rational subjects. And so the epistemic oughts that apply to them will apply to them not simply by virtue of a role that they occupy (even necessarily), but by virtue of their essence. The role oughts that apply to born slaves are, in this respect, unlike the epistemic oughts that apply to rational subjects. And we can notice the difference if we compare the oughts listed above as examples of oughts that apply to organisms by virtue of their species to oughts that can apply to those same organisms by virtue of some role into which they might be cast (even as a result of their birth):

> The tiger nurses its young for about three to six months, to give the cubs time to develop their teeth; this particular (normal maternal) tiger ought to nurse its young for at least another month.
>
> Compare the above to: this particular tiger is playing a role in the movie that I'm filming now; he ought to gain about 60 pounds in order to play the role convincingly. (And I bred him and raised him simply in order to have a suitable actor for the role.)
>
> The caterpillar eats host plants like anise, parsley, and carrot; this particular (normal mature) caterpillar ought to be eating anise, parsley, carrot, or other host plants – don't keep feeding it cactus.
>
> Compare the above to: my housecat likes to eat caterpillars; this particular caterpillar ought to get a little closer so that my housecat can get at it. (And I bred this caterpillar simply in order that my cat might eat it.)
>
> Bermudagrass grows under high pine-tree shade; this particular patch of (normal) Bermudagrass ought to have more exposure to sunlight than is available when you pitch the tent over it.
>
> Compare the above to: having a lawn covered with dense Bermudagrass increases your property value; this particular patch of Bermudagrass in my front yard ought to be a bit more densely packed. (And that patch exists only because I grew it there to raise my property value.)

In each of the pairs above, there is a clear difference between the normative force of the ought that applies to the individual organism by virtue
of its species and the ought that applies to it by virtue of some role that it
occupies, perhaps even necessarily. While Feldman was right to claim that
epistemic oughts apply to believers by virtue of their being believers (or,
more to the point, I would say, rational systems), he was wrong to regard
such oughts as role oughts. Such oughts do not apply to rational subjects
by virtue of some role that they might occupy, even necessarily: they apply
to rational subjects by virtue of their essence.

Individual rational subjects who can do so *ought to* think and act in just
the way that the rational subject *does* think and act. Since the rational subject is ideally rational, individual rational subjects who can do so ought to
think and act in the ways that an ideally rational subject thinks and acts.
This implies that epistemic oughts are, as Kornblith says, ideals. If these
ideals are to help guide our cognitive performance, it must be neither trivial
nor impossible to attain them. The avoidance of triviality and impossibil-
ity places some constraint on the content of the epistemic oughts to which
we are subject. But, as the examples of (a), (b), and (c) above illustrated, it
does not place enough of a constraint on that content to rule out all sorts
of arbitrary norms like (c). So what can rule out arbitrary norms like (c)?

To see how we should answer this question, consider an analogous question. Which of the following could be a norm for the circulatory system:

(a′)   Your heart should pump blood at a rate sufficient to nourish and
       oxygenate your cells as quickly as they need to be nourished and
       oxygenated.
(b′)   Your heart should pump blood at a rate of 50–70 beats per minute
       (depending upon age).
(c′)   On weekdays, your heart should pump blood at a rate sufficient to
       nourish and oxygenate your cells as quickly as they need to be nour-
       ished and oxygenated; on weekends, your heart should pump blood
       at a rate of 50–70 beats per minute (depending upon age).

Here again, while (a′) and (b′) are plausible candidates for norms governing the circulatory system, (c′) is not. Why is that? It is because the
goal state that the circulatory system operates to achieve does not vary
with the day of the week. Perhaps the circulatory system does not successfully achieve the goal state it operates to achieve. Perhaps the circulatory system does, in fact, work slightly differently on weekdays and on
weekends: perhaps it is more efficient some days of the week than others.
But these claims don't imply that what goal state the circulatory system is

operating *in order to achieve* varies with the day of the week. It is a reasonable assumption – though of course an empirically defeasible one – that what goal state the circulatory system is operating in order to achieve is invariant with the day of the week.

I propose that we answer our original question about (a), (b), and (c) in analogous manner. The goal state that the rational subject operates to achieve does not vary with the day of the week. Perhaps the rational subject does not successfully achieve the goal state it operates to achieve. Perhaps the rational subject does, in fact, work slightly differently on weekdays and on weekends: perhaps it is more efficient on some days of the week than others. But these claims don't imply that what goal state the rational subject is operating in order to achieve varies with the day of the week. It is a reasonable assumption – though an empirically defeasible one – that what goal state the cognitive system is operating in order to achieve is invariant with the day of the week.

I have given an account of the epistemic ought on which it is a particular kind of proper function ought, a particular kind of ought that applies to us by virtue of our being believers, and a particular kind of regulative ideal. This account seeks to fill the explanatory gaps left by the insights of Wolterstorff, Feldman, and Kornblith. But the key to my account is the idea that the epistemic "ought" is a relation between an individual rational subject, on the one hand, and the kind of homeostatic system of which it is essentially an individual, on the other. My account rests on a highly substantive assumption, namely, that there is a particular biological kind of homeostatic system, the individuals of which operate so as to achieve the goal state of *operating rationally*. I leave it open that there are many such kinds: I leave it open, say, that elephants, tigers, earthworms, and roses are all, unbeknownst to us, rational subjects who reason and communicate in ways presently undetectable by us. I leave it an open question which particular biological species (or genera) are essentially rational subjects. I have also, for now, left it an open epistemic question precisely how we might go about finding an answer to the preceding question. To address that question would require addressing the larger questions: how do we figure out what goal state is essential to a particular kind of homeostatic system, and when an individual organism has that goal state?

5   Conclusion: back to "ought" and "can"

We began by considering whether, in epistemology, "ought" implies "can." Then we offered an account of the epistemic "ought," an account that builds on the insights of earlier views while filling the explanatory lacunae left by those views. But what does our account tell us about the question with which we began: whether, in epistemology, "ought" implies "can"?

On our account, the epistemic "ought" marks a relation between an individual epistemic subject and the operations that the epistemic subject performs in the endeavor to achieve rationality: if kind K performs operation O in order to achieve G, then each individual K who can do so *ought* to O in order to achieve G. But if this is how to understand the epistemic "ought," it follows that a particular rational subject who can do so ought to O if and only if the rational subject (that *type* of homeostatic system) *does* O. In other words, the epistemic "ought" applies to an individual organism only if (i) the corresponding "does" applies to the organism's species, and (ii) the corresponding "can" applies to the individual organism itself. Thus, we can sum up our view in a slogan: what the kind *does* is just what the individuals of that type *ought to do* if and only if they *can*. The epistemic "ought" implies, and is implied by, "does" and "can." Applying this general point to the case of rational subjects: what the rational subject does is just what individual rational subjects ought to do if and only if they can.

Of course, not every member of a species possesses all the capacities that are exercised in the operation of that species: perhaps the individual possesses the capacity in an immature form, or in a disordered or damaged or degraded form, or simply lacks the capacity altogether. Perhaps it is true of such individuals that they ought to have those capacities: the blind cat ought to be able to see, but cannot; the three-legged dog ought to be able to run, but cannot. Even if this is so, however, it does not follow that disabled individuals ought to be able to do just what normally abled individuals ought to do: the cat ought to pounce on the mouse, but not if he is blind; the dog ought to run to fetch the ball, but not if she is lame. Similarly, to the extent that an individual rational subject possesses the capacities that are exercised in *operating rationally*, it is also true to that same extent that she ought to operate rationally. So, to put these pieces together: what makes a particular individual subject to the epistemic "ought" is that she is a normally capable rational subject. It is only by virtue of having the full complement of rational capacities that a creature is subject to the epistemic "ought."

I conclude that the epistemic "ought" does imply "can," but this very same "can" also implies "ought."

CHAPTER 4

Naturalism and norms of inference

Carrie Ichikawa Jenkins

1 Introduction

All of the following (and perhaps other things) are subject to distinct-ively epistemic norms: your beliefs, your credal states, and the inferences you make. Such distinctively epistemic normativity is not[1] to be identified with moral, pragmatic, or any other non-epistemic kind of normativity. A belief, for example, can be highly epistemically justified although it harms one practically and is morally neutral.

This chapter is about epistemic norms of inference. Suppose that a sub-ject S makes a token inference from [P & P→Q] to Q. To focus ideas, I'll take this to be a matter of her transitioning from a belief in the premise to the adoption of a new belief in the conclusion which she now holds on the basis of her belief in the premise (which is retained throughout).[2] This inference (*as distinct from S's belief in the premise and/or conclusion*) is avail-able for distinctively epistemic normative assessment. The inference itself might be described as epistemically good or bad, warranted or unwar-ranted, justified or unjustified, appropriate or inappropriate, correct or incorrect, permissible or impermissible, and so on.

Norms of inference can also be classified by analogy with the more familiar distinction between doxastic and propositional justification with respect to propositions. Roughly speaking, when we say that a subject has a justified belief that *p*, we are attributing doxastic justification. When we say that she has justification to believe that *p*, whether or not she does so,

I am grateful to audiences at the Northern Institute of Philosophy, Brown University, and the University of St Andrews, who provided valuable feedback on earlier versions of this material. I am particularly indebted to Abrol Fairweather, Jonathan Jenkins Ichikawa, Masashi Kasaki, Edwin Mares, Koji Tanaka, and Crispin Wright for comments which led to substantial improvements.

[1] Without serious argument at least.
[2] I don't mean to suggest that all inference must look like this, but it will help to focus on this kind of concrete case.

we are attributing propositional justification. Similarly, when we say that a subject *justifiedly infers* from p to q, we are attributing the analog of doxastic justification. When we say that she has *justification to infer* from p to q, whether or not she does so, we are attributing the analog of propositional justification.

In this chapter I will be considering only the analog of doxastic justification[3] for inferences, and I will be considering only token inferences.

I will talk throughout of epistemically 'solid' inference, stipulating that solidness is to be understood by analogy with the epistemic status of *knowledge*. That is to say, a solid inference is epistemically on a par with a knowledgeable belief: solid inference is to inference as knowledge is to belief. One reason I focus on inferential solidness in this sense is that, like knowledge, it plausibly requires justification *and then some*. Knowledge requires truth as well as doxastic justification (not that truth is the only additional requirement, but it is one of them). Solid inference, by analogy, requires something like *the conclusion's having a sufficiently high probability conditional on the premise(s)*, as well as the inferential analog of doxastic justification. Because solidness is in that respect strictly harder to achieve than mere justification, much of what I say here may be relevant to the project of applying notions of epistemic justification[4] to the case of inference as well. Note that solidness as I am characterizing it does not require that a subject's *beliefs* (in the premise or conclusion or anything else) have any particular epistemic status.[5]

Some inferences plausibly derive their normative status from that of other inferences or beliefs of the subject. For example, on some occasions when I infer in accordance with modus ponens, my inference might be solid at least partly in virtue of my knowledgeable belief in the proposition *Modus ponens is valid*. And when I make a multi-stage inference from p to s via intermediate conclusions q and r, the complex inference plausibly derives its epistemic status at least in part from the epistemic statuses of the constituent inferences from p to q, q to r, and r to s. In this chapter, however, I want to focus attention on the epistemic status of *basic* inferences: that is, inferences whose epistemic status is *not* derived from those

---

[3] Not because I assume it is in any substantive sense *prior* to the analog of propositional justification; merely because it is the topic in which I'm presently interested.

[4] And perhaps other notions, such as warrant, insofar as they are distinct from that of justification.

[5] The characterization leaves open the possibility that in some epistemic situations there may be multiple incompatible solid inferences available to a subject; for example, in some situations it might be that *either* a ponens inference *or* a corresponding tollens inference would be solid if performed. Thanks to Jonathan Jenkins Ichikawa here.

of the subject's other inferences or beliefs.[6] I won't make assumptions as to exactly which inferences are basic for whom; though I will use an example to make things concrete, nothing hangs on the choice of example. I discuss my reasons for thinking that *some* inferences must be basic in section 4 below.

The project of this chapter is to make some first steps towards an interesting, promising, and naturalistically respectable way of understanding the epistemology of basic inference that is compatible with virtue-theoretic approaches to epistemology.[7] The project has two parts. First I outline an interesting, etc. strategy for understanding *what* it is for a basic inference to be solid (i.e. what solidness for basic inferences consists in). Then I outline an interesting, etc. strategy for understanding *how* it is that some basic inferences come to have the positive status of solidness.

My approach here is to consider in the first instance the epistemic status of inferences rather than that of agents who infer. But I will indicate some of the places where I think there may be connections with the epistemic status of agents. In focusing for the most part on the status of inferences rather than that of agents, I do not mean to suggest that one kind of status is conceptually or metaphysically prior to the other. I should emphasize that the project is highly speculative. These thoughts are offered by way of opening a conversation, not by any means attempting to have its last word.

2 Epistemic norms, naturally

Naturalism, for the purposes of this chapter, I will take to be the view that a broadly scientific world-view is correct, and there exists nothing supernatural or otherwise spooky.[8] I won't attempt here to be more precise about what this comes to, although I acknowledge there are many dimensions in which the characterization just given is vague.

---

[6] In this respect, my project is similar to investigations into other kinds of epistemic foundations, such as discussions of basic (non-derived) knowledge, and as such will be of merely hypothetical interest to non-foundationalists. Note that an inference's being basic in my sense is compatible with its epistemic status being derived from that of an agent.

[7] Some components of the view developed are separable from naturalism; for example, blocking Carroll-style regress by appeal to the epistemic status of concepts in the manner described in section 5 below is separable from my naturalistically motivated empiricism concerning that status, and from the naturalistic identification of normative with natural facts described in section 2. Thanks to Edwin Mares for helping me get clear on this.

[8] I say more about 'naturalism' and naturalisms in Jenkins 2013. In particular, I explore some of the ways this term is used that are different from my usage here.

Normativity can raise concerns for naturalists about spookiness or non-naturalness. A naturalist might wonder which part of natural science studies how things should be (as opposed to how they are). This kind of question arises regardless of whether we are talking about the normative status of an agent, a belief, or an inference. If normativity is *not* dealt with by natural science, the worry goes, then perhaps normativity must be regarded as a spooky or non-natural aspect of the world, belief in which is in tension with naturalism. In response to such concerns, one kind of naturalist strategy is to identify target normative facts with uncontroversially natural facts, the idea being that if normative facts are identical with natural ones, then it is unproblematic for naturalists to believe in them.

This is certainly not the only strategy available to naturalists who want to accommodate normativity, but it's the one I'll engage here. Two quick points about this strategy as I'm envisaging it. First, the relevant identity claim is intended in the spirit of locating, rather than doing away with, the relevant normative facts. Second, while identity is a symmetric relation, the kind of identity claim employed by this strategy is offered with an asymmetric purpose in mind: the identification is supposed to demystify the normative, rather than mystify the natural. We are to understand the identity claim by drawing upon our pre-existing grasp on what the natural facts are like as our basis for understanding what the normative facts are like, not the other way around.

Consider again a subject S making a token inference from [P & P→Q] to Q. Let's stipulate that this inference is *basic* and epistemically *solid*. The question I want to address now is: with what kind of natural fact might the normative solidness fact be plausibly identified? I want to suggest that it might be a fact of the following conjunctive form:

(1)   Q is conditionally probable to a degree higher than .n on [P & P→Q] *and*

(2)   S is responsive to (1) in inferring as she does.

If this is correct, one connection with the epistemic assessment of agents who make inferences immediately suggests itself: *responsiveness to (1) is a virtue of an inferring agent.* Three obvious questions about this suggestion: what is n? What is *responsiveness*? And what *kind of probability* is intended?

My response to the first question is that the strategy as I'm outlining it here is schematic, and different values for n are compatible with the approach. In fact, I would be particularly interested in exploring versions of the approach on which the value of n can be determined in part by such things as the subject's circumstances or interests, and versions on which what kind of fact is ascribed by a person describing S's inference as 'solid', including what value of *n* the fact thus ascribed involves, can be determined in part by the speaker's context of utterance.

My response to the second question is similar. The proposal-schema on the table is *consistent* with a strong form of internalism on which responsiveness requires that S must be capable of citing (1) as a reason for making the inference if challenged, although I myself would be more interested in a more externalist version on which responsiveness requires instead a non-deviant explanatory connection (of which S need not be aware) between (1) and S's inferring as she does.[9] Again, variable determination along this dimension by the subject's circumstances and/or the context of evaluative utterance is also an option. The possibilities for understanding *responsiveness* here may be understood as corresponding to choices about what we should count as virtues in an inferring agent.

My response to the third question is by now predictable. Inserting a notion of objective chance will give rise to one version of the proposal, while inserting various notions of subjective probability will give rise to others. And as with the first two questions, contextually variable determination could be in play here too.

It is important to be clear that the strategy described here is a fact-identification strategy and *not* a conceptual analysis strategy, nor a strategy that (directly) engages the question of what epistemically normative words mean. It is not a commitment of the proposed identification of a solidness fact with a natural fact of the form specified in (1)&(2) above that anything like (1)&(2) can be *read off the semantics* of the epistemically normative language. Similarly, it is not a commitment that any epistemically normative *concept* can be analyzed so as to reveal the connection with facts of the form of (1)&(2). The proposed approach is rather in the spirit of a view more familiar from ethics, whereby moral facts may be identified with natural facts without commitment to any corresponding semantic or conceptual reduction. (See, e.g., Sturgeon 1985; Railton 1986; Boyd 1988; Brink 1989.)[10]

A more traditional approach to naturalism about epistemic norms of inference would be one inspired by Quinean naturalism about epistemic norms of belief (see, e.g., Quine 1969, 1986). According to Quine, epistemic normativity is entirely instrumental: epistemology is "the

---

[9] Cf. the externalist account of *knowledge* outlined in Jenkins 2008a: ch. 3.
[10] I sketched how this approach might be applied to epistemic norms of *belief* in Jenkins 2007a.

technology of truth-seeking ... a matter of efficacy for an ulterior end, truth" (1986: 665) and "the normative here, as elsewhere in engineering, becomes descriptive when the terminal parameter is expressed" (664–65).

A Quine-inspired naturalizing strategy for norms of inference might seek to identify the normative fact that an inference is solid with the natural fact that the inference promotes the goal of truth.[11] But I am putting a different strategy on the table, one which identifies the normative fact with a different kind of natural fact. Epistemological naturalism does not *have* to involve Quinean normative instrumentalism; that is to say, it does not have to identify epistemologically normative facts with instrumental facts (facts about what promotes what goals). Identifying epistemically normative facts about inferences with facts of the form of (1)&(2) above avoids this instrumentalism. And avoiding instrumentalism means avoiding problems it engenders; if (for example) one identifies epistemically normative facts as facts about what promotes the goal of truth, then one faces hard questions about the epistemic evaluation of people who *lack* the goal of truth but seem to be epistemically evaluable nevertheless. (See, e.g., Kelly 2003 for discussion of this problem.)

3   An open question argument, and related issues

However, versions of the *Open Question Argument* (OQA) are liable to be raised as objections to the naturalizing strategy under development here. This is a style of argument familiar from ethics, where it appears (initially in Moore 1993) as an objection to the identification of *ethically* normative properties with natural properties. Applied to the strategy of this chapter, an OQA might be formulated as follows:

> *Premise:*   Granting that [the appropriate fact of the form of (1)&(2)] obtains, it is still an open question whether S's inference is solid.
> *Conclusion:*   The (1)&(2) fact is not identical to a normative fact.

A question that must immediately be asked about any OQA is what is meant by the claim that the normative question is "still open" after the relevant natural fact is granted. If the claim in this case is that the question of solidity is "open" in the sense that it does not follow *as a matter of semantic or conceptual analysis* from the obtaining of the (1)&(2) fact that S's inference is solid, then the OQA's conclusion does not follow, since

---

[11] It is not entirely clear whether Quine intends fact-identity claims, and/or any semantic or conceptual theses.

believing in the identity of these facts does not commit one to any corresponding semantic or conceptual claims.

What must be meant by the premise, then, is that settling the (1)&(2) fact *does not settle* the normative fact. But to say that is to beg the question against the view that these facts are identical. An argument is needed; something which just assumes that the identity thesis is mistaken is not dialectically available to be used as a *premise* in an objection to that thesis.

In the light of such considerations, the OQA (here and in other incarnations) might be best regarded trying to pump an intuition: perhaps an intuition to the effect that there just isn't enough normative "oomph" to the natural facts under consideration. For those of us who lack that intuition, however, it is not moving when construed in this light. (And for those who do share it, the question arises of how that intuition should be weighed against other considerations, such as the intuitive appeal of the naturalism which motivates the fact-identity attacked by the OQA. Considering one intuition in isolation doesn't settle matters.)

In my 2007a (§V) I also discussed another style of argument in the vicinity of epistemic OQAs, based on Kornblith's claim that "an account of the source of epistemic norms must explain why it is that I should care about such things" (Kornblith 1993: 363). But I argued that this is not a fair demand to make of an account whose remit is a *metaphysics* of epistemic normativity, and also that the 'should' in Kornblith's demand admits of multiple interpretations (epistemic, pragmatic ...), on any of which the question is committing to questionable presuppositions.

It now seems to me, however, that there are also other issues nearby worth investigating. It may not be fair to expect a metaphysician of epistemic normativity to provide an account that explains *why we should care* about epistemic norms, but the account should at least be consonant with the fact that a lot of people *do* care about them. It is also worthwhile to reflect on why *some but not all* natural facts are identical to epistemically normative facts, and we should expect a metaphysics to cohere with some plausible explanation of this point.[12]

In these two regards, identifying solidness facts with facts of the form (1)&(2) looks quite promising. The view is certainly consonant with the fact that many people care about norms of inference, for people care (whether or not they can articulate this care) about the conditional probability of their own and others' conclusions on their premises, and people

---

[12] Particular thanks to my audience at the Northern Institute of Philosophy for discussion of this issue.

care about their own and others' sensitivity to that kind of probabilistic relationship. This care might in turn be explained as an upshot of the fact that people care about truth and truth-seeking, thus preserving something of the spirit of Quinean naturalism, although epistemic normativity is no longer being treated as a kind of instrumental normativity.

As for why some but not all natural facts are identical with epistemically normative facts, here one might again turn to an explanation in terms of truth and truth-seeking. It may be that what *accounts* for the epistemically normative status of certain natural facts is their relationship to truth and truth-seeking. That is to say, it may be *because* of the epistemically normative status of truth that facts like (1)&(2) get to be epistemically normative while others do not. This explanatory connection, however, does not entail that the epistemically normative facts are themselves instrumental (that is, identical to facts about the promotion of a goal). If it suggests anything, it suggests that the epistemically normative facts are *non-fundamentally* (derivatively) normative and/or that the epistemic value of facts of the form (1)&(2) comes from something *extrinsic* to them.[13] To explain the epistemic value of facts of the form (1)&(2) in terms of these facts' relationship to truth and truth-seeking may be to say something about the explanatory source of their normative status, but it is not to say that they are facts about goals or the promotion of goals.

4   Epistemology of inference

Some inferences are *basic* in the sense that their epistemic status is not derived from that of the subject's other inferences or beliefs. Multi-step inferences composed of smaller inferences plausibly derive their status at least in part from those of the component steps, but it is not (psychologically) plausible that *all* inferences are built out of smaller steps in this way. Perhaps there are other ways for the status of one token inference to depend on that of another (e.g. if one remembers a previously made inference of a similar kind and infers on that basis), but this chain of dependence has to ground out somewhere in an inference whose status does not depend on that of another inference. Call such inferences *semi-basic*. (They are basic as far as dependence on the status of other inferences

---

[13] I am here adapting a version of the distinction between instrumental and extrinsic normativity described by Korsgaard in her 1983. As Korsgaard puts matters, to call some goodness instrumental is to say that it is not valuable or valued "for its own sake or as an end," whereas to call some goodness extrinsic is to say something about the "location or source of the goodness rather than the way we value the thing" (170).

goes, though their status may still depend on that of some of the subject's *beliefs*.)

Problems in the vicinity of the Lewis Carroll regress (Carroll 1895) threaten if basic inferences are not accepted once semi-basic inferences are. Here is a version of the regress tailored for the current setting:

(1) Suppose that a subject S solidly and semi-basically infers from her belief that [P & P→Q] to a new belief that Q.

(2) (Assume for reductio) for this inference to be solid, S must be (at least tacitly) relying on a belief to the effect that Q is conditionally probable to a degree higher than .n on [P & P→Q].

(3) (From (2)) the solidness of S's original inference is a matter of (or derived from) the knowledgeability of this further belief linking premise and conclusion.

(4) But if S is reliant on this additional belief in this way, S is in effect inferring from her belief that [P & P→Q], *together with* her belief to the effect that Q is conditionally probable to a degree higher than .n on [P & P→Q], to the new belief that Q.

(5) And for this inference to be solid S must be (at least tacitly) relying on a belief to the effect that its conclusion is conditionally probable to a degree higher than .n on its premise.

(6) (From (5)) the solidness of this larger inference of S's is a matter of (or derived from) the knowledgeability of this further belief linking its premise and conclusion.

(7) But if S is reliant on this additional belief in this way, S is in effect inferring from her belief that [P & P→Q], her belief to the effect that Q is conditionally probable to a degree higher than .n on [P & P→Q], *and* her belief that Q is conditionally probably to a higher degree than .n on those first two premises, to the new belief that Q.

(8) Etc.

Is this regress vicious? My best guess is that it is. I find it psychologically implausible to attribute infinitely many different beliefs of the kind required to everyone who ever makes a solid semi-basic modus ponens inference. I also have foundationalist intuitions about epistemic status which are incompatible with regarding this sort of regress as virtuous.

The regress is generated by the assumptions that give rise to lines (2)–(4) (and (5)–(7), and so on): that (i) in inferring, S is tacitly relying on a further *belief*; that (ii) this reliance means the *epistemic status* of the inference is a matter of, or derived from, that of the further belief; and that (iii) this means the further belief must be treated as an additional *premise*.

Rejecting any one of these assumptions would be enough to block the regress. But once we allow (i) it is not so easy to see how to block something in the vicinity of (ii) and (iii). The strongest response to the regress requires that we deny (i), and correspondingly (2).

BonJour (in, e.g., his 2005) argues that regresses in this vein can only be blocked by taking the subject at some point to have an *immediate, non-propositional, rational insight* into the acceptability of some inferential move she makes, as opposed to relying on a further *propositional* insight (which is what a belief would be). So BonJour would block the regress by rejecting (i). In some ways, his strategy looks to me to be on the right track. Immediacy seems important, since appealing to a *non*-immediate insight risks reintroducing epistemic regress when we ask upon what the insight is based. And appealing to any additional *propositional* insight risks suggesting that this proposition ought to be added as a premise in S's inference.

That said, it's worth noting that there are alternatives to appealing to non-propositional insight.[14] On such a view as that developed in Wright 2004, a subject may enjoy epistemic warrant to trust in some proposition *p*, without believing *p*, without having any evidence that *p* is true, and without in any sense having 'earned' a warrant to trust that *p*. Building on this thought, one might suggest that in some such cases, where the trusted proposition states a probabilistic connection between two other propositions *q* and *r* (the premise and conclusion respectively in a putative inference), such unearned warrant to trust in *p* can give rise to a corresponding derivative warrant to trust in the inference from *q* to *r*. This strategy would not require the subject to have any *non-propositional* insight, nor indeed would anything non-propositional have to figure in the structure of her epistemic justification at all. There would still be room for maneuver against the thought that the trusted proposition ought to be regarded as an extra *premise* in the original inference: the trusted proposition need not be something the subject believes, for example, and it could be argued that a premise,[15] by contrast, would need to be believed.

However, I am not persuaded that the Wright 2004 position on unearned warrant is viable (for reasons detailed in Jenkins 2007b). And there are further difficult questions facing the development of it sketched above. For example, would any of the propositions in which unwarranted trust is available *have the right form* to play the required role with respect

---

[14] Thanks to Crispin Wright for discussion of this point.
[15] As opposed to a supposition or an assumption.

to the epistemic status of corresponding inferences? And can the purported difference between a premise and a merely trusted proposition do all the required work? On this score, it is worth noting that a version of the regress might be reinstated which works not by claiming that the trusted proposition is in effect an additional premise in the inference, but by claiming that it is an additional *premise or quasi-premise*, where quasi-premises are merely-trusted propositions which play a very similar role in inferences to premises except that they need not be believed by the subject.

In my opinion, the strategy of appealing to a non-propositional insight offers a more promising way to avoid the risks inherent in invoking epistemic reliance on something that looks too much like an additional premise. Thus far, then, I am in favor of BonJour's strategy of appealing to *immediate, non-propositional, rational insights* to block Carroll-style regress: I am on board with regard to both immediacy and non-propositionality. The other two terms in the italicized phrase, however, I am not convinced about.

The word 'insight' suggests a kind of awareness in the subject that does not seem to me to be necessary for blocking the regress. While it is true that at some point S needs to *make an inferential move* from premise to conclusion in a way that is non-propositional and enjoys immediate epistemic status, I don't think there need be anything of which S need be *reflectively aware* in so doing.

And finally, I do not want to say that the immediate non-propositional status that accrues to basic inferential moves must be *rational* (as opposed to *empirical*). BonJour's argument against empiricist options is that "[a]ny purely empirical ingredient [in the justification of an inference] can, after all, always be formulated as an additional empirical premise" (1998: 5). But it is unclear why BonJour thinks there is a difference between empirical and rational 'ingredients' in this regard. What matters is that the justification should be for something non-propositional: that is, what makes it unsuitable to be added as an additional premise. Empirical justification for something non-propositional, such as an inferential move, should still be on the cards.

5 Concept grounding and inference

In this section I'll sketch the outlines of an epistemological account of how some basic inferential moves have the epistemic status of solidity. Consonant with (many forms of) naturalism, this will be an empiricist proposal, and is a development (and application) of some of the core ideas about the epistemology of arithmetical *knowledge* that I sketched in Jenkins 2008a. (Although it is an empiricist proposal, I actually think that is consistent with calling the postulated epistemic status a priori,[16] although this does not much matter in the current context.) I should stress that I don't present this as an account of the *only* way for basic inferential moves to be solid, but as a suggestion about how one possible way might look.

The central ideas are:

(1) Sometimes, one can be *guided* to make an inference by the way one's concepts are. (This is perhaps most easily made plausible in the case of concepts of logical connectives.)

(2) If those concepts are in good standing epistemically (that is, *fit to be trusted* as guides), then provided nothing goes wrong, an inference which is guided by them will, as a result, also be in good standing epistemically.

(3) The epistemic good standing of concepts can be empirically underwritten.

(4) Hence the resultant epistemic good standing of inference can be empirically underwritten.

Let me develop these four thoughts in order. To focus on a concrete instance of (1), let me suggest that sometimes a subject S can be guided in making a modus ponens inference by her concept of the (indicative) conditional.[17] A *concept* in the sense I intend here is a sub-propositional mental representation. In Jenkins 2008a I developed a view on which a subject's concepts may guide her to adopt certain (arithmetical) *beliefs*, and when this goes well the resultant beliefs are in good standing epistemically (in the best case, they amount to knowledge). Here I am suggesting that something similar can work for inference too.

The specific proposal I want to lay out here is that something about S's concept of the conditional guides her to infer from [P & (P→Q)] to Q. I won't here fill in many details of just how concepts manage to play this kind of guiding role; such details presumably go beyond the remit of armchair philosophy in any case. The minimal details I do want to specify are that the guiding relationship is envisaged as causal, but that it will also be subject to further constraints to rule out cases of "deviant" causation. The

---

[16] Cf. Jenkins 2008a: §9.5.

[17] Perhaps other concepts are also doing some guiding work, but the concept of the conditional is at least one key part of what guides S to infer as she does.

best way to specify what these further constraints need to achieve without attempting an inappropriate level of detail may be by way of analogy: the suggestion is that just as in normal cases of perceptual knowledge S's belief is *guided by her experience*, so in certain normal cases of solid inference S's inference is *guided by her concepts*. (NB: to say this much is not yet to make a distinctively empiricist claim about the solidity of these inferences. This part of the view can be shared by non-empiricists.)

The guiding relationship as I envisage it need not be something of which S is reflectively aware, or even capable of becoming aware. S need not (although she *might*) consciously perform an introspective examination of her conditional concept to guide her in making a modus ponens inference. She might alternatively experience the process as at matter of just *thinking about the conditional* and feeling compelled on that basis to infer as she does. Or she might be completely unaware of thinking about anything other than the premise and conclusion of the inference (and maybe, in some cases, even those).

The first part of (2) to unpack is the idea of concepts (sub-propositional mental representations, as opposed to *beliefs*) being in good standing epistemically: that is, fit to be trusted as guides. In Jenkins 2008a I developed the idea of concepts being fit to be trusted as guides with regard to *what to believe*. I suggested that when concepts have that trustworthy status, and we trust them to guide our beliefs, then (provided nothing goes wrong with that process) the beliefs we end up with can count as knowledge. I won't reiterate details of the proposal here, but the core thought is that our concepts are trustworthy guides for us with regard to what to believe when (and only when) they (and the relationships between them) constitute a trustworthy on-board conceptual *map of the world's structure*. Just as I can learn by examining a trustworthy map that the University of British Columbia is west of Simon Fraser University, I can learn by examining a trustworthy conceptual map that (say) all vixens are foxes, or that $2 + 2 = 4$. The trustworthiness of the guide, in both cases, is what accounts for the epistemic good standing of the resultant belief. I described concepts as being *grounded* when they are trustworthy in this way.

Groundedness, thus defined in relation to belief, is the notion of epistemic good standing for concepts that I have worked with to date. The current suggestion, however, is that we extend the core idea of groundedness to cover inference as well. On the envisaged view, as well as guiding one to believe (say) that $2 + 2 = 4$, one's concepts may also guide one to infer (say) according to modus ponens. And just as the good standing or trustworthiness of one's concepts can lead to a *knowledgeable* belief provided nothing goes wrong, so it can lead to a *solid* inference under similarly favorable conditions. I shall hereafter refer to concepts which are trustworthy guides to *inference* as grounded* concepts.

The idea of appealing to grounded* concepts to account for the solidity of inferences is not, so far, distinctively empiricist. It becomes so when we add in parts (3) and (4) of the proposal. My putative epistemology involves what I have elsewhere called an *input step*: sensory input grounds* S's concepts: that is, makes them trustworthy guides with regard to how to infer. S then allows her empirically grounded* concepts to guide her with regard to how to infer. (This may or may not be something of which S is aware.) There is then an output step: so guided, S makes an inference from [P & P→Q] to Q. Crucially for the empiricist element of the proposal, this inference counts as solid precisely because it is made with guidance from empirically grounded* concepts.

The appeal to empirically grounded* concepts as guides to inference is meant to address what I understand to be a lacuna in certain other approaches, of which Boghossian's will serve here as an exemplar. Boghossian has outlined what he calls "a concept-based account of the nature of our *entitlement* to certain very basic inferences"[18] (Boghossian in press: §1). His view is that the availability of such entitlement is to be explained in some way by appealing to the following argument schema (Boghossian 1996: 386; 1997: 348):

(1) If C is to mean what it does, then A has to be valid, for C means whatever logical object in fact makes A valid.
(2) C means what it does. Therefore,
(3) A is valid.

In his 2003a, however, Boghossian says that (1)–(3) is not to be thought of as an inference one can make which justifies (3), but rather as "constitutive" of one's entitlement to accept (3) and trust the inference rule A. He describes (2003a: 26) a view on which one in fact has no positive warrant for trusting the rule, but is "not epistemically blameworthy" in so doing, because one must be disposed to reason according to the rule in order to have thoughts that involve C (that is, in order to possess the concept of C). This can't be the end of the story, however; for all this view tells us so far, it may be epistemically blameworthy *to have such thoughts*, or to

---

[18] I should note, though, that Boghossian probably means something more restrictive by "inference" than I intend here, if the account of inference described in Boghossian in press is supposed to capture what he is discussing in his 1996, 1997, and 2003a.

employ such concepts. It may be that these concepts are defective ones that we cannot employ without "irremediable error" (cf. Field 2006: 85; Boghossian also considers this worry in the later sections of his 2003a). If they are, it is no defense against a charge of being epistemic blameworthy in trusting A that one could not think C-thoughts without doing so.

In Boghossian's subsequent discussion of what he calls "defective" concepts, he proposes that one has warrant to trust in inference A in exactly those cases where we are (as a matter of fact) dealing with a *non-*"defective" concept C. He appears to claim in particular that concepts of one's own "primitive logical constants" are non-defective because one has "no choice" but to employ them and hence adopt any attendant commitments to trust in corresponding inferences. Boghossian here seems to assume some sort of epistemic ought-implies-can principle to generate the epistemic blamelessness he requires. This strategy is open to query, both with regard to whether it is true that one has "no choice" and with regard to whether lack of choice *does* in fact generate epistemic blamelessness (i.e. whether any ought-implies-can principle of the required kind is true). But there is also another problem to which I would like to draw attention here.

Unless there is some underlying difference in our epistemic situation between the defective and the non-defective cases, it is unsatisfying simply to say that when the concepts are non-defective there is no epistemic blame. For it doesn't rule out the possibility that our possession of non-defective concepts has come about in a way that would interfere with epistemic evaluation. It seems that even a concept that one has "no choice" but to employ could be employed for reasons that interfere with its epistemic status, just as someone who voluntarily chooses to kill someone whom they would have been forced to kill had they not so chosen may be subject to moral criticism for performing that action.

If one merely *happens* to have landed upon a concept that is non-defective, however one does it, then by Boghossian's lights one is doing better epistemically than if one had similarly happened to land upon a defective one. But unless more is said, this is at risk of being as philosophically unsatisfying as the claim that if one merely *happens* to land upon a true belief, however one does it, one is doing better epistemically than if one had happened to land upon a false one.

By contrast, empirically grounded* concepts are trustworthy guides to inference because they are sensitive to sensory input. There is nothing accidental about their having this status. This is the respect in which the present story is intended to fill a gap in extant concept-based accounts of the epistemic status of inference: one doesn't merely *happen* upon trustworthy, epistemically valuable concepts if those concepts are grounded*. One has them for the right reasons. Such concepts have their epistemic status because of their responsiveness to empirical input, and the same goes for inferences performed with guidance from them.

It is important to note that an inference which is solid for the reasons sketched in this section can still be *basic* in the sense that its epistemic status is not derived from those of S's other inferences or beliefs. Its status depends on that of S's *concepts*, but that's not the same. Such an inference also need not be mediated in any psychological sense by any of S's other inferences or beliefs.[19] So this sort of proposal promises a new empiricist strategy for blocking Carroll-style regresses of the kind discussed in section 4 above.

6   The metaphysics of inference norms + the epistemology of inference

If everything is going well, our concepts can be expected to guide us towards making inferences that meet the (naturalistically specifiable) conditions for solidness. For if our concepts are grounded* through empirical contact with the natural world, then they are sensitive to how that world really is. It's that sensitivity that explains why they can then be relied upon to guide us to infer in ways that preserve truth (truth being a matter of how the world really is), or at least do so with a high enough probability.

But to say that it is because of empirical contact with the world that we make epistemically respectable inferences, such as modus ponens inferences, is not to say that we *perceive logical structure*, in anything like the sense in which we perceive oranges. That would be an overly simplistic way of describing what is envisaged here.[20] The proposal is rather that *somehow or other* our concepts are sensitive to the world (including perhaps the world's logical structure, if it has any) because the world *affects* us, and our concepts, through experience. This sensitivity may turn out to be best construed holistically: on a holistic picture, the world's structure determines the structure of our experience *in toto*, and the structure of our experience *in toto* renders certain concepts useful for making best sense wholesale of all that experience. In the case of concepts which serve

---

[19] There are, however, ample opportunities for developing stories on which the acquisition of, and/ or responsiveness to guidance from, grounded* concepts count among the epistemic virtues of an agent. The epistemic status of a solid basic inference may consistently be regarded as derived from that of the agent performing it.

[20] Cf. Jenkins 2008a: §5.3.

to guide inference (as on the hypothesis under consideration our conditional concept does), the story then goes: this usefulness is best explained as being (at least partly) due to the fact that the concepts in question guide us towards inferences that preserve truth with sufficiently high probability. Concepts that guide us towards making inferences which do *not* have this quality would not be similarly useful to us.

I say that *if* everything is going well, our concepts can serve as guides to solid inference in this way. I should conclude by making explicit that there are always possibilities of error. We may in some cases rely on concepts which are not in fact grounded*. Or the relevant concepts may be grounded* but we may not be properly guided by them in inferring as we do: we might get distracted, or be misled by other influences. If something like this goes wrong, the resulting inference is not so solid.

But assuming that in general the mere possibility of error is not sufficient to make skepticism appropriate, the fact that things *can* go wrong is consistent with the claim that when they go right we do make solid inferences.

CHAPTER 5

Indirect epistemic teleology explained and defended

David Copp

Many of the epistemic judgments we make are normative. We judge that
we are justified to believe such and such. We judge that a certain belief
is irrational or that another belief is so evidently correct that it would
be irrational to deny it. We judge that certain things are known. These
judgments are normative in much the way that our moral judgments are
normative. When all goes well, and in appropriate circumstances, our epistemic beliefs of these kinds guide our reasoning and guide as well our
assessments of one another's epistemic performance. In a similar way,
when all goes well, and in appropriate circumstances, our moral beliefs
guide our decision-making and guide as well our assessments of one
another's moral performance. Meta-epistemics addresses philosophical
issues that arise in accounting for the normativity of our epistemological
thinking and discourse that are analogous to those that are addressed in
meta-ethics concerning our moral thinking and discourse. These include
familiar issues in metaphysics, philosophy of language, and philosophy of
mind. Suppose we assert, "The widespread belief that global warming is
a hoax is unwarranted." Does the predicate "unwarranted" here ascribe a
property to the belief in the way that the predicate "widespread" ascribes
a property? If so, what is the nature of this property? Is it a natural property? Is it identical or reducible to or constituted by or at least superve-
nient on some more basic naturalistic properties? Perhaps the predicate
does not ascribe a property at all. If not, then what is its semantics? Is the
state of mind of a person who holds that a given belief is unwarranted of
the same kind as the state of mind of someone who judges that the belief
is widespread, or is it of some different kind?

This chapter was presented to the annual meetings of the Pacific Division of the American Philosophical
Association in Seattle, April 2012, and to graduate seminars at San Francisco State University and the
University of California, Davis. I am grateful to the participants for very useful discussion. I am espe-
cially grateful to Kyle Adams, Selim Berker, Abrol Fairweather, Timothy Houk, Michael Hunter, Noel
Joshi-Richards, Adam Morton, Ram Neta, Josh Schechter, Adam Sennet, and Paul Teller.

There is no need to exaggerate the similarities between the philosophical issues in meta-ethics and the philosophical issues in meta-epistemics. For my purposes, it is enough to see that moral judgments and typical epistemic judgments are both normative even if they are perhaps normative in different ways. This provides reason to think it might be fruitful to generalize a meta-ethical theory and to apply the result to the epistemic case (*mutatis mutandis*). To be sure, to give one example, a philosopher who is a non-cognitivist about moral judgment is not thereby forced to accept non-cognitivism about epistemic judgment. But one might reasonably think that a meta-ethical theory would be given some support if it could plausibly be extended to the epistemic case (*mutatis mutandis*) and that such a theory would be undermined at least to some degree if it could not plausibly be extended to the epistemic case. It certainly seems right that a theory that purports to provide a general account of the nature or sources of normativity should apply to the epistemic case as well as the moral case.

In earlier work I have proposed a realist and naturalistic account of normativity that is intended to be fully general (Copp 2009). I call the account, "pluralist teleology." In earlier work, I have applied the account in meta-ethics (Copp 2007). My goal in this chapter is to apply it to the epistemic case. As I will explain, when pluralist teleology is applied in this case, the upshot, given plausible empirical assumptions, is a form of indirect epistemic teleology that I call IET. As should become clear in what follows, although I do not stress this point, IET is a kind of social epistemology. By bringing IET under the umbrella of pluralist teleology, I hope to do several things. First, I hope to provide a new motivation for epistemic instrumentalism. Second, I hope to show that an epistemic instrumentalism that is grounded in pluralist teleology has unexpected resources for addressing some important objections. Third, I hope to make some progress in assessing the plausibility of pluralist teleology. The chapter thus aims to develop the version of indirect epistemic teleology that is supported by pluralist teleology and to explore how it might answer at least some of the more important objections.

In section 1, I lay out the basic ideas of pluralist teleology. In section 2, I explain that IET is the view that results from applying pluralist teleology to the field of epistemic normativity. In section 3, I situate IET in relation to both meta-epistemic issues and issues in normative epistemology. In section 4, I discuss the concept of justification and other epistemic evaluative concepts. In section 5, I consider objections to IET and briefly explore the ability of the theory to respond to the objections. Section 6 is a brief concluding section.

1 Pluralist teleology

According to pluralist teleology, normative facts are facts about solutions to, or ways to ameliorate, certain generic problems faced by human beings in the circumstances they face in their ordinary lives.[1] These are problems that we can better cope with when we subscribe to appropriate systems of norms, so I call them *problems of normative governance*. Since there are more than one problem of this kind, the theory is pluralist. It implies that there are different kinds of reasons and different sources of normative requirement. There are for example epistemic reasons, moral reasons, and practical or prudential reasons. The theory treats each of these different kinds of normative consideration as corresponding to a different problem of normative governance. Let me explain what I mean by a problem of normative governance, first in general terms, and then by means of two examples, the "problem of sociality," and the "epistemic problem."

There is a problem of normative governance just in case there is a state of affairs or set of facts such that, first, other things being equal, these are general facts about the circumstances of human life and about human beings' biological and psychological nature that interfere with or hinder humans' ability to meet their basic needs and to serve their values – no matter what they value, within a wide range of possible things to value – or would so hinder them if they did not subscribe to appropriate norms.[2] Second, humans' ability to cope with this state of affairs is affected by their actions and choices. Third, the state of affairs is better coped with when humans comply with an appropriate system of standards than would otherwise be the case. Situations of this kind are what I call the problems of normative governance. Intuitively, a problem of normative governance is a generic kind of situation that limits our ability to achieve what we value or to get what we need.

The *problem of sociality* is familiar. Human beings need to live in societies in order to meet many of our basic needs and to be in a position to achieve the things we value. Yet there are a variety of familiar causes of discord and conflict which can undermine cooperation and make a society less successful than it otherwise could be at enabling people to pursue what they value with a reasonable prospect of success. This situation qualifies as

---

[1] I explain the theory in Copp 2009. Throughout this section I draw on that paper.
[2] Take it that something is needed by human beings just in case, given the circumstances of human life and the physical and psychological nature of human beings, human beings must have this thing in order to achieve what they value, no matter what they value, within a wide range of possible things to value.

a problem of normative governance in this sense. First, other things being equal, given this situation, unless it is mitigated in some way, members of the society are less able than would otherwise be the case to achieve what they value. Second, our ability to cope with the situation is affected by our actions and choices. We can work together to try to address causes of conflict, for example. Third, our ability to cope with the situation would be enhanced if we subscribed to an appropriate system of standards. Plainly widespread subscription to a moral code can help to ameliorate the problem, provided that the code calls for people to be willing to cooperate, and generally to avoid discord and conflict. To *subscribe* to a norm in the sense I have in mind is roughly to have a general intention to conform to it and also to be disposed to experience a negative emotional response if one fails to conform. Hence, subscription to a moral code, other things equal, would enhance and reinforce any tendency a person already had to live in accord with its requirements. Of course, some moral codes would do better than others at ameliorating the situation.

According to pluralist teleology, roughly, the moral truth is a function of the content of the moral code the currency of which in society would do most to ameliorate the problem of sociality. Call this the *ideal code*. The idea, to a first approximation, is that there is a moral requirement to do something if and only if, and because, the ideal code requires us to do it. And there is moral reason to do something if and only if, and because, the ideal code calls on us to do it. This, in a nutshell, is the account I have called the "society-centered" theory.[3] It says, in effect, that morality is the solution to the problem of equipping people to live comfortably and successfully together in societies.[4] The basic idea was proposed by J. L. Mackie, who remarked that morality is best understood as a "device" needed to solve a "problem" faced by humans because of "certain contingent features of the human condition" (1977: 121). The society-centered theory is intended to explain the normative standing of morality. The ideal code has normative authority insofar as subscription to it helps to ameliorate a problem of normative governance, namely, the problem of sociality.

There is a plurality of problems of normative governance. A problem of normative governance is posed by interference with our ability to achieve what we value, interference that is caused, other things being equal, by

---

[3] Various complications would need to be addressed in a full development of this view. I address some of the complications in Copp 1995: 199–200, 213–45 and 2007: 25–26, 55–150, 203–83.
[4] For details, see Copp 2007, especially the Introduction, and Copp 1995.

certain kinds of generic facts about the circumstances of human life and about our biological and psychological nature. Problems of normative governance are distinguished on the basis of the different kinds of facts that interfere with our ability to achieve what we value and also on the basis of the kinds of ameliorative strategies that are available.

Pluralist teleology holds that the existence of normative facts is due to the existence of problems of normative governance. It is due to the fact that certain generic problems faced by human beings interfere with our ability to meet our basic needs and to achieve what we value. We need to subscribe to appropriate norms in order to alleviate these problems. The nature of the normative facts depends, roughly, on the content of the norms subscription to which would do most to alleviate the problems. Pluralist teleology says, then, that the nature of the normative *epistemic* facts depends, roughly, on the content of the set of norms subscription to which by believers would do most to alleviate the *epistemic* problem.

2   Indirect epistemic teleology

I turn, then, to the *epistemic problem*. To achieve what we value and to meet our needs, we need *information*. The problem is that our untutored processes of belief-formation are not in general reliable in all the circumstances where we need them to be, given the kind of things we value and need. According to pluralist teleology, roughly, the truth of normative epistemological claims depends on the content of the set of epistemic standards such that people's generally subscribing to it would do most to ameliorate the epistemic problem. This, in brief, and to a first approximation, is the view I call indirect epistemic teleology. It says, crudely, that the "point" of epistemological evaluation is to help to ameliorate a problem we face in achieving what we value and meeting our needs due to our need for information. Let me explain.

The *truth* of our beliefs is not precisely what is at issue. When I write of "information" regarding a subject matter, I mean to refer to beliefs that are sufficiently accurate given our interests. For example, I do not have any interest in knowing *precisely* what time it is. For most purposes, it would be sufficient to have a belief about the time that is accurate to within plus or minus five minutes. I will describe such a belief as "information." The epistemic problem arises because, to achieve what we value and to meet our needs, we need *relevant information*, beliefs about matters that are relevant to achieving our values and meeting our needs that are

sufficiently accurate to enable us to do as well as we can in the circumstances to achieve our values and meet our needs. What we need are *needs-
and-values-relevant beliefs that are sufficiently accurate*.

The epistemic problem, then, is basically that our untutored processes
of belief-formation are not in general reliable at providing us with sufficiently accurate needs-and-values-relevant beliefs. The accuracy of a person's beliefs depends in large part on the epistemic standards the person
subscribes to. An *epistemic standard* is a norm regarding the circumstances
in which to form, retain, modify, or question a belief. Examples are the
norm, Trust your senses other things being equal, and the norm, Trust
your memory other things being equal. To subscribe to such a standard
is, roughly and inter alia, to be disposed to reason in accord with it or to
form or maintain beliefs in accord with it. So understood, subscription
need not involve awareness of the standard or of how it might be formulated, for it is a matter of one's dispositions. Subscription to some epistemic standards would serve us better than subscription to others. Ideally,
a person's processes of belief-formation would be regulated by the set of
standards, subscription to which by the person would do *most* to ensure or
enhance the likelihood that she will have sufficiently accurate needs-and-
values-relevant beliefs.[5] We can think of this as the *optimal* set of epistemic
standards.

It is important that problems of normative governance are *generic* problems. They are problems of a general kind faced by people in general. For
instance, although the specific form that the problem of sociality takes in a
given society might differ from the form it takes in a different society, both
societies face the same generic problem. Again, some people might value
things that do not require cooperation. Someone might value chaos, for
example. Yet it remains the case that there is a generic problem for human
beings.[6] Similarly, the epistemic problem is a generic problem. This will be
important in what follows because it underwrites a constraint on the content of the optimal set, the "generic solution constraint." It means that the
content of the optimal set is not tailored to the special talents or difficulties of specific people in specific circumstances. More generally, the optimal set of epistemic norms is to be a set of norms subscription to which
by human beings in general in the ordinary circumstances of human life

---

[5] That is, subscription to the standards must do more than subscription to any alternatives would do,
or do at least as much. I simplify by ignoring certain obvious complications. See note 3 above.
[6] Similarly, our vulnerability to disease is a generic problem for human beings even though some people are immune to specific diseases.

would do most to alleviate the generic epistemic problem.[7] Accordingly, it also means that the optimal set is a set of norms that can form the epistemic culture of a society. Let me explain.

People come to subscribe to epistemic standards as a result of the influence of parents, peers, and teachers. We learn from others and teach others, and what we learn and teach implicitly includes epistemic standards as well as substantive propositions. In typical cases, individuals come to subscribe to the standards of the local culture. Ideally, then, the local epistemic culture would be such that the influence of our parents, peers, and teachers brings us to subscribe to the *optimal* standards. In the ideal case, the local epistemic culture would *include* the optimal set of standards for individuals. (Indeed from this point forward I will often not distinguish between the optimal epistemic culture and the optimal set of epistemic standards.) There is the further point that much, if not most, of what we know or believe about the world either has been taught us by others, or has been learned by us in a way that depended on using what we have learned from others. We are taught the local language; we learn to read; we are provided with books; our parents teach us various things. The accuracy of what we learn from these sources depends at least in part on the nature of the epistemic standards with currency in the local culture, for the nature of these standards affects what is taken to be known in the local culture. The optimal epistemic culture would then be the set of epistemic standards such that general subscription to them would do most to ensure or enhance the likelihood that what is locally believed about the matters about which we need information is sufficiently accurate. It would include what I earlier described as the optimal set of epistemic standards. It presumably would also include standards for evaluating other people's epistemic performance and it might include standards providing for an epistemic division of labor, as I will now explain.

It might be optimal for the epistemic culture to include norms aimed at people in specialized roles.[8] For instance, scientists and engineers and judges presumably ideally would regulate their professional work by standards that they set aside in their more ordinary activities, such as deciding

---

[7] In effect, then, the optimal set of norms is defined relative to the set of worlds that are relevantly similar to the actual world. Say that the "realistic possible worlds" are the worlds in which the laws of nature are as they actually are and in which the general facts about human psychology and cognitive capacities are as they actually are. Say that a set of norms is "robustly optimal" just in case its currency in the epistemic culture would do as well as the currency of any other at enabling humans to cope with the epistemic problem in all realistic possible worlds. I ignore this complication in the text. See Henderson and Horgan, 2001.

[8] I thank Ram Neta for helpful discussion of the ideas in this paragraph.

which cereal to purchase. Parents might ideally apply different epistemic standards in evaluating their children's thinking than in evaluating the thinking of other adults. The optimal epistemic culture plausibly would include norms for the regulation of belief-formation in certain kinds of activity that would not optimally regulate belief-formation in other kinds of activity. Scientists ideally would be socialized into the optimal epistemic norms that apply specifically to scientific investigation, but those who are not scientists presumably would have no need to learn such norms. A randomly chosen person presumably would not subscribe to every norm in the optimal culture.

The content of the optimal set of epistemic norms is an empirical matter. It depends on which set of norms is such that people's generally subscribing to it would do most to alleviate the epistemic problem. But there are certain constraints on the content of the optimal set that are grounded in the nature of the epistemic problem and in the nature of problems of normative governance more generally. I have already mentioned the generality constraint, but there is also the "learnability constraint." The norms in the optimal set must be norms that people would be capable of internalizing and conforming to, and, because of this, general human cognitive and psychological limitations constrain their content. They cannot be so complex or numerous that people with ordinary cognitive capacities would be incapable of internalizing them or conforming to them. They must be norms that can be learned by people in the ordinary way. This is the learnability constraint. There may be additional constraints of this kind.

The view that emerges, then, when we apply pluralist teleology to the epistemic case, is a kind of epistemic teleology. According to this view, the truth of normative epistemological claims depends on the content of the optimal set of epistemic standards, the set of standards, general subscription to which would do most to alleviate the epistemic problem. It also depends on the content of the epistemic concepts, such as the concepts of knowledge and justification, and on how these concepts can best be explained in terms of the optimal epistemic standards. I will illustrate this point in sections 4 and 5, where I discuss the concept of justified belief.

3 Locating indirect epistemic teleology

Pluralist teleology therefore leads me to IET, the kind of indirect epistemic teleology that I will be defending. IET is a *meta-epistemic* theory. It is not a rival to virtue epistemology or to deontological or evidentialist accounts of justification. It is compatible with various proposals about the analysis of justified belief and about the epistemic virtues. In the first instance, the important thing about IET is that it offers a cognitivist, realist, and naturalist account of normative epistemological judgment.

The theory is a kind of *indirect* epistemic teleology. It offers a teleological account of the justification of epistemic norms or standards, but the standards that are thereby justified might not be teleological in content. Their content is an empirical issue; it turns on the nature of the standards that would be included in the optimal epistemic culture. But it seems unlikely that these standards would evaluate beliefs on an instrumental basis. The standards that meet the teleological test could turn out to apply in the first instance to intellectual dispositions or habits or styles of reasoning, and if so the theory would support a kind of virtue epistemology. Alternatively, the standards that meet the test could support evidentialism, or some other non-virtue-theoretic approach. The theory does not deal directly with such issues.

IET is structurally analogous to a kind of rule-consequentialism in ethics. Insofar as the object of moral appraisal is people's actions, rule-consequentialism can be counted as *indirect* since the moral status of actions in such a theory is only indirectly based on consequentialist considerations; rule-consequentialism assigns a normative status to actions on the basis of whether they are in accord with moral standards that meet a relevant consequentialist test.[9] Similarly, in IET, it is epistemic standards that are appraised teleologically, not our specific beliefs or our specific styles of reasoning. The epistemic status of beliefs or intellectual dispositions or styles of reasoning is assessed on the basis of whether they are in accord with a set of standards that meets the relevant teleological test.

IET is intended in the first instance as a theory of epistemic normativity. If we are naturalists, it might seem puzzling how it could be that we *ought* to reason in certain ways or that we have *reason* to have certain beliefs. Pluralist teleology is intended to explain how normativity fits into the natural world (Copp 2009). It says that normative facts are facts about solutions to or ways to ameliorate problems of normative governance. Intuitively, the view is that normative facts are analogous to engineering facts. This approach to explaining epistemic normativity differs from two more familiar strategies that naturalists have proposed.

---

[9] Rule-consequentialism is ordinarily classified as a normative ethical theory rather than as a meta-ethical theory. But for reasons I cannot here attempt to explain, I think it is most plausible when formulated as a kind of meta-ethical view.

One strategy argues that we have practical (or "pragmatic") reason to value true belief, whatever else we might value, because we need true belief to enable us to pursue our goals effectively (Kornblith 1993: 372–73; Kornblith 2002: 156). Such an account is intended to show, without invoking anything "mysterious," that everyone has reason to value truth, whatever else she values. This strategy bears a family resemblance to the approach I am proposing, and it may well be true that everyone has practical reason to value true belief. But I believe that we need to explain the normativity of standards of practical reason just as much as the normativity of morality and the normativity of epistemology. IET does not rest the normativity of epistemic standards on the claim that we have practical reason to value true belief nor does it aim to reduce the normativity of epistemology to the normativity of practical reason. Instead, it rests the normativity of epistemic standards on the general account provided by pluralist teleology together with an account of the epistemic problem. Similarly, pluralist teleology aims to account for the normativity of standards of practical reason by invoking an account of a relevant problem of normative governance (Copp 2009).

A different strategy proposes a kind of "proper functionalism."[10] It sees our cognitive system as a natural functional system with the function, roughly, of leading us reliably to form true beliefs. The strategy rests on the claim that the human cognitive system was selected for in the evolutionary development of the species on account of its having had the property of leading humans reliably to form true beliefs. It holds that the *good* of a functional system is a matter of its functioning well. So if the natural function of our cognitive system is to lead us reliably to form true belief, then the system functions well and is good to the extent that it leads us reliably to form true beliefs. I reject this strategy because, it seems to me, the issue whether a given process of belief-formation is epistemically appropriate is independent of the details of the evolutionary development of our species. Perhaps human beings popped suddenly into existence, out of thin air. According to IET, nothing turns on whether this is so. Nothing in epistemology turns on whether our cognitive system is the way it is due to its having been selected for. To me, this seems the correct way to approach epistemology.

[10] We find this idea or close cousins of it in Velleman 2000, Neta 2007, and Graham 2012a.

4 Justified belief: a proposal

To derive any normative epistemological claims from IET, one must make empirical assumptions regarding the content of the optimal set of epistemic standards and one must also make assumptions about the content of epistemic concepts. The theory as such is neutral on these points. It would not be a straightforward matter to take IET and devise on its basis an analysis of the epistemic evaluative concepts. I believe that the theory is nevertheless of interest to normative epistemologists because it supports certain constraints on the content of the optimal set of standards, including the generic solution constraint and the learnability constraint, and these constraints have normative import. I will illustrate this point by discussing the concept of justified belief in this and the next sections of the chapter.

Given IET, it would be natural to propose that a belief is justified just in case it was formed or maintained in conformity with the relevant optimal epistemic standards. This account is similar to the "two-stage" reliabilism that has been proposed by Alvin Goldman (1992 and 2001). In Goldman's theory, considerations of truth-conduciveness enter into the selection of the "right" set of epistemic norms, where, as Goldman (2011) states the view, a belief is justified "if and only if it is arrived at (or maintained) in conformity with the right set of norms." Yet there are complications. For one thing, there is the possibility that two or more sets of epistemic standards could turn out to be tied for the role of being best suited to ameliorating the epistemic problem. For another thing, the optimal set of epistemic standards might contain importantly different kinds of standards. As I will explain, we can distinguish between the optimal set of J-relevant epistemic standards and the optimal set of the remaining standards. I will suggest that justified belief is to be understood in terms of the optimal set of J-relevant standards. Finally, there are a variety of epistemic evaluative concepts, including the concepts of fruitful belief, appropriate belief, and virtuous belief, which need to be distinguished from the concept of justified belief.

It is important, moreover, to understand the ways in which IET differs from Goldman's reliabilism. First, and most obviously, whereas reliabilism aims to provide an account of justified belief, IET is a meta-epistemic theory that aims to provide a framework for devising an account of justified belief along with accounts of other evaluative epistemic notions. IET as such is not committed to any particular analysis of justified belief. Second,

Goldman's "two-stage" reliabilism is similar to IET in that it proposes a teleological test for evaluating proposed epistemic standards or norms and directly appraises items of this kind rather than epistemic processes or methods. Yet IET differs from Goldman's approach in that it supports the two-stage view by embedding it in an overall theory of normative judgment. Third, in reliabilism, the criterion relevant to epistemic appraisal is the goal of believing truly and avoiding false belief. In Goldman's two-stage view, the goal is truth-conduciveness. According to IET, however, the optimal epistemic standards are those, subscription to which in the ordinary circumstances of human life would do most to enable humans to ameliorate or solve the epistemic problem. Truth as such is not directly relevant. The important point is that one's own needs-and-values-relevant beliefs and the local needs-and-values-relevant stock of beliefs be sufficiently accurate to enable one to do as well as can be at achieving what one values and meeting one's needs.

This being understood, it will be useful to consider here a version of Goldman's account of justified belief. I think that an examination of a view like Goldman's in the context of IET will support my view that IET offers a fruitful way to think about epistemic issues. I begin with the following proposal, which is based on Goldman's work (see Goldman 2011): A belief is justified if and only if it is arrived at (or maintained) in conformity with the optimal set of epistemic norms. But this is only an initial preliminary account.

The account needs to be "rigidified." Imagine a world where an evil genius causes our senses to be systematically misleading. People in this world arguably are still justified to trust their senses, but the norm calling on us to trust our senses arguably would not be optimal by the standards of IET because subscribing to it in the evil genius world would lead us systematically to have false beliefs. Goldman (2011) suggests that this challenge can be solved if we say that "the right system of epistemic norms is made right in virtue of facts and regularities obtaining in the actual world." Call this the "rigidifying move." The rigidifying move is completely natural, given IET. For IET says that the normative epistemic facts are determined by the content of the optimal set of epistemic norms. And facts about the actual world determine which set of norms is (actually) optimal. Moreover, according to IET, the (actually) optimal set of norms is the set relative to which one is to assess the truth value of normative epistemic propositions. We evaluate epistemic practices in all possible worlds, considered as hypothetical or counterfactual possibilities, relative

to the actually optimal set of norms. So epistemic claims, including counterfactual and modal claims, are evaluated relative to the actually optimal
set of epistemic norms. In general, an epistemic claim that is made in a
given context is evaluated relative to the set of epistemic norms that is
optimal in that context. Obviously the claims *we* make are made in the
actual world, so they are to be evaluated relative to the set of epistemic
norms that is *actually* optimal. Given this, IET implies that if the actually optimal set of epistemic standards includes the standard, Trust your
senses, then even if there were an evil genius, people would still be justified to trust their senses.[11]

The optimal set of epistemic norms includes importantly different
kinds of norms. We can distinguish between what I will call "J-relevant
norms" and the remaining norms or "R norms," where I will argue that
the R norms are not relevant to the justification of belief. Once I explain
this distinction, it will be obvious that we need to amend the preliminary
account accordingly. I propose that a belief is justified if and only if it is
arrived at (or maintained) in conformity with the optimal set of *J-relevant*
epistemic norms. Call this "the Proposal."

A norm is a J-relevant norm just in case both (a) it requires or permits
forming or maintaining beliefs under certain conditions, where a believer
can in principle be in the position of attending to the norm and assessing whether the norm permits or requires the belief, and (b) its formulation does not use or invoke any normative epistemic notions. Here are
four examples. Reason in accord with the rules of logic. Trust your senses,
other things being equal. Trust the testimony of others, other things being
equal. Believe whatever is generally believed in your society, other things
being equal. Let me assume for the sake of argument that these norms
are included in the optimal set. There might also be a norm, Treat other
things as equal with respect to any epistemic norm N unless you are in
circumstances where some norm you accept calls on you not to believe in
accord with N. So if there is conflict between the evidence of your senses
and something that is generally believed in your society, other things are
not relevantly equal. This means that the rule to trust your senses permits a driver to decide it's not the case that there is a lake ahead, even if
it looks to her that there is one, if it is widely believed that there are no
lakes in the area. (Perhaps she is driving in a desert.) These norms are all
J-relevant under my characterization. And the Proposal says that justified

---

[11] I have used a rigidifying move in formulating the truth conditions for moral claims. See Copp
2007: ch. 4.

beliefs are ones that believers form or maintain in conformity with optimal J-relevant norms.

The remaining optimal epistemic norms, the R norms, do not figure in our account of justified belief. There are at least two kinds of R norm. First, there are norms that, if they are optimal, undergird truths about the epistemic virtues. Second, there are norms that, if optimal, undergird truths about epistemically appropriate or useful beliefs as contrasted with epistemically justified beliefs.[12] Some R norms of both of these kinds use the concept of justified belief, and for this reason could not figure in our account of justified belief, not even if they are included in the optimal set. Other R norms are such that believers cannot use them to assess whether to continue to believe as they do. An example might be the norm, Believe only the truth. Even if norms of this kind are in the optimal set, they are not J-relevant.

First are R norms that concern or assess believers' cognitively relevant dispositions or attitudes to reasoning or belief-formation. For example, there is a norm that calls on people to be disposed to reason in accord with the rules of logic. If this norm is in the optimal set, then being logical is an epistemic virtue. It might similarly be an epistemic virtue to trust the testimony of others, other things being equal, to be epistemically careful and conscientious, and to have justified beliefs – to believe in conformity with the optimal set of J-relevant norms. It is plausible that the desire for the truth is fundamental to epistemic virtue (Montmarquet 1993), and it is similarly plausible that a norm calling on us to desire the truth would be included in the optimal set of epistemic norms. By taking these ideas on board, IET can explain the truth conditions of judgments about the epistemic virtues.

Second are R norms that might undergird truths about epistemically appropriate or useful belief. Consider, for example, the norm, Children are to believe what children at their stage of cognitive development would standardly believe even if such beliefs are not justified. Or consider the norm, Parents are to trust the testimony of their children more than they would be justified to. A third example might be the norm, People are to be more confident of their talents than they are justified to be. A fourth might call on scientists to follow the norms of scientific investigation but to be reluctant to give up their theories even if they would be justified to do so.[13] If these norms are in the optimal set, then it is appropriate for

---

[12] I thank Josh Schechter and Ram Neta for helping me with these issues.
[13] These examples were suggested by Ram Neta in conversation.

children to have rather naïve beliefs, for parents to trust the honesty of their children, for people to be excessively confident, and for scientists to be somewhat stubborn in holding on to their theories. None of this means that such beliefs are justified, however, for the norms in question are not J-relevant. For example, consider the norm, Be more confident of your talents than you are justified to be. This is not a J-relevant norm because it uses the concept of justified belief, and moreover believers cannot use it to assess whether to continue to believe as they do. Norms of this kind may be in the optimal set, but they are not J-relevant.[14]

I should mention as well that we need to distinguish between the notion of justified belief and the notion of epistemically faultless belief. Consider, for example, the epistemic culture in medieval Europe, which, let us say, required people to believe what was written in the Bible. People in medieval Europe who formed and maintained their beliefs in conformity with their epistemic culture surely were epistemically blameless for believing what nearly everyone else believed and for reasoning in conformity with the norms that they learned from their parents and teachers. Yet these norms presumably were not optimal. The important point is that people who form or maintain their beliefs in accord with the local epistemic culture in cases of this kind may be epistemically faultless.[15] Justified beliefs are beliefs justified in terms of the optimal J-relevant standards. My Proposal is an account of justified belief rather than of faultless belief. Perhaps faultless beliefs are beliefs that are formed and maintained in a way that does not depend on any epistemic vice, but I am uncertain how to analyze faultless belief.

My proposed account implies that the J-relevant norms are such that, in principle, a person can be in the position of attending to the norms and assessing whether they permit her to continue to believe as she does. This applies even in simple cases of perceptual beliefs. Suppose I open my eyes and see right away that the orange tree is in blossom. Obviously I didn't arrive at my belief as a result of any process of reasoning that involved my attending to any norm. However, there is a J-relevant norm, Trust your senses other things being equal, and we are assuming that this norm is in the optimal set. I could in principle be in a position to attend to the norm and to decide whether it permits me to continue to believe that the tree is in blossom. If the norm does permit me to continue to believe this, then if

---

[14] The examples suggest that the optimal epistemic culture might provide for a division of epistemic labor. I mentioned this possibility before.

[15] Goldman (1988) distinguishes between "strongly" and "weakly" justified belief, where weakly justified beliefs are epistemically faultless even if not strongly justified.

other things are equal, the belief is justified according to the Proposal. For I have trusted my senses as the norm requires and maintained the belief accordingly. As we might say, the belief is maintained in *conformity* with the set of optimal internal epistemic norms.[16] Of course, my proposed account does not require that I must *actually* be aware of or attend to the norms or *actually* be in a position to assess whether they permit me to continue to believe as I do. My belief might be justified even if I am not aware of any relevant epistemic norms so that I am not actually in a position to assess whether I am permitted to continue to have the belief in light of such norms.

5　Objections and replies

In this section, I will consider a few objections to my Proposal about justified belief. Objections of this kind are not objections to IET as such since IET as such is not committed to the Proposal. The objections do however raise worries about IET to the extent that the proposal seems to be well motivated in light of the basic approach of IET. We will see that in many cases IET offers a natural way to deal with the objections.

Perhaps the most familiar problem with process reliabilism is the generality problem. There is a range of J-relevant norms of different degrees of generality. Trust your eyes. Trust your eyes on Tuesday. Trust your senses. Trust your senses except your sense of touch. What is the relevant degree of generality for the J-relevant norms in the optimal set? The *learnability constraint* can be invoked to answer this question. Human cognitive and psychological limitations constrain the content of the optimal norms. They must be norms that can be learned by people in the ordinary way. They cannot be so complex or numerous that people with ordinary cognitive capacities would be incapable of internalizing them.

Some epistemologists have wanted to explain why it is epistemically more valuable to have justified true belief than merely to have true belief.[17] True belief would do as well at enabling us to serve our values and meet our needs as true justified belief, and, after all, the epistemic problem is of interest because it is a problem for our ability to serve our values and meet

---

[16] To believe in conformity with a norm is not simply to believe what the norm calls on one to believe. In the example, I trust my senses and this explains why I believe that the tree is in blossom. I don't here offer an analysis of believing in conformity with a norm. However, plainly, one who believes what a norm in the optimal set requires her to believe but believes it on the basis that her Ouija board says to believe it would not count as believing in *conformity with the norm*.

[17] See Pritchard 2007, cited in Greco and Turri 2011.

our needs. Note, however, that justified beliefs are formed and maintained in conformity with norms that tend to lead us to have beliefs about needs-and-values-relevant matters that are sufficiently accurate to enable us to do as well as we can in the circumstances to achieve our values and meet our needs. Because of this, it seems plausible that a norm calling on us to have justified beliefs would be in the optimal set. If this is right, then according to IET, it is epistemically virtuous to have justified beliefs. A person who has *justified* beliefs exhibits more in the way of epistemic virtue than one who merely has true beliefs (see Greco and Turri 2011).

The *generic solution constraint* and the *rigidifying move* can be invoked to answer the Mr. Truetemp objection, which is due to Keith Lehrer (1990). Truetemp has a device installed in his head that causes him to have accurate beliefs about the local air temperature. Truetemp knows nothing about this device, so, from his point of view, his beliefs about the temperature seem to pop up with no obvious explanation. The worry is that these beliefs might count as justified even if Truetemp has not tested their accuracy. According to my Proposal, however, beliefs are justified only if they are formed or maintained in conformity with the optimal set of J-relevant norms, and it is implausible that this set includes a norm that says to believe whatever pops into your head. One might respond that the optimal set of norms *for Mr Truetemp* would include a norm that says to believe any proposition *about the temperature* that pops into your head.[18] The generic solution constraint rules out this response, however, because it says the optimal set is not tailored to the special talents of specific people in specific circumstances.[19] Also, the rigidifying move says that epistemic claims are to be evaluated relative to the *actually* optimal set of epistemic norms. The actually optimal set of norms would not include a norm that says to believe any proposition about the temperature that pops into your head.

The bootstrapping problem is a challenge for versions of reliabilism that take a belief to be justified if it is produced by a reliable process (see Vogel 2000; Cohen 2002; Fumerton 2008). Bootstrapping of this kind is not a problem for my Proposal because my Proposal does *not* say that a belief is justified if it is produced by a reliable process. It says that a belief is justified if and only if it is arrived at or maintained in conformity with the optimal set of J-relevant norms. Nevertheless, as Ram Neta has shown me,

---

[18] I owe this objection to Selim Berker, personal correspondence.
[19] This is not to deny that Truetemp could learn that beliefs about the temperature that pop into his head tend to be highly accurate. In this case he could be justified by ordinary induction in relying on his intuitions about the temperature.

a version of the bootstrapping problem does arise for the Proposal.[20] Neta proposed the following example: suppose that, relying on her memory, Hilary believes that (1) Lincoln was assassinated in 1865. Her belief plausibly is justified according to the Proposal, assuming that the optimal set of J-relevant norms includes a norm permitting us to trust our memory, other things being equal. Hilary also believes that (2) she remembers that Lincoln was assassinated in 1865. The Proposal may also imply that this belief is justified, for we can assume that a norm permitting us to trust introspection is included in the optimal set. Now Hilary infers from (1) and (2) that (3) her memory is reliable on this occasion, and this belief will presumably also count as justified since she sees that it follows from beliefs (1) and (2). The problem is that Hilary has no independent evidence of the reliability of her memory. She is invoking her belief that Lincoln was assassinated in 1865 to check her memory but her only reason to believe that he was assassinated in 1865 is her memory. One cannot justify a belief that one's memory is reliable simply by relying on one's memory.

I think that we *are* typically justified to believe that our memory is reliable other things being equal. But Neta's bootstrapping argument does not account for this. What accounts for it is that the norm, Trust your memory other things being equal, is plausibly in the optimal set of J-relevant norms, and, at least typically, the belief that one's memory is reliable other things being equal would be in conformity with this norm. To believe what one's memory tells one, other things being equal, is to believe in conformity with the norm, for so to believe is to trust one's memory. And to believe that one's memory is reliable other things being equal is *also* to believe in conformity with the norm, for to believe this is to believe that one can trust one's memory, other things being equal. So if Hilary has a belief about her memory's reliability, then if she trusts her memory, she must believe her memory is reliable, other things being equal. If this is right, then on the Proposal, the belief that one's memory is reliable other things being equal would typically be justified, but not on the basis of bootstrapping.[21]

The claim here is that the *default* is that we are justified to believe that our memory is reliable other things being equal. Similarly, the default is that we are justified to believe that our senses are reliable other things

<hr/>

[20] In personal correspondence.
[21] Hence the Proposal is not subject to Fumerton's worry about views that would justify the legitimacy of a kind of reasoning by using that very kind of reasoning. See Fumerton 2008: 405. It also avoids Vogel's objection that if reliabilism rejects bootstrapping as illicit then it cannot answer Cartesian skepticism. See Vogel 2000: 618–19.

being equal. This does not mean that Hilary can use Neta's bootstrapping argument to defend her memory if her memory is challenged. If Hilary comes across evidence that Lincoln was not assassinated in 1865, "other things are not equal." So in face of the evidence, even if Hilary has a memory that Lincoln was assassinated in 1865, she presumably would not be justified to believe this. In short, the Proposal is not subject to the bootstrapping objection. One might object of course to the idea that we are default justified to believe that our memory is reliable, or that our senses are reliable, but that is another matter.

The final objection I shall consider is due to Selim Berker.[22] He calls it the objection from the "separateness of propositions." IET takes the justification of a given belief to be determined by the content of a set of norms subscription to which is instrumental to our having sufficiently accurate needs-and-values-relevant beliefs. The problem is that there apparently can be a set of norms, subscription to which would contribute to this outcome due to factors that are intuitively completely irrelevant to whether beliefs held in conformity to the norms are justified.

First is the useful belief problem. For an arbitrary proposition <p>, there may be possible circumstances in which believing that <p> would contribute causally to the relevant outcome such that the norm, Believe that <p>, plausibly would be included in the optimal set of J-relevant norms. But then the belief that <p> apparently would count as justified by the Proposal even though intuitively it might seem completely unjustified. Imagine that heart-destroyer is a highly dangerous stress-related disease such that one's chance of surviving it, and of going on to acquire a useful stock of sufficiently accurate needs-and-values-relevant beliefs, is significantly enhanced if one is completely confident that one will survive. In this circumstance, the set of optimal norms plausibly would include the norm, If you get heart-destroyer be completely confident that you will survive. But then, according to the Proposal, one would be justified to believe that one will survive heart-destroyer regardless of the medical circumstances, simply because the optimal norms require one to have this belief.[23]

Second is the bogus norm problem. There might be an epistemic norm N such that subscription to it contributes to the relevant outcome for reasons that have nothing intuitively to do with whether what one believes, when believing in conformity with N, is justified. For example, consider

---

[22] Berker 2013 and Berker unpublished manuscript. In presenting Berker's arguments, I draw on personal correspondence as well as these papers.

[23] The example is based loosely on Roderick Firth's case in which an important mathematician, John Doe, is suffering from a terminal illness. See Firth 1981. See Berker unpublished manuscript.

a norm, subscription to which is likely to lead us to have true beliefs simply for statistical reasons having nothing to do with anything that would be intuitively relevant to whether a given belief is justified. An example might be the norm, when considering whether a number greater than 100 is prime, believe it is not prime. Any arbitrary number greater than 100 is much more likely not to be prime than to be prime, so it is likely that beliefs formed in conformity with this norm are true. Yet a person who believes that some number is prime simply because it is greater than 100 is not justified in so believing.[24] For another example, note that those who are enormously confident in their intellectual abilities might tend to do much better than the rest of us at forming sufficiently accurate needs-and-values-relevant beliefs. If so, then the norm, Be enormously confident in your intellectual abilities, might be in the optimal set. If so, the belief that one is superior intellectually to most other people apparently would count as justified according to IET no matter how dense one is.[25]

These worries are not obviously apt.[26] First, if the belief that <p> is merely useful in the way suggested, the probability that it is true might still be very low, and if so, the norm calling on us to believe that <p> might not be in the optimal set. Even if it is in the optimal set, the belief that <p> might not count as justified given that other norms in the set might call on us not to believe that <p>. Second, a merely useful rule of thumb might not be in the optimal set. The rule calling on us to believe that numbers greater than 100 are prime is not optimal, since it obviously could be improved on. The example of the number 102 makes this very clear; it is easy to tell that 102 is not prime. If the optimal set contains a rule of thumb for detecting primes, it must be optimal – subject to the learnability constraint – and beliefs formed in accord with an optimal rule of thumb plausibly *would* be justified.

A more general response to the worries invokes the learnability constraint and the generic solution constraint as well as the point that justification is defined in terms of the *optimal* set of norms. The norms in the optimal set must be norms that people with ordinary cognitive capacities would be capable of learning, internalizing, and conforming to, and because of this, general human cognitive and psychological limitations constrain the content of the optimal set. The norms in the set cannot be too numerous or complex. Most important, they must be such that

---

[24] The example was given by Berker in personal correspondence. See Berker 2013.
[25] The example is due to Berker, in personal correspondence.
[26] I thank Paul Teller for helpful discussion of the issues addressed in this paragraph.

their being internalized and conformed to would optimally enhance our ability to cope with the epistemic problem. Moreover, we cannot predict in advance exactly which specific subject matters might turn out to be needs-and-values-relevant. For these reasons, it is not plausible that the optimal set would include rules of thumb for specific subject matters or norms mandating that specific propositions be believed. Instead, the optimal set plausibly would be a set of generic subject-neutral rules specifying on what basis to form beliefs or what sources of belief to trust, such as the norm, trust your senses other things being equal.

In this section, I have considered a few objections to my proposed account of justified belief. In response, I have invoked the rigidifying move, the learnability constraint, and the generic solution constraint. Given these constraints, my contention is that the optimal set plausibly would be a set of generic subject-neutral rules specifying on what basis to form beliefs or what sources of belief to trust. It is implausible that the optimal set would include norms that would allow bootstrapping or that would mandate specific beliefs or reliance on specific statistical generalities. The optimal set might include a norm mandating that, other things being equal, we trust our senses or our memory or our intellectual capacities, and if so, then beliefs formed accordingly are justified. I do not see this as an objection. No doubt there are objections that I have not anticipated. My goal in this section, however, has merely been to explore a few important objections to the Proposal and to show that IET gives us resources with which to answer the objections.

6   Conclusion

In previous work I have proposed a general theory of normativity, pluralist teleology. My chief goal in this chapter has been to test pluralist teleology by exploring whether it can plausibly be applied to normative epistemic judgments. The intuition lying behind the theory is that the normative facts are, roughly, facts about solutions to or ways to ameliorate certain generic problems of normative governance that are faced by human beings. When applied to normative epistemology, this view leads to a kind of indirect epistemic teleology that I call IET. In this way, pluralist teleology provides a new motivation for indirect epistemic teleology. The central issue, however, is whether IET is plausible and whether it provides us with a useful tool for exploring issues in normative epistemology. To assess this, I proposed a tentative account of justified belief. IET is not committed to the details of this account, but it does seem to be well motivated on instrumentalist grounds. I then explored a number of important objections to the account and I argued that IET points the way toward responses to the objections. It therefore seems to me that the kind of indirect epistemic teleology I have proposed is both promising and plausible. This fact offers some support for pluralist teleology.

CHAPTER 6

Moral virtues, epistemic virtues, and the Big Five

Christian Miller

Recent discussions of the empirical adequacy of traditional moral and epistemic virtues have increasingly advanced the claim that most people do not possess any such character traits. This claim in turn is thought by some to have significant implications in normative ethics for the plausibility of Aristotelian virtue theory, and in epistemology for the plausibility of virtue-responsibilism.

Yet when one turns to the actual literature in personality psychology, recent work suggests that times have never been better for the empirical reality of traits. In particular, work on the Big Five personality traits (or Five-Factor model)[1] has come to dominate the field, with thousands of relevant papers appearing in just the past five years.[2] Indeed, in contrast to the talk of "paradigm crises" and "burying personality psychology" which surrounded the early years of the situationist movement in psychology, today one finds very optimistic language from psychologists themselves about a "quiet revolution"[3] and "renaissance"[4] with "real science"[5] and "real

This chapter draws from material in Miller 2014: ch. 6. I am very grateful to Owen Flanagan and Abrol Fairweather for inviting me to contribute to this volume. Thanks also to Dan McKaughan, Adam Pelser, Adam Kadlac, and Ray Yeo for helpful comments. Support for this work was funded in part by a grant from the John Templeton Foundation. The opinions expressed in this chapter are my own and do not necessarily reflect the views of the Templeton Foundation.

[1] It is now common to use the labels 'Big Five' and 'Five-Factor model' interchangeably and I will do so in what follows (see, e.g., Pytlik Zillig *et al.* 2002: 847 n. 1, and Nettle 2007: 9). But it is worth noting that some psychologists reserve the first label for research in the lexical tradition and the second for research in the questionnaire tradition (see, e.g., Goldberg and Saucier 1995: 221; Caprara and Cervone 2000: 68; Ashton and Lee 2005: 1326). These two traditions are clarified in section 2.

   Other common labels are 'Big Five personality dimensions', 'Big Five taxonomy', or simply 'the Big Five'. I will use these various expressions interchangeably. The label 'Big Five' derives from Goldberg 1981.

[2] As Costa and McCrae write, the Five-Factor model, "has become a dominant paradigm in personality" (1995: 21). Of particular interest are the data on the number of publications related to Big Five personality traits as reported in John *et al.* 2008: 116.

[3] Goldberg 1992: 26.   [4] McCrae and Costa 2003: 21, and Nettle 2007: 9, 35.
[5] McCrae and Costa 2003: 21.

progress toward consensus"[6] after "decades of floundering."[7] Yet this work is almost never discussed in the philosophy literature on character.[8] The goal of this chapter is to provide the first detailed assessment in philosophy of the Big Five approach, specifically on the question of whether it provides empirical support for the widespread possession of the moral and epistemic virtues. My conclusion will be that it does not. The first part of the chapter briefly reviews some of the recent discussions in philosophy concerning the empirical adequacy of the virtues. The second part provides an overview of the Big Five approach in personality psychology. The final sections then offer three reasons for why this approach does not offer any support for thinking that most of us are indeed virtuous people.

1   The empirical adequacy of the moral and epistemic virtues

The virtues of interest in this chapter are traditional ones such as courage, compassion, and intellectual humility. They will be understood as causal dispositions which, when triggered in the appropriate way, can give rise to occurrent beliefs and/or desires of the relevant kind. So if someone is deeply compassionate, for instance, then when she realizes that her friend needs help, she can form compassionate desires which ultimately can give rise to helpful behavior.[9]

There are virtues with respect to all the various normative domains such as athletics, aesthetics, and religion, but the focus here will be just on the moral and epistemic virtues. And nothing will depend on how these particular virtues are distinguished. On one view, for instance, the epistemic virtues are fundamentally distinct from the moral ones, whereas on another view the epistemic virtues are all a certain kind of moral virtue. Fortunately nothing will hang on this in what follows.[10]

In a now well-known literature, a number of philosophers have drawn on work in psychology to argue for some version of the following claim:

---

[6] McCrae and Costa 2003: 20.
[7] McCrae and Costa 2008: 159. For additional examples of such language see Pervin 1994: 103; Goldberg and Saucier 1995: 221; McCrae and Costa 2003: 3. See also McAdams 1992: 329–30.
[8] For very brief discussions of the Big Five taxonomy in philosophy, see Doris 2002: 67–71; Prinz 2009: 120–22; Snow 2010: 11–12; Slingerland 2011: 397.
[9] For much more on character traits as dispositions to form occurrent mental states, see Miller 2014: ch. 1.
[10] For extensive discussion of these issues, see Zagzebski 1996: 137–65, and Baehr 2011: appendix. See also Roberts and Wood 2007: 59–60.

(CM)   Given the psychological evidence, we are justified in believing on the basis of that evidence that most people do not possess the traditional moral virtues to any degree.[11]

Some of the leading studies cited in this connection have been the Milgram shock experiments, the Darley and Batson Princeton Theological Seminary study, and the Isen phone-booth study.[12] In *Moral Character: An Empirical Theory* (Miller 2013), I offer a great deal of additional support from other areas of psychology for this claim.

More recently, a similar claim has also surfaced in the epistemology literature:

(CE)   Given the psychological evidence, we are justified in believing on the basis of that evidence that most people do not possess the traditional epistemic virtues to any degree.[13]

Here some of the relevant studies have used the Duncker candle task or been inspired by the Asch conformity experiments from the 1950s.[14] (CE) is also a claim that I find highly plausible.

Yet these two claims seem to be called into question by the emerging evidence from personality psychology. Before we turn to that work, it is worth saying something about what the *philosophical* significance is supposed to be of (CM) and (CE). Here we get different answers in the moral and epistemic cases.

Let me start with (CM). According to Gilbert Harman and John Doris, (CM) is important because it poses a threat primarily to Aristotelian versions of virtue ethics.[15] Some Aristotelians seem to commit themselves to the widespread possession of the virtues, in which case their position turns out to be empirically inadequate. Others merely hold that the virtues are rarely possessed. But then, according to Doris, Aristotelian virtue ethics would lose various advantages it is meant to have over rival Kantian and consequentialist positions.[16] So the upshot is that (CM) leads to the formulation of an allegedly difficult dilemma for the Aristotelian.

How about the philosophical significance of (CE)? The main implication here is supposed to be for responsibilist versions of virtue epistemology, which also address traditional problems in epistemology in terms of

---

[11] See in particular Harman 1999, 2000, and Doris 1998, 2002.
[12] For a review of these studies, see Doris 2002: ch. 3.
[13] See especially Alfano 2012.
[14] For a review of some of the relevant studies, see Alfano 2012: 235–45.
[15] See in particular Doris 1998 and Harman 1999. I say "primarily" because they claim that other normative theories which invoke the traditional virtues in central ways can also come in for criticism.
[16] See Doris 1998.

the epistemic virtues such as love of knowledge, intellectual humility, and intellectual generosity.[17] Examples of such traditional problems include providing an analysis of the concepts of knowledge or justification, and Linda Zagzebski's influential work on these problems serves as perhaps the leading example of this kind of responsibilist virtue epistemology.[18] I will use the label RVE for virtue epistemological approaches which are both responsibilist and address traditional problems in epistemology.[19]

So how is (CE) meant to bear on RVE? Mark Alfano has sketched one way of making the connection.[20] To use his terminology, given that most philosophers accept:

Non-skepticism: Most people know quite a bit.

Then this claim plus (CE) lead to the rejection of:

RVE about knowledge: Knowledge is true belief acquired and retained through responsibilist intellectual virtue.

For given this analysis of knowledge together with the empirically supported claim that most people lack the intellectual virtues, it seems to follow that most people do not in fact know very much. A similar argument could be used for versions of RVE which analyze other epistemic notions, such as justification, evidence, or warrant, in terms of the believer's actual possession of the epistemic virtues.

As I have already indicated, I think there is good reason to accept both (CM) and (CE). So if I were to defend either Aristotelian virtue ethics or RVE, I would focus my attention on the details of the arguments that are being formulated on the basis of these two empirical

---

[17] For detailed discussion of individual epistemic virtues, see Roberts and Wood 2007.
[18] See Zagzebski 1996.
[19] More precisely, following the recent taxonomy provided by Jason Baehr (2011: ch. 1), the main implication here is supposed to be for those versions of virtue epistemology which are both responsibilist (as opposed to reliabilist) and conservative (as opposed to autonomous). *Responsibilist* virtue epistemology (VE) appeals to the epistemic virtues such as intellectual courage or humility in order to address one or more topics in epistemology. A *conservative* advocate of responsibilist VE addresses certain traditional problems in epistemology, such as providing an analysis of the concepts of knowledge or justification, in terms of one or more epistemic virtues. *Autonomous* responsibilist VE, on the other hand, puts the epistemic virtues to work in various non-traditional areas of epistemology, such as better understanding the epistemic praiseworthiness of a believer (see Roberts and Wood 2007 for an example of this approach). Note, though, that conservative responsibilist VE need not be the only view for which important philosophical implications may arise given (CE). Baehr, for instance, argues for normative connections between responsibilist character virtues and reliabilist faculty virtues, which may thereby implicate the latter in this discussion as well. See his 2011: ch. 4.
[20] See Alfano 2012: 234.

claims. For instance, elsewhere I have challenged Doris's dilemma argument by defending the plausibility of a virtue ethicist's claim that the moral virtues are rarely possessed.[21] In the case of responsibilist virtue epistemology, I might instead question Alfano's formulation of the analysis of knowledge. Zagzebski herself, for instance, is quite explicit that on her account knowledge does not require the actual possession of any epistemic virtues.[22]

But there is another, much more direct route to defending these philosophical positions, one which can avoid any complicated philosophical maneuvering. It is to undermine (CM) and (CE) right from the start. Indeed, the leading work in personality psychology over the past thirty years appears to do precisely this. So let me turn to the Big Five taxonomy.

2   An overview of the Big Five approach

There are two commonly cited avenues of research which each arrived at the Big Five taxonomy.[23] The first is represented most prominently in the work of Lewis Goldberg, who claims that over time our language has come to be shaped by the different patterns of behavior people exhibit, and so can serve as a reliable guide to categorizing those patterns. As he formulates the so-called lexical hypothesis:

> The most promising of the empirical approaches to systematizing personality differences have been based on one critical assumption: Those individual differences that are of the most significance in the daily transactions of persons with each other will eventually become encoded in their language … [this] has a highly significant corollary: The more important is an individual difference in human transactions, the more languages will have an item for it.[24]

---

[21] See Miller 2014: ch. 8.
[22] See Zagzebski 1996: 234–36, 243–44, 275–81, as well as Baehr 2011: 39. Zagzebski does, however, require the possession of the relevant virtuous motive (at least momentarily), and so Alfano may redirect his critical focus to the empirical adequacy of such motives. For criticism of Zagzebski along these lines, but without appealing to the psychology literature, see Battaly 2008: 652–53, 658–59, and Baehr 2011: 39–45. For defenses of RVE from empirical criticisms, see Axtell 2010.
[23] See, e.g., McCrae and John 1992: 181–87, and Goldberg 1993: 30. In what follows I focus on areas of overlap and agreement in the conclusions arrived at from these two avenues of research, but there are some differences in the details (e.g. Goldberg 1993: 30–31).
[24] Goldberg 1981: 141–42. Goldberg also notes in the same place that, "we should find a universal order of emergence of the individual differences encoded into the set of all the world's languages" (142).

Building on this assumption, Goldberg spent much of his career analyzing lists of trait adjectives in ordinary language, having participants rate the degree to which they (or their peers) are describable by those adjectives, doing factor analyses on the data, and testing the generalizability of the findings across methods and data sources.[25] For instance, here are three of the trait adjectives from Goldberg's 1992 100 Unipolar Markers:[26]

Fearful
Fretful
Generous.

Participants have to rate how accurately the trait describes them on a one (extremely inaccurate) to nine (extremely accurate) scale. Responses to this and other questions can then be factor analyzed to see which adjectives are highly correlated with each other, thereby suggesting an underlying factor or latent variable which is more basic and which can account for these relations.[27] For instance, fearful and fretful might tend to cluster together, but not generous. The first two can then be related to an underlying factor often labeled 'neuroticism'. Note that the evidence that would be gathered in this example (and in many of the actual studies) is self-report data involving categorizing oneself using broad trait labels.

The second prominent avenue of research which led to the Big Five taxonomy focused not on using trait adjectives, but on having participants fill out personality questionnaires. There are many such questionnaires in use today, including the NEO-FFI, HEXACO, TDA, BFAS, and BFI, but the leading measure continues to be the NEO-PI-R, developed by Robert McCrae and Paul Costa.[28] Here are a few examples from their instrument:[29]

---

[25] See, e.g., Goldberg 1992, 1993.
[26] Goldberg 1992: 41.
[27] Factor analysis is the leading statistical approach in the Big Five literature. As Mark Leary nicely describes it, "Factor analysis attempts to identify the minimum number of factors or dimensions that will do a reasonably good job of accounting for the observed relationships among the variables" (2004: 188–89). For a helpful introduction, see Leary 2004: 187–92. See also Block 1995; Caprara and Cervone 2000: 81–84; McCrae and Costa 2003: 33.
[28] A search of the PsychLit database between 1980 and 1998 revealed more than 400 mentions of the NEO in citations, with the next questionnaire mentioned no more than 50 times (Pytlik Zillig *et al.* 2002: 850). It initially began as the NEO (pertaining to three of the elements of the Big Five – Neuroticism, Extraversion, and Openness), but in 1985 was expanded to measure agreeableness and conscientiousness. A revised version ('R') was published in 1992 (Costa and McCrae 1992). The NEO-FFI is a sixty-item short form of the NEO-PI (Costa and McCrae 1992). For the HEXACO, see Ashton and Lee 2001, 2005. For the TDA, see Goldberg 1992. For the BFAS, see DeYoung *et al.* 2007. For the BFI, see John *et al.* 2008.
[29] From the NEO-PI-R Item Booklet-Form S, p. 3.

I am easily frightened
I don't get much pleasure from chatting with people
I don't take civic duties like voting very seriously.

where participants respond on a one to five scale ranging from *strongly disagree* to *strongly agree*. These items are longer than mere trait adjectives, thereby (the thought is) serving to mitigate the errors that might result if participants define a trait adjective such as 'deep' or 'imperturbable' in different ways.[30]

Numerous factor analyses have been run on self-report data using the adjective and questionnaire scales. Comparisons have also been made between self-reports and friend, spouse, and expert reports.[31] Analyses have been made between the NEO-PI-R and other personality instruments not tied specifically to the Big Five, such as the California Q-Set, Wiggins's revised Interpersonal Adjective Scales, Jackson's Personality Research Form, the Guilford–Zimmerman Temperament survey, the Eysenck Personality Questionnaire, the Myers–Briggs Type Indicator, the MMPI, the Comrey Personality Scales, and the California Psychological Inventory.[32] The trait adjectives and NEO scales have also been translated into dozens of languages and extensive data have been gathered using non-American subjects.[33] The results of all of this work have seemed to many personality psychologists to point in the direction of five basic dimensions of personality. Here are the most commonly used labels for these dimensions:[34]

Extraversion	(also labeled Surgency, Energy, Enthusiasm)
Agreeableness	(also labeled Altruism, Affection)
Conscientiousness	(also labeled Constraint, Control of Impulse)
Neuroticism	(also labeled Emotional Instability, Negative Emotionality, Nervousness)
Openness	(also labeled Intellect, Culture, Originality, Open-Mindedness)

[30] These two adjectives are taken from Goldberg's 100 Unipolar Markers (Goldberg 1992: 41). For related discussion, see Block 1995: 197; McCrae and Costa 1997: 510; Piedmont 1998: 28–29.

[31] See, e.g., McCrae and Costa 1987 and Piedmont 1998: 52–56, ch. 5.

[32] For specific studies, reviews, and discussion, see McCrae and John 1992: 180–83; McCrae and Costa 1996: 62–64, 2003: 52–56; Wiggins and Trapnell 1997: 747; John *et al.* 2008: 139–40. See also the comparison of the NEO-PI-R, TDA, and BFI in John *et al.* 2008: 130–38.

[33] See, e.g., McCrae and Costa 1997; Piedmont 1998: 43–46, 73–74; Caprara and Cervone 2000: 73–75; and McCrae *et al.* 2000: 176–77.

[34] See, e.g., Wiggins and Trapnell 1997; McCrae and Costa 1987: 83, 1997: 509, 2003, 2008: 159; Piedmont 1998: 43; and especially John *et al.* 2008: 120.

The idea, then, is that in a typical group there will be people who differ in their ratings on each of these five dimensions. Some, for instance, might be high on extraversion, which can be interpreted as involving an energetic approach towards social interaction manifested in, for instance, the behavior of attending more parties and introducing themselves to strangers.[35] Others might be quite introverted instead. And perhaps some of the extraverts and introverts are also highly conscientious, as manifested by, for instance, showing up on time or cleaning the house regularly.

So a person's rating on the Big Five dimensions is believed to correlate with certain patterns of thought and actual behavior, as well as with consequences for oneself and others. And studies have indeed suggested that this is the case.[36] For instance, high conscientiousness has been linked to avoidance of risky behaviors[37] and success on job performance criteria.[38] High neuroticism, on the other hand, positively correlates with job dissatisfaction and criminal behavior.[39]

The Big Five are not the only personality traits in the picture, even if they are the broadest and most comprehensive.[40] Advocates typically have hierarchical models of personality traits in mind, where the Big Five are subdivided into different 'facets' that are less broad and so are claimed to have increased accuracy. Unfortunately there is little consensus about how many facets there are or even what to call them.[41] Indeed on my reading of the literature, the number of facets at times seems to be a matter of convenience as dictated by the researcher in question.[42] But to cite one

---

[35] John *et al.* 2008: 120.
[36] For helpful reviews, see Caspi *et al.* 2005: 470–76; Ozer and Benet-Martínez 2006; and John *et al.* 2008: 141–43. Even Cervone *et al.*, who are highly critical of the Big Five approach, concede that, "There can be no question that measures of context-free, average-level personality constructs often are correlated to a nonzero degree with measures of important psychosocial outcomes" (2007: 7). The magnitude of these correlations, though, is still up for debate (Doris 2002: 67–68).
[37] Bogg and Roberts 2004.
[38] Mount and Barrick 1998.
[39] Ozer and Benet-Martínez 2006.
[40] Although even this is controversial, as there are recent debates about an even higher level of 'meta-traits'. For references to this literature, see DeYoung *et al.* 2007: 880.
[41] "[T]here is no consensus about what might constitute even the beginning of a compressive list of narrow traits" (Ozer and Benet-Martínez 2006: 403). See also Caspi *et al.* 2005: 456.
[42] As McCrae and Costa note, "The finer distinctions within domains, however, are more arbitrary ... no one has come up with a compelling theoretical or empirical basis for identifying facets ... 30 constructs seemed to be pushing the limit for most users to grasp" (2003: 47). And, "Unlike five and seven, there is nothing magical about the number six. It was chosen because we saw the need to make at least that many distinctions within domains and because inclusion of more than six would soon lead to intellectual overload" (Costa and McCrae 1995: 26–27). See also Costa and McCrae 1995: 24–25; Block 1995; Piedmont 1998: 30, 40–41, for further discussion.

example in order to focus the discussion, here are the thirty facets from McCrae and Costa's version of the Five-Factor model:[43]

Neuroticism
   Anxiety, Angry Hostility, Depression, Self-Consciousness, Impulsiveness, Vulnerability
Extraversion
   Warmth, Gregariousness, Assertiveness, Activity, Excitement Seeking, Positive Emotions
Openness to Experience
   Fantasy, Aesthetics, Feelings, Actions, Ideas, Values
Agreeableness
   Trust, Straightforwardness, Altruism, Compliance, Modesty, Tender-Mindedness
Conscientiousness
   Competence, Order, Dutifulness, Achievement Striving, Self-Discipline, Deliberation.

In the 240-item NEO-PI-R, eight items are designed to measure each of these facets. For instance, "I keep my belongings neat and clean" and "I like to keep everything in its place so I know just where it is" are two items for the consciousness facet of order.[44] I especially want to highlight the moral connotations of facets such as 'altruism' and 'modesty'. Similarly with respect to epistemic considerations, 'fantasy' has to do with imaginativeness, 'ideas' with intellectual curiosity, and 'values' with open-mindedness.[45]

There is obviously much more that could be said in reviewing the details of and supporting evidence for the Big Five.[46] But in the remainder of this chapter, I want to focus on three important reasons for why the Big Five taxonomy, however well supported it might be, does not offer any

---

[43] Costa and McCrae 1995: 28. It is important to be clear about the following point made by Goldberg: "proponents of the five-factor model have never intended to reduce the rich tapestry of personality to a mere five traits … Indeed, these broad domains incorporate hundreds, if not thousands, of traits" (1993: 27). See also McCrae and John 1992: 190. To complicate matters even more, DeYoung et al. (2007) have argued for the existence of ten 'aspects' between the Big Five domains and the facets. Each Big Five trait has two aspects, i.e. for agreeableness these are compassion and politeness (884).

[44] Costa and McCrae 1992: 73.

[45] See Costa and McCrae 1992: 17, and Piedmont 1998: 87–89.

[46] For helpful reviews and historical background related to the Big Five, see McCrae and John 1992; Goldberg 1993; Wiggins and Trapnell 1997; Piedmont 1998; Caprara and Cervone 2000: ch. 3; McCrae and Costa 2003: chs. 2 and 3; John et al. 2008.

empirical support for the widespread possession of the traditional moral and epistemic virtues.

3 First concern: Big Five traits are only summary labels

Thus far I have been careful to not say anything about the metaphysical status of the Big Five traits and their facets. This is for good reason, as there is sharp disagreement among advocates about how to understand them. On the one hand, they could be viewed as causally efficacious psychological dispositions in people's minds which, when triggered, can give rise to occurrent beliefs and desires of various sorts. As noted earlier, this is how character traits have traditionally been understood, and I examine a version of this approach for Big Five traits in the next section.

On the other hand, the Big Five traits and their facets could be seen solely as descriptive labels for people, without claiming that they have any underlying mental reality, causal powers, or explanatory psychological role to play. In other words, they are just terms to classify people in certain ways – it is useful to describe some people as more extraverted than others, for instance, rather than appealing to the 17,953 trait terms in the English language.[47] On this approach it is very helpful and efficient to have a way of grouping traits into only five categories,[48] but there is no need to go further and posit actual traits of extraversion or conscientiousness corresponding to these categories which are part of the causal explanation for individual differences between people.

The labeling approach to understanding the Big Five traits strikes me as the right way to go. After all, it does seem clear enough, especially in light of the empirical evidence supplied by advocates of the Big Five, that people *can* be helpfully classified as more or less extraverted, conscientious, and the like, so long as we are clear that these are just broad labels meant to reflect average or general patterns of thought and behavior.[49] This same approach can even apply to the facets which use virtue concepts. I see

---

[47] This list was famously compiled by Allport and Odbert 1936, although it needs considerable updating given new trait labels which have emerged in subsequent years.

[48] See, e.g., Hogan 1996: 170–73, and McCrae and Costa 2003: 36.

[49] Even the most outspoken critics of the Big Five approach are willing to concede this much. Hence Walter Mischel admits that it "was never disputed [that] some people are more friendly than others, some are more open-minded, some are more punctual, and so on. Such aggregate information is useful for many goals" (2009: 268) and again that, "The descriptive use of trait terms and constructs as summaries of behavior tendencies has never been at issue" (Mischel and Shoda 1994: 157). Remarks of his along these lines go all the way back to Mischel 1968: 50–52. Similarly, Dan McAdams concedes that, "the five-factor model provides a workable framework for organizing a plethora of simple, comparative, one-dimensional, and virtually nonconditional observations about others (or about the

nothing wrong with classifying some people as more altruistic or modest than others, for instance, where this just amounts to saying that comparatively speaking they seem to exhibit a more altruistic or modest *general pattern of behavior* over the course of their lives. Acknowledging this does not in any way commit one to saying that these people actually *are* compassionate or modest or have those traits as part of their minds. Many more premises would be needed to get to that conclusion.

At the same time, what these trait labels are *not* expected to do, on this way of understanding Big Five traits as mere summary labels, is to reliably predict how a person will act from moment to moment.[50] A person high on extraversion might still act quite introverted in certain situations, and vice versa. Nor does this approach offer any kind of causal explanation for why some people differ from others in these respects. As Daniel Ozer and Steven Reise note, the Big Five taxonomy, "provides a useful taxonomy, a hierarchical coordinate system, for mapping personality variables. The model is not a theory; it organizes phenomena to be explained by theory."[51] Coming up with an adequate theory would involve examining the actual psychological processes that are going on in the minds of each person one at a time, i.e. the actual beliefs and desires (broadly construed) that they are forming. In recent work I have tried to examine some of these processes in detail, and have argued that they do not correspond to the psychological processes we should expect from virtuous traits like compassion.[52]

Indeed, it should come as no surprise that the survey data being collected in Big Five research does not tell us much about the underlying causally relevant character traits of the participants in question. One reason for this is that, at least for the items of the survey instruments I have examined, the questions are not nearly extensive enough to evaluate the possession of a moral or epistemic virtue. Without this crucial first step in place, there would be no basis upon which to claim that people actually *have* virtues like modesty.

---

self) into five general classes" (1992: 352). And Gian Caprara and Daniel Cervone write that, "If the five-factor model were construed solely as a description of individual differences in the population in surface-level tendencies, there would be little controversy" (2000: 76). Similar remarks can be found in Mischel and Shoda 1998: 250; Cervone 1999: 331; Caprara and Cervone 2000: 80.

[50] See also McAdams 1994: 338; McCrae and Costa 1995: 234, 2003: 26–27, 2008: 174–75; Mischel and Shoda 1998: 250; Nettle 2007: 44.

[51] Ozer and Reise 1994: 360–61. Similarly McAdams claims that "the Big Five are more accurately viewed as five basic *trait categories*, rather than five basic traits" (1994: 339, emphasis his).

[52] See Miller 2013, 2014.

To see this, consider how McCrae and Costa understand the facet of 'altruism' under agreeableness.[53] This facet is characterized as follows:

> High scorers on the Altruism scale have an active concern for others' welfare as shown in generosity, consideration of others, and a willingness to assist others in need of help. Low scorers on this scale are somewhat more self-centered and are reluctant to get involved in the problems of other[s].[54]

McCrae and Costa measure altruism with these questionnaire items (where 'R' denotes a reversed item):[55]

Some people think I'm selfish and egotistical. (R)
I try to be courteous to everyone I meet.
Some people think of me as cold and calculating. (R)
I generally try to be thoughtful and considerate.
I'm not known for my generosity. (R)
Most people I know like me.
I think of myself as a charitable person.
I go out of my way to help others if I can.

I grant that responses to these items tend to be highly intercorrelated, and that they give us good reason to postulate a label called 'altruism', provided that this term is understood broadly as pertaining to a general tendency to be helpful.[56] What should be clear, however, is that these items do not provide nearly enough information to properly assess whether someone has a *moral virtue* such as compassion, even setting aside worries about the accuracy of self-reports. For instance, four of the items have to do with how other people think of me, not how I am. Two have to do primarily with manners and politeness, and one concerns social liking. Only the last item relates directly to helping behavior, and none of them gets at the motivation behind helping.[57]

By way of comparison, here are the four questions that Michael Ashton and Kibeom Lee use in the 100-item version of their HEXACO-PI-R to measure altruism (on a one to five scale between *strongly disagree* and *strongly agree*):[58]

---

[53] Agreeableness itself is characterized in part as follows: "The agreeable person is fundamentally altruistic. He or she is sympathetic to others and eager to help them, and believes that others will be equally helpful in return" (Costa and McCrae 1992: 15).
[54] Costa and McCrae 1992: 18.
[55] Costa and McCrae 1992: 72.
[56] As it seems to be in Caspi *et al.* 2005: 459.
[57] In fact, DeYoung *et al.* claim that "no good markers for Compassion appear in the NEO-PI-R" (2007: 885).
[58] Available at http://hexaco.org/downloading.html (accessed May 13, 2011).

(97)   I have sympathy for people who are less fortunate than I am.
(98)   I try to give generously to those in need.
(99)   It wouldn't bother me to harm someone I didn't like.
(100)   People see me as a hard-hearted person.

If 'altruism' is supposed to be anything like the virtue of compassion, kindness, or the like, then these items will not get us very far in assessing whether a given person has it.[59] The third item has to do with harming rather than helping behavior, and so pertains to the virtue of non-malevolence. The last item concerns people's perceptions, not how one actually is. The first two items start to unpack motivation, but are not sharply focused enough to examine whether it is altruistic. Finally, none of these items has anything to do with helping *behavior*.[60]

Ashton and Lee are well known for arguing that the Big Five trait list is insufficient, and needs to be expanded to include a sixth personality dimension of 'honesty/humility', with four facets of sincerity, fairness, greed-avoidance, and modesty.[61] All of these labels sound robustly moral, and I will not go over the questionnaire items for each of them. Let me just pick fairness:[62]

(12)   If I knew that I could never get caught, I would be willing to steal a million dollars.
(36)   I would be tempted to buy stolen property if I were financially tight.
(60)   I would never accept a bribe, even if it were very large.

[59]   They characterize the facet as follows: "The *Altruism (versus Antagonism)* scale assesses a tendency to be sympathetic and soft-hearted toward others. High scorers avoid causing harm and react with generosity toward those who are weak or in need of help, whereas low scorers are not upset by the prospect of hurting others and may be seen as hard-hearted" (http://hexaco.org/scaledescriptions. html, accessed May 13, 2011, emphasis theirs). Of course, if they do not intend altruism to be a moral virtue, then I have no objection to the claim that altruism (so understood) is universally possessed.

[60]   For different emphases on belief, desire, and action in the items used in various questionnaires to assess Big Five traits, see Pytlik Zillig *et al.* 2002.

[61]   See Ashton and Lee 2001, 2005. For criticism of the need for this sixth dimension, see McCrae and Costa 2008: 167, and DeYoung *et al.* 2007: 881, 885. One puzzling feature of this list is that none of these labels seems to have any connection to honesty (with respect to telling the truth), and the same is true of the sixteen specific items used to measure these facets. But leave that point aside.

[62]   "The *Fairness* scale assesses a tendency to avoid fraud and corruption. Low scorers are willing to gain by cheating or stealing, whereas high scorers are unwilling to take advantage of other individuals or of society at large" (http://hexaco.org/scaledescriptions.html, accessed May 13, 2011, emphasis theirs). Again, if they do not intend fairness to be a moral virtue, then I have no objection to the claim that fairness (so understood) is universally possessed.

(84)   I'd be tempted to use counterfeit money, if I were sure I could get away with it.

Someone who scores high on item (60) and low on the other three, could seem to be a fair (perhaps better, honest) person in *some* respects, or at least he might think that he is.[63] But note that this is a far cry from actually being fair in a morally virtuous sense. For instance, perhaps the person would not do these wrong actions in order to avoid feeling guilty in the future. Or in order to try to earn rewards in the afterlife. Or in order to enjoy the satisfaction that comes with thinking of oneself as a moral person. None of these motives would be virtuous ones, and without clarification here we have no basis for attributing the virtue to him.

The concerns above are specific ones about particular questionnaires. Of course, new surveys could always be developed, and they could have additional items which are directly aimed at meeting these concerns.[64] But that would still leave a more fundamental problem in place, namely that these are measures designed to collect report data (self, friend, expert, spouse, or whatever) on how people tend to be in general. Yet there are serious concerns about how much such report data can tell us about a person's moral or epistemic virtues. For instance, with respect to a virtue such as compassion, the relevant questionnaire items from measures like the NEO-PI-R, HEXACO-PI-R, and DeYoung's Big Five Aspect Scales are not going to be able to supply crucial information such as:

(i)   How many helping-relevant situations the person actually encountered during, say, the past month.

---

[63] Although even this might be challenged. For instance, a dishonest person wants to appear honest to others, and so might score high on item (60) and low on the other three, which would lead to a highly erroneous assessment of him. Thanks to Dan McKaughan for pointing this out to me.

[64] For instance, in recent work Colin DeYoung and his colleagues (2007) have divided the Big Five trait of agreeableness into two 'aspects', compassion and politeness, and use the following scales for compassion (887, with 'R' denoting a reversed item):

> Am not interested in other people's problems. (R)
> Feel others' emotions.
> Inquire about others' well-being.
> Can't be bothered with others' needs. (R)
> Sympathize with others' feelings.
> Am indifferent to the feelings of others. (R)
> Take no time for others. (R)
> Take an interest in other people's lives.
> Don't have a soft side. (R)
> Like to do things for others.

Cumulatively these questions strike me as doing a far better job than those pertaining to 'altruism' in the text above.

(ii)   Of the situations he was in during the past month, how many did he accurately recognize as being helping-relevant versus how many did he fail to recognize as helping-relevant.

(iii)   How many of these situations he thought (whether accurately or not) were helping-relevant.

(iv)   Which of those situations he actually helped in and which he did not.

(v)   Of the situations in which he helped, the degree to which he was actually helpful in those particular situations.

(vi)   What his motivation for helping or not helping in any of those situations actually was.

(vii)   Whether when he did help during the past month he in fact was helpful in general, as opposed to only thinking that he was helpful.

(viii) To what extent, if any, he was either subconsciously or consciously misreporting or even distorting his answers to the survey questions.

In particular, I want to especially emphasize the concern that most of us have psychological processes going on in our minds which we may not be aware of and which can undermine our possession of the virtues, *even in spite of* what we ourselves (and our peers) think about our characters. These processes can be highly influential in causing behavior, and yet may not often be appreciated or even recognized – hence our shock at the results found by Milgram and other famous studies in psychology.[65]

So *even if* there ended up being good statistical reasons based on new survey data to posit additional facets of the Big Five corresponding to the traditional moral and epistemic virtues – such as compassion – it would *still* be a fundamental mistake in my opinion to then infer that the people in question actually have those virtues. Whether they do indeed have the virtues is ultimately a matter of what dispositions to form beliefs and desires there are in their minds as well as the relations between those dispositions. These psychological facts should best be assessed not on the basis of surveys and quick paper-and-pencil devices, but rather (if at all possible) on the basis of longitudinal studies of actual behavior in relevant situations designed to shed light on the possession of the virtue in

---

[65] For additional concerns with self-reports and the Big Five, see McAdams 1992: 340, 349–54; Block 1995: 209; Buss 1996: 195–97; Hogan 1996: 175–78; Prinz 2009: 121. For more general concerns about self-report data and moral character, see Miller 2013 ch. 8.

question.[66] Hence at the end of the day, I am suspicious about how far research on the Big Five in personality psychology can really take us in understanding our actual moral and epistemic characters.

4   Second concern: problems for the leading causal trait model of the Big Five

In adopting this account of the nature of Big Five traits as mere summary labels, I am in agreement with the majority of personality psychologists who publish in this area. Oliver John, Richard Robins, Lewis Goldberg, Gerard Saucier, Robert Hogan, Jerry Wiggins, Paul Trapnell, Laura Naumann, and Christopher Soto, for instance, can all be found saying similar things.[67]

There is a notable exception, however. McCrae and Costa, two of the leading personality psychologists today, do not accept the summary label view, and instead advocate a robust causal interpretation of the Big Five traits.[68] To unpack their position, let me begin by noting that they have recently developed a Five-Factor *Theory* (FFT), which is designed to provide a comprehensive theoretical account of personality and the relationship between different variables such as external influences, the self-concept, genetics, behavior, emotional reactions, and personality traits. For my purposes, the key point of the FFT is their distinction between what they call "basic tendencies" and "characteristic adaptations."[69]

Basic tendencies include, among other things, the personality traits themselves. Insofar as they are basic tendencies, they are objectively existing, causal dispositional features of individuals. Furthermore, personality traits are not culturally acquired or individually cultivated according to FFT, but rather are 'endogenous', i.e. they arise from our DNA.[70] Indeed,

---

[66] For much more on methodological principles to use in studying moral character, see Miller 2013 ch. 8.

[67] John and Robins 1994: 138–39; Goldberg and Saucier 1995: 221; Hogan 1996; John *et al.* 2008: 140. See also the helpful discussion in Mischel and Shoda 1994, 1998: 249–51; Wiggins and Trapnell 1997: 744–58; McCrae and Costa 2008: 160.

[68] This was less clear in their earlier work because of ambiguities in the way they were using the term 'trait', as Wiggins and Trapnell helpfully show (1997: 745). But their acceptance of a causal view becomes unambiguous with the development of the Five-Factor Theory, as discussed in what follows. Ralph Piedmont (1998) also accepts what seems to be the entirety of the Five-Factor Theory (74–77), and explicitly rejects the summary view (38–39). The same can be said for Daniel Nettle (2007). David Buss (1996) also seems to accept a causal model of Big Five traits, although within a different theoretical framework from that provided by McCrae and Costa.

[69] For the Five-Factor Theory, see McCrae and Costa 1995, 1996, 2003: ch. 10, 2008; and McCrae *et al.* 2000.

[70] McCrae and Costa 2003: 190, 2008: 164–65.

they are universally held such that, "All adults can be characterized by their differential standing on a series of personality traits that influence patterns of thoughts, feelings, and behaviors … Traits are organized hierarchically from narrow and specific to broad and general dispositions; Neuroticism, Extraversion, Openness to Experience, Agreeableness, and Conscientiousness constitute the highest level of the hierarchy."[71] So the claim is not only that individual differences between people can be usefully categorized using the Big Five, but that all people *actually have* such traits to some degree or other in virtue of our biological hardwiring. Indeed, McCrae and Costa go on to argue that our possession of them shows very little change during the lifespan.[72]

What then are 'characteristic adaptations'? McCrae and Costa describe them this way: "Over time, individuals react to their environments by evolving patterns of thoughts, feelings, and behaviors that are consistent with their personality traits and earlier adaptations."[73] They are 'characteristic' because they depend on the individual's basic tendencies, but they are also 'adaptations' to the specific details of what the individual is confronting at the moment.[74] For instance, to use one of their own examples, a person's specific desire to go see a show at the local opera for the first time would not itself be a basic tendency, but it can be influenced by her degree of Openness.[75]

If the list of five broad traits and thirty facets did not include any moral or epistemic virtue terms, then as far as my project in this chapter is concerned there would be no conflict. But in fact it does – 'altruism' and 'modesty', for instance, have already been highlighted in the moral case, and 'fantasy' (imaginativeness), 'ideas' (intellectual curiosity), and 'values' (open-mindedness) have been highlighted in the epistemic case.[76] Recall the claim from the first section of the present chapter that most people

[71] McCrae and Costa 2003: 190. Similarly they write that "all the traits …. are found in varying degrees in all people, with distributions that approximate the familiar normal curve" (25). See also McCrae and Costa 1996: 72, 1997: 509.
[72] For more on basic tendencies and the specific claims mentioned above, see McCrae and John 1992: 184, 195, 199, 201–2; McCrae and Costa 1995: 238, 1996: 66–74, 2003: 187–205, 2008: 163–66; McCrae et al. 2000.
[73] McCrae and Costa 2003: 190.
[74] McCrae and Costa 2003: 191, 2008: 163–64.
[75] McCrae and Costa 2003: 191–92. For more on characteristic adaptations, see McCrae and Costa 1995: 238, 247, 1996: 69–74, 2003: 187, 190–92, 2008: 163–66.
[76] Nor is this unique to their list of thirty facets. See also 'Ruthless', 'Stingy', and 'Generous' in McCrae and Costa 2003: 4. 'Kind', 'Cruel', 'Stingy', 'Hard-Hearted', and 'Forgiving' show up in John et al. 2008: 128. Goldberg's 100 Unipolar Markers include 'Kind', 'Generous', and 'Helpful' (1992: 41). 'Callous', 'Stingy', 'Humble', and 'Generous' appear on the list of trait adjectives in McCrae and Costa 1987: 85. 'Forgiving', Generous', 'Kind', and 'Sympathetic' are on the adjective

do not have any moral or epistemic virtues such as modesty, even to a minimal degree. So this claim seems to be threatened by a view such as McCrae and Costa's which says that all people have causally efficacious virtues such as modesty to some degree or other.

With this background in place, let me raise some questions about their proposal, while continuing with the example of the trait of modesty. First of all, how should the actual trait itself be understood on McCrae and Costa's theory? Clearly it has to be explained in terms which appeal to something other than just modest behavior, as otherwise the view would be circular. Modest behavior would be explained by the trait of modesty, but the trait itself had better not be characterized just as the trait which gives rise to modest behavior.

But while McCrae and Costa have written extensively on the nature of traits, I am still not sure what their answer is supposed to be.[77] Let me consider two options. On the one hand, they could treat the Big Five traits and their facets as psychological primitives, i.e. as dispositions which are not grounded in more basic mental state dispositions, but which simply arise genetically and have their own distinctive metaphysical existence and causal role in everyone's minds. In philosophy it is standard to view character traits as causal dispositions which are constituted by more specific dispositions to form particular beliefs and desires (broadly construed).[78] For instance, philosophers tend to understand the trait of compassion as constituted, at least in part, by a variety of dispositions to form beliefs about what would be helpful to do, and desires to help another person for his or her own sake. But on this first interpretation of McCrae and Costa's model, they would be rejecting this picture and instead positing traits which are not grounded at all in dispositions to form such mental states.

At times this seems to be their considered view. For instance, they write that, "Motives, wishes and attitudes are not personality traits, nor are patterns of motives, wishes and attitudes," and, "Personality traits, in our model, account (in part) for the motives, habits, and attitudes that directly affect behavior."[79] If this is indeed their position, then I am not sure

---

list pertaining to Agreeableness in McCrae and John 1992: 178. And plenty of other examples could be cited.

[77] The most extensive discussion that I am aware of which is related to this topic can be found in McCrae and Costa 1995.

[78] For an extensive review of this topic, see Miller 2014 ch. 1. For broad versus narrow understandings of 'desire', see Schueler 1995.

[79] McCrae and Costa 1995: 236, 242. Similarly this first option would be in line with their claim that, "In FFT, traits are not patterns of behavior, nor are they the plans, skills, and desires that lead to

I can make sense of it. Traits would become mysterious entities, with their own ungrounded causal powers.[80] They also would seem to be redundant, since people can have specific dispositions to form beliefs and desires having to do with, say, helping others, and those dispositions can account for the patterns of behavior we observe just fine without having to postulate a separate entity altogether which also does the same causal work. Finally, I am not sure how worries about circularity would be avoided, since traits on this approach would then be characterized only in terms of the patterns of thoughts and behavior to which they give rise. But then those very same patterns of thoughts and behavior would in turn be explained by these traits.[81]

Suppose on the other hand that McCrae and Costa go on to provide a more fundamental *psychological* account of a trait like modesty, say in terms of relevant underlying dispositions to believe and desire in a modest way. The quotations above could then be interpreted as stating that traits are not themselves *occurrent* mental states, but rather are dispositional properties which are grounded in causal mental state dispositions to *form* occurrent "motives, habits, attitudes," and the like.

I can understand this second option and I grant that it is not circular.[82] But at the same time I claim that the resulting position is not empirically

patterns of behavior. They are directly accessible neither to public observation nor to private intro-spection. Instead, they are deeper psychological entities" (McCrae and Costa 2008: 163). See also the statements that: "traits provide a structural basis for goals and motives" (McCrae 1994: 152); that "The questionnaires that trait psychologists write include questions about specific thoughts, feelings, and behaviors, but they are of interest chiefly as indicators of a deeper level of personality" (McCrae 1994: 151); and that "motive concepts … can explain patterns of behaviour … and can themselves be explained as expressions of basic tendencies" (McCrae and Costa 1995: 246–47). To be fair, these quotations do not *entail* the first option, and could be made compatible with the second option for the reasons outlined in the next note.

[80] Immediately after the passage cited in the text above, McCrae and Costa go on to write that "the crucial word in our definition of traits is *tendencies*, because this term denotes the dispositional core of the trait construct" (1995: 236, emphasis theirs). So it could be that when they say traits are not mental states, what they have in mind are occurrent mental states, and so they are claiming that traits are causal *dispositions* to form occurrent motives, wishes, and the like. This idea I have no difficulty with at all, and I go on to discuss it next in the text above. But unfortunately I cannot tell for sure whether this really is their view.

[81] For their response, see McCrae and Costa 1995: 241–43. For a recent, detailed development of the circularity concern with a focus on McCrae and Costa's view, see Boag 2011: 230–36. See also Cervone 1999: 313–14; Caprara and Cervone 2000: 114–15; Nettle 2007: 36–40. Even if they are identified with certain biological structures in the brain (Nettle 2007: 38–39), traits still seem to be characterized in the first place solely in behavioral terms, thereby leading to circularity worries. And in any event, McCrae and Costa reject such an identification of traits with biological structures: "We do not equate basic dispositions with biological constructs, nor have we offered a psychobiological theory of personality" (1995: 239). For a response to the circularity worry on behalf of McCrae and Costa, see John et al. 2008: 146.

[82] Thereby blocking at least some of the concerns raised by Boag 2011.

adequate. For what evidence has been offered that most people actually do have dispositions to form beliefs and desires of a modest, or compassionate, or intellectually humble, or any other virtuous sort? There is no such evidence, as far as I am aware, in the Big Five literature in personality psychology. And when one looks to other areas of psychology, I have argued elsewhere that at least in the moral case, there is overwhelming evidence that most people *do not* have the requisite mental state dispositions and have them function in the ways needed in order to qualify as even minimally virtuous.[83] So I do not think this second option is a very promising way for McCrae and Costa to go either, if they want to claim that there is empirical support for the universal possession of virtues such as modesty.

Let me end this section by offering a diagnosis for where, in my view, McCrae and Costa's approach has gone wrong. Grant for the moment something that I have already rejected, namely that the survey instruments such as the NEO-PI-R provide thorough and careful questions which help to classify someone as modest to a certain degree. What I find objectionable is the inference from (i) someone's being described as, say, weakly modest using a survey instrument like the NEO-PI-R, to (ii) the conclusion that the best explanation for this is that the person *actually has* the trait of modesty to a weak degree. This is what is called a 'top-down' explanation in personality psychology – a factor is found and labeled, such as modesty, as a result of interrelated patterns of survey data gathered from groups of people. This factor is then explained by positing an actual trait that the person is supposed to possess, namely modesty.

In contrast, the method that I think we should employ when empirically examining a person's character is to start by understanding the particular psychological processes and mental state dispositions (dispositions to form beliefs and desires, broadly understood) which are present in each person's mind, and then on *that* basis determine whether they constitute a character trait or not. If they do, then it can be decided next on normative (rather than empirical) grounds whether the trait is, say, an epistemic virtue or a vice.

My approach thus starts with the individual, not with the group of participants, and thereby tries to avoid the common complaint from social psychologists that, "trait theorists, who so often have focused on individual differences, have so rarely focused on individuals,"[84] thereby giving rise to a "psychology of the stranger."[85] More precisely, the top-down approach to

---

[83] See Miller 2013, 2014.   [84] Pervin 1994: 110.   [85] McAdams 1992: 348–54, 1994.

trait explanation starts with measures of individual differences in groups, measures which typically use highly simple and broad items like self-ratings on 'generous' or 'I am easily frightened'. As Dan McAdams notes, the measures are used "to get a general, superficial, and virtually nonconditional picture of your personality."[86] The top-down approach then posits that a given person has the trait in question, but in doing so sheds little light on the psychological organization and processes that are at work in that person. What beliefs and desires generally, and specifically what goals, plans, values, schemas, strategies, and the like are in that person's mind, all remain a mystery, whereas I hold that mental states (and the dispositions to form them) should be at the center of any understanding of moral and epistemic character traits, and indeed of personality psychology more generally.[87]

To be fair, it could very well turn out on my approach that some people *really do have* traits like intellectual curiosity or modesty. But the way to discover this is *not* to start with broad labels of a person's behavior, typically supplied by self-reports or other paper-and-pencil devices, and then reason to the existence of an underlying trait. Rather mine is a 'bottom-up' approach to traits – start with the particular psychological mechanisms that play a causal role in a person's mind during specific situations, and construct an empirical account of character traits out of them.[88]

Now one response could be that McCrae and Costa never intended the Big Five traits and their facets to be interpreted as moral or epistemic *virtues* in any traditional normative sense. Fair enough. If so, then as far as my project in this chapter is concerned, I have no objection *even to a causal interpretation* of the Big Five traits, so long as advocates of the view are clear about how they are using their terms. 'Modesty' and 'altruism'

---

[86] McAdams 1992: 350.
[87] Hence I am in basic agreement with Seymour Epstein when he writes about Big Five traits that, "Their units are useful for describing what people are like (structure) but not for how they operate (process)" (1994: 120). Similarly according to Jack Block, "no matter how satisfying on descriptive or other grounds the variable-centered structure of the [five-factor model] may be, it cannot represent a personality structure. Personality structures lie within individuals … it does not offer a sense of what goes on within the structured, motivation-processing, system maintaining individual" (1995: 188). And Lawrence Pervin claims that, "If we focus exclusively on individual differences, and if we aggregate only over situations, I fear that we will miss the essence of personality – the dynamic interplay among the parts of a system that can be characterized by varying degrees of complexity, organization, and integration" (1994: 110). Many other psychologists have made similar complaints. See in particular Mischel and Shoda 1994, 1998: 250.
[88] For related discussion of these two approaches to understanding structural units of personality, and in particular for concerns about whether top-down models of between-person differences should be applied to understanding individual within-person psychological structures, see in particular Cervone 1999.

would then not be used to stand for ordinary moral virtues, and similarly 'ideas' and 'values' would not stand for ordinary epistemic virtues, even though that clearly seems to be how psychologists intended all of these terms to be understood in the past.[89]

5 Third concern: the Big Five and responsibility

In recent years, a number of ambitious claims have been made about the Big Five taxonomy. Highly problematic in my view are claims to the effect that the Big Five taxonomy or Five-Factor model offers a complete picture of personality. Hence we find McCrae and Costa writing that:

> Much of what psychologists mean by the term 'personality' is summarized by the FFM.[90]

> [T]he structure of personality ... that must be explained is, for now, best represented by the five-factor model.[91]

But they are not the only ones making such claims:

> Taken together, they [the Big Five] provide a good answer to the question of personality structure.[92]

> My opinion is that the five-factor model of personality ... is largely sufficient for characterizing normal and abnormal personality functioning.[93]

> [If] we have truly discovered the basic dimensions of personality – it marks a turning point for personality psychology.[94]

---

[89] See, e.g., McCrae and Costa 1987, where they explicitly state that the two Big Five traits of Agreeableness and Conscientiousness in general are traits which are judged and evaluated from a moral point of view (88; see also McCrae and John 1992: 197). Surely the same would apply to their facets, too. For an opposing view which sees the moral and epistemic virtues as distinct from Big Five traits, see Ozer and Benet-Martínez 2006: 403, 405–6. See also Caspi *et al.* 2005, who seems to equate 'altruism' just with levels of prosocial behavior (459). And Piedmont writes that, "When interpreting scores from the NEO-PI-R it is important to ... not impose any value judgments on the scores. One frequent mistake ... has been to see some of these qualities as better than others ... Personalities should not be thought of as 'good' or 'bad'" (1998: 57). See also Nettle: "any level of any of the big five is advantageous in some ways whilst being disadvantageous in others. Thus, there is no intrinsically better or worse personality profile to have" (2007: 244–45; see also 70). Also relevant is Prinz 2009: 121.

[90] McCrae and Costa 2008: 159.

[91] McCrae and Costa 1987: 89. See also McCrae and Costa 1997: 509, and the references in Block 1995: 187.

[92] Digman 1990: 436. [93] Widiger 1993: 82.

[94] McCrae and John 1992: 177. Similarly, Piedmont writes that, "we have increased confidence that the five-factor model is indeed a comprehensive description of individual difference variables" (1998: 46). See also Ashton and Lee 2001: 335 (with respect to their Big Six) and Nettle 2007: 9.

Big Five advocates have been chastised for badly overreaching here, and rightly so.[95] Surely other variables such as beliefs and desires, including particular values, goals, motives, self-concepts and the like, are also crucial to personality.

But this has not stopped Big Five advocates from making bold claims about the completeness of their pictures of *traits*. For instance Costa and McCrae write that:

> One of the chief merits of the FFM is that it offers a comprehensive yet manageable guide to personality traits.[96]

> [T]he FFM is intended to be a comprehensive taxonomy of all personality traits.[97]

These claims seem to me to lead to a dilemma for any virtue ethicist or virtue-responsibilist who wants to appeal to the Big Five in order to secure the empirical adequacy of the relevant virtues.

Suppose, on the first horn of the dilemma, that we accept a summary label interpretation of the Big Five traits and their facets. Then to claim that these traits provide a comprehensive taxonomy of *all* personality traits leaves no room for precisely the character traits which are central for these philosophers. Traits like compassion and intellectual curiosity, for instance, are understood by Aristotelian virtue ethicists and by virtue-responsibilists as causal efficacious dispositions which underlie certain behavioral patterns, not as labels for the behavioral patterns themselves. Hence ironically this version of the Big Five approach would serve as additional support for philosophers like Gilbert Harman and John Doris who challenge the empirical reality of the moral and epistemic virtues.

---

[95] See in particular McAdams 1992, Pervin 1994, Block 1995, and, more recently, Mischel 2009: 285. For more cautious statements by Big Five advocates, see John and Robins 1994: 137, 139; McCrae 1994: 149; Goldberg and Saucier 1995: 223; McCrae and Costa 1995: 235; Piedmont 1998: 51; and John et al. 2008: 140.

[96] McCrae and Costa 1996: 57; see also 61.

[97] Costa and McCrae 1995: 25. As Jerry Wiggins and Paul Trapnell write, "Interest in the five-factor model derived mainly from the claim that five dimensions might provide an adequate preliminary taxonomy for *all* nontrivial personality traits – those whose importance in human interaction has resulted in a descriptive label in the natural language (e.g., dominant), as well as those reflected in the constructs of personality researchers (e.g., Machiavellianism)" (1997: 756–57, emphasis theirs). For similar claims, see also McCrae and John 1992: 176; Piedmont 1998: 31, 58; and McCrae and Costa 2003: 3, 52. As noted, opposition to the sufficiency of the Big Five exists among personality psychologists. Ashton and Lee (2001, 2005) have argued for a Big Six taxonomy that includes honesty-humility, which they take to thereby be a comprehensive taxonomy (Ashton and Lee 2001: 350). As they write, "the NEO-PI-R does not contain any facets that directly assess greed and status-seeking, nor does it contain any facets that directly assess dishonest tendencies of the kind measured by overt integrity tests" (Ashton and Lee 2005: 1344). Paunonen and Jackson (2000) claim

On the other hand, suppose instead that we accept McCrae and Costa's causal interpretation of the Big Five traits and their facets. And now consider another aspect of their approach which I only briefly alluded to earlier. On McCrae and Costa's view all personality traits in general are said to arise genetically and serve as largely (if not entirely) fixed and uncontrollable 'basic tendencies' of our personalities.[98] In their visual diagram of the personality system, for instance, "Most readers will probably be startled by the conspicuous absence … of an arrow from *external influences* to *basic tendencies*. This is not an oversight; FFT deliberately asserts that personality traits are endogenous dispositions, influenced not at all by the environment."[99] And they claim that after 30 years of age, people's personality traits are, "set like plaster."[100]

If this is the case, then McCrae and Costa's view leaves little room for the kind of character traits which are of central importance to Aristotelian virtue ethicists and virtue-responsibilists. For on this approach personality traits are such that we have no moral and epistemic responsibility in acquiring them in the first place, at least on many leading accounts of responsibility.[101] Nor is there much, if anything, we can do to shape them subsequently in our lives.[102] So both their acquisition and continued maintenance are outside our control, thereby raising questions about

that ten additional factors need to be added to the Big Five, including integrity and religiosity. Buss (1996) focuses on individual differences in sexuality and on 'sex-linked' trait terms (203–4). See also Goldberg 1993: 31; Block 1995: 205; Piedmont 1998: 219; and Caprara and Cervone 2000: 74.

[98] For relevant discussion, see McCrae *et al.* 2000 and McCrae and Costa 2003, 2008. This claim includes the thirty facets and not just the Big Five domains, and so includes the morally relevant facets of 'modesty' and 'altruism' as well. See, e.g., McCrae *et al.* 2000: 174, 176, 182. See also the development of this kind of position in Nettle 2007: ch. 8.

[99] McCrae *et al.* 2000: 175, emphasis theirs. They go on to write that, "the generalization that personality traits are more or less immune to environmental influences is supported by multiple, converging lines of empirical evidence that significant variables in life experience have little or no effect on measured personality traits" (174–75). See also McCrae and Costa 2003: 193. The surrounding discussion in both places does qualify these statements, but not in a way that significantly bears on the above.
   Of course, the claims above by McCrae and Costa can seem highly problematic, but this is not the place to engage in a detailed assessment of them. For helpful criticism of their view, see, e.g., Roberts 2009: 139, 141–43.

[100] Costa and McCrae 1994. Furthermore, on their view while there might be some change in personality traits over time (people tend to increase slightly in agreeableness and conscientiousness, for instance), this change is *not* due to environmental influences (not primarily, at least, if at all), but rather to genes being activated at various points in time.

[101] For more on the relationship between moral character traits and responsibility, praise, and blame, see Miller 2014: ch. 1.

[102] To be fair, McCrae and Costa would say that we have some control over the *manifestation* of the trait. Extraverts, for instance, have control over whether they go to a particular party or not. So responsibility can still be found with respect to what one *does with* one's personality traits. But there would be no accountability for traits one possesses in the first place. Nettle elaborates this

the appropriateness of praise and blame for any thoughts and actions to which they directly give rise.[103] Yet for the philosophical views in question, responsibility, praise, and blame are central to their understanding of what it is to be a virtuous person, to think in a virtuous way, and to act from having the virtues.[104] It is hard to see how such philosophers could be enthusiastic about an empirical framework for thinking about character which does not allow any room for these notions.

Now there is a straightforward way to avoid the dilemma I have formulated in this section. It is to find empirical support for the Big Five traits and their facets understood *both* (i) as causal dispositions rather than mere summary labels, and (ii) as traits for which we can be appropriately responsible for their acquisition and/or maintenance. Then we would indeed have support for the kind of traits that would be of interest to Aristotelians and virtue-responsibilists. I see no reason in principle why such empirical support could not be found. The only problem at present is that it has not yet been found. So as of now, we have a third respect in which research in personality psychology on the Big Five has not done enough, at least for the time being, to establish the widespread possession of the moral and epistemic virtues.

6 Conclusion

In this chapter I have considered in some detail whether the extensive research in personality psychology on the Big Five traits undermines the

---

idea as follows: "Whilst no one can hold me responsible for the dispositional traits that I have, since those are not of my choosing, I am morally and legally responsible for the behaviour patterns I develop as an expression of those traits. There are morally good, morally neutral, and morally bad behavioural expressions of all traits, and I am responsible for cultivating ones that are at least morally neutral" (2007: 244). For related discussion, see Piedmont 1998: 38–39 and Nettle 2007: 239–48.

[103] And yet McCrae and John write about agreeableness and conscientiousness that, "Like A, C is a highly evaluated dimension; indeed, A and C are the classic dimensions of character, describing 'good' versus 'evil' and 'strong-willed' versus 'weak-willed' individuals. Perhaps it was these moral overtones that often led scientific psychologists to ignore these factors" (1992: 197). Similarly, McCrae and Costa ascribe personality traits to animals (2003: 204), but it is not clear that animals have any character traits, especially moral ones. Cervone *et al.* (2007) make the related point that since the same factor structure is replicated in non-human animals this, "means that it did not capture unique psychological features of persons" (4).

[104] For relevant discussion, see Zagzebski 1996: 102–6; Prinz 2009: 121–22; Baehr 2011: ch. 2. As Baehr writes, if "we were to learn of someone that his open-mindedness and intellectual tenacity, say, are *entirely* a matter of the way he was parented or the community in which he was raised – if we learned that the person does not himself figure in any notable way in an explanation of why he has these traits – then I take it that we would not regard him as possessing genuine intellectual character virtues" (27, emphasis his).

claim that most people do not possess the traditional moral and epistemic virtues to any degree. As far as I can tell, it does not. Hence, empirical support for the widespread possession of these virtues will have to come from elsewhere. At this point in time, I do not know where that would be.

To be clear, as I noted in this chapter's first section, the lack of empirical support for these virtues does not by itself challenge the truth of either Aristotelian virtue ethics or virtue-responsibilism in epistemology. Additional premises are needed to make any such argument, and the ones I have seen so far are contestable.

However, this lack of empirical support *does* provide a new challenge for the advocates of these views.[105] The challenge is to provide a detailed and empirically informed account of how we should go about *cultivating* the moral and epistemic virtues in ourselves and others, given their apparent absence in most of us. Such a discussion needs to move beyond traditional platitudes about the importance of a proper moral education and the role of habituation over time, and actually get knee-deep in the relevant empirical studies.[106]

This is just a challenge, of course, and not an objection to the truth of the views in question. But it is a challenge that should not be taken lightly.

[105] This challenge can be broadened to include autonomous versions of responsibilist virtue epistemology as well, such as that advocated by Roberts and Wood 2007, and perhaps versions of reliabilist virtue epistemology too. For these distinctions, see note 19 above.
[106] I review some of the relevant studies in Miller 2014: ch. 9.

CHAPTER 7

Epistemic dexterity
A Ramseyian account of agent-based knowledge

Abrol Fairweather and Carlos Montemayor

1 Introduction: metaphysical epistemology

Virtue epistemology is widely known as a deeply normative form of epistemology, and indeed it is.[1] However, less attention has been given to the fact that it is also deeply metaphysical and empirically committed.[2] Two metaphysical projects within virtue theory that will be discussed at length below involve (a) *individuating disposition types* and (b) providing an account of the *because of* relation that must obtain between an agent and their epistemic success in order to achieve states of knowledge. Regarding disposition types, one well-known challenge to process reliabilism is the Generality Problem (Conee and Feldman 1998). This is a challenge to properly individuate processes that has proven difficult for standard reliabilism, but virtue epistemology would appear to give us a principled way to distinguish the processes that matter, namely those that constitute (or are elements of) epistemic virtues. But a virtue epistemologist will then need a nuanced dispositional taxonomy to ground solid responses to generality-type worries and to claim any advantage over process reliabilism on this score. In virtue ethics, virtues are usually associated with character traits, but virtue epistemologists refer to a greater range of disposition types: Sosa goes for faculties (1991), competences (2007), and most recently dispositions related to action, agency, and risk assessment (2010). Greco (1993) appeals to skills and abilities (2010), Zagzebski (1996) and Baehr (2011) use traditional Aristotelian character traits, and

An earlier version of this chapter was presented at the "naturalized virtue epistemology" session of the Pacific APA, 2012 meeting, by one of us, and then at a workshop on mind and epistemology at UNAM. We are grateful for comments received in those sessions.

[1] See Zagzebski 1996; Riggs 2007; Sosa 2010; Pritchard 2012, and many others for the normative dimension of VE.

[2] See contributions from Ram Neta and Peter J. Graham in this volume for an overtly metaphysical virtue theory, as well as David Copp and Allan Hazlett in this volume for overtly semantic approaches.

all of these broad dispositional kinds have a range of narrower instances. While we can see a competing metaphysics of virtue epistemology here, each account is articulating some form of disposition. Dispositions are the basic metaphysical category at work in virtue-theoretic epistemology.[3]

Regarding the *because of* relation, this is essential to the success of virtue epistemology in addressing both the value problem with accounts of *agent credit* for true belief and Gettier problems by properly connecting an agent to their achievements in ways that (seem to) preclude the special mix of good luck and bad luck that generate Gettier-type problems.[4] The requirement that a success be sufficiently 'due to' the virtue in the agent engenders a commitment to causal-explanatory facts connecting an agent to their successful outcomes *through the exercise of an ability.*[5] While the intuition is clear and promising, an adequate account of what it is for an epistemically assessable state of an agent to be *sufficiently due to the abilities of the agent* has been elusive. Getting clear on the *because of relation* is necessary for any account of properly manifesting an epistemic virtue, and thus for any virtue epistemology with a robust commitment to a metaphysics of dispositions. Since virtue epistemology is agent-based, causal-explanatory facts connecting an agent to their successful outcomes will involve some form of epistemic agency, motivation, or other "agent-level" states with causal salience in success.[6]

These are largely metaphysical issues, and they constitute a certain conceptual core of virtue epistemology. Consider Duncan Pritchard's (2012) claim that there are two "master" intuitions about what turns true belief into knowledge:

(a) The ability intuition: *knowledge requires cognitive ability, in the sense that when one knows one's cognitive success should be the product of one's cognitive ability.*

(b) The anti-luck condition: *when one knows one's cognitive success (i.e. one's believing truly) is not a matter of luck.*

---

[3] Since not all dispositions are virtues, a "dispositionalist epistemology" need not be virtue theoretic. Any virtue epistemology will be metaphysically dispositionalist in a broad sense, as motivational elements are often construed dispositionally in more internalist accounts of virtue.

[4] See Pritchard 2012 for an argument that virtue epistemology alone cannot achieve both, and must appeal to an independent anti-luck condition.

[5] See Greco and Groff 2013 on the "new Aristotelianism."

[6] This is not to say that all elements of epistemic virtues must be person-level states, just that the necessary conditions for knowledge will non-trivially refer to some person-level states involved in cognitive achievements. Implicit knowledge clearly plays important roles in action selection and other person-level activities. We claim only that some agent-level states must play some significant causal-explanatory roles in order for any virtue epistemology to be truly 'agent-based' rather than 'belief-based'.

The ability intuition (hereafter just ABILITY) tells us that a true belief is well formed when "it is the product of a cognitive ability, in the sense that when one knows one's cognitive success should be the product of one's cognitive ability" (Pritchard 2012). Any skill or ability is a disposition to do something *reliably*, and thus ABILITY is essential to any reliabilist virtue epistemology. The anti-luck condition (hereafter just LUCK) requires that cognitive dispositions must be suitably integrated with the agent's other belief-forming dispositions "if we are to think of these dispositions as genuinely reflecting the agent's cognitive agency" (Pritchard 2012). ABILITY and LUCK appear to be two faces of a single intuition, since any cognitive success achieved from ability will typically *not* be a success due to luck. However, Pritchard argues that this is actually false because "these two intuitions in fact impose independent epistemic demands on our theory of knowledge, and that it is only once one recognizes this fact that one can offer a successful resolution of the analytical project" (Pritchard 2012) Pritchard argues that virtue epistemology nicely provides for the ability condition, but cannot offer an adequate anti-luck condition and is thus not a self-standing general epistemology.

While Sosa and Greco do not accept Pritchard's conclusion, they recognize similar core demands for virtue epistemology. Greco (2010) defines knowledge as a certain form of *success from ability*, and Sosa (2007) defines knowledge as a certain form of *apt performance*. The common project uniting these (and arguably all) virtue epistemologists is to properly understand the nature of cognitive abilities and their explanatory role in epistemic success. Differences between virtue epistemologists emerge in deciding what to include in the disposition types we are to call epistemic virtues, what forms of epistemic success to recognize and the different ways the former might sufficiently *explain* the latter. This is the *core project* of virtue epistemology, at least on the metaphysical side. There might be some concerns about pursuing this kind of *metaphysically thick* virtue theory in epistemology. Pritchard argues that the core project cannot succeed without borrowing essential elements from outside of virtue theory, while Sosa and Greco have accounts that aspire to achieve precisely this, but which face difficulties of their own in the process discussed below.

We seek a novel guide here in F. P. Ramsey's (1927) "success semantics," initially proposed as a theory of truth rather than knowledge by Ramsey, and recently for mental content by Bence Nanay (2012). We propose modifications to Ramsey's success semantics that are amenable to naturalistic analysis and which addresses the core project of virtue epistemology described above in ways that avoid problems facing both

Sosa's and Greco's accounts. The Ramseyian account is especially fruitful as an account of epistemic agency and nicely unifies a number of disparate and at times unstable areas in virtue epistemology. *We argue that a modified success semantics provides a naturalistic grounding for the core project of virtue epistemology.* Below we examine John Greco's recent account of "success from ability" defended in *Achieving Knowledge.* While we agree with much of Greco's account, and it is perhaps the most plausible current version of virtue-reliabilism, his contextualism about causal salience creates a problematic rift between the metaphysical and normative aspects of his theory. We diagnose the problem facing Greco below, and then defend an improved account drawing on Ramsey's success semantics.

2   Greco, dispositions, norms in virtue epistemology

In his recent book, John Greco (2010) proposes a reliabilist virtue epistemology for knowledge that explicitly requires that the *abilities* of agents serve as the *causes* of their epistemic achievements. Greco's focus on "success from ability" as the driving image for epistemic inquiry is also seen in Sosa (2007), Turri (2011), Pritchard (2012), and others, and thus captures a unifying intuition for a number of important perspectives in epistemology. Greco also has one of the most thorough virtue-theoretic accounts when it comes to the semantic and psychological underpinnings of reliabilist virtue epistemology. In this section, we critically assess some of the psychological and semantic commitments of Greco's account and provide an alternative proposal that, like Greco's, will ground epistemic assessment in agent-level mental states in the context of *action*, but requires more robust causal and motivational connections between an agent and their successful outcomes than Greco. This account shows all the merits of Greco's (2010) theory without the problematic assumptions discussed below. In the process, we will introduce a new name to contemporary virtue epistemology, Frank Ramsey. One promising aspect of Ramsey's emphasis on action rather than beliefs or propositional attitudes is that it offers the reliabilist a nice way to partially achieve responsibilist epistemic aims. Ramsey (1931) was the first person to espouse reliabilism, but did not have opportunity to develop the idea. Combining this reliabilist commitment with a suitably modified "success semantics" provides a powerful account of epistemic virtue, and promises to provide a naturalistic way of "thickening" standard reliabilism. Success semantics is an 'action-first' form of assessment that nicely unifies contexts, interests, motives, and abilities in a dispositionalist framework and holds greater promise than Greco's contextualist account discussed below.

Greco construes the 'because of' relation in terms of *causal explanatory salience* and insists that the semantics must be of the subject-sensitive contextualist sort. In particular, *Greco proposes that practical interests will specify which features of a situation are explanatorily salient in the production of true belief.* These features will show a range of agent-responsibility, but also worrisome departures from abilities and virtues. If the practical interests that determine explanatory salience do not happen to give priority to abilities over environments in a given case, then the success cannot be knowledge. This is a different way of shifting the context, because here the stakes are not shifting the standards for determining whether our reasoning was rigorous enough, but now on whether the achievement was "causal enough," so to speak. Greco is quite clear that his contextualism is for causal salience, not stakes and standards. While this route has some advantages for fully deliberate knowledge, there is a lot of knowledge that should not be as variable as Greco would have it under contextualist readings of causal salience.

How is it that context, interests, purposes, and the abilities of agents fit together into an account of epistemic virtue? Greco says that the contexts relevant for the evaluation of causal explanatory salience are 'practical environments'. For instance, to determine that someone is a good baseball player one needs to specify what kind of practical considerations are relevant. Is the player participating in the major leagues or a neighborhood game? The causal etiology of belief must be fully specified by the abilities of the agent, but in order to specify such etiology there will be practical considerations that will determine whether such abilities are causally salient. Greco says:

> In cases of knowledge, S believes the truth because S believes from intellectual ability – S's believing the truth is explained by S's believing from ability. But the success of this explanation requires more than that ability is involved. It requires that S's ability has an appropriate level of explanatory salience. (Greco 2010: 75)

Greco admits that his account of explanatory salience in terms of causal relevance is far from being a detailed account of the etiological basis of knowledge, because it does not offer a theory of causal explanation or the pragmatics of causal explanation-language, which, he says, are poorly understood in general. Nonetheless, he argues that, although sketchy and provisional, his account can solve a great many traditional difficulties in epistemology (e.g. Gettier problems, barn façade cases, etc.).

The strategy to answer questions regarding lucky or accidental true belief is to emphasize that the agent's abilities are *not* the direct cause of the belief (they are not causally and explanatory salient in the production of such belief). The absence of the abilities as causes rules out knowledge attribution or epistemic responsibility. Greco connects all these ideas as follows:

> What does all this have to do with contextualism? In short, the present thesis is that knowledge attributions are a kind of credit attribution, and that credit attributions in general involve causal explanations: To say that a person S is creditable for some state of affairs A, is to say that S's agency is salient in an explanation regarding how or why A came about. Now add a further, plausible thesis: that the semantics of causal explanation language requires a contextualist treatment. (Greco 2010: 105–6)

This is certainly a theoretically plausible account of epistemic virtue. It has many advantages, as Greco's book makes clear. But one may have concerns about the contextualist commitments of the proposal, *particularly with respect to causal explanations* and the notion of 'practical environment'. More specifically, the saliencies entailed by practical interests of agents may not match neatly (or at all) with the type of considerations that are usually salient in causal explanations. Some practical environments may make the agent's motivations salient more than others, although presumably the agent's causal relevance will be an invariant feature of these contexts where practical interests and the motivations of the agent will vary. If this is the case, which of the contexts should we pick? We will argue that Greco's account is inadequate to answer this question because it parses the semantically relevant features for the evaluation of epistemic virtue too coarsely. The question that has broad implications for naturalized virtue epistemology is whether the right solution for a reliabilist can also account for the epistemic value of an agent's motivations that responsibilists often make central to epistemic evaluation.

There are two aspects of Greco's account that make it particularly problematic. One is the role given to the practical environment, which is not how causal explanation is construed in general, at least not from a naturalistic point of view. It seems that Greco's move is justified by the unique type of cause that epistemic virtues require: agents, rather than generic physical events (or even *sub-personal* components of the agent that are not cognitively integrated). But then, why insist that it is the semantics of *causal explanation* that matters? Either it is robust causal explanation (as understood in metaphysics and philosophy of science) that matters or it is a more practically oriented, folk understanding of the salience of an event in producing an effect (a folk theory of causality) that matters. We will argue that it cannot be either, because they compromise the psychological plausibility of the resulting success attributions. An advantage of the Ramsey-inspired semantics examined in section 4 is that it explicitly incorporates a psychologically plausible restriction on knowledge attributions.

The other problematic aspect of Greco's proposal is that the causal salience of abilities on his account can be entirely unrelated to the motivational cognitive processes of the agent. While this is a worry for simple reliabilism, Greco is aware that motivation and some form of subjective justification is an important ingredient of a virtue-theoretic account of knowledge. For this reason, he suggests that an Aristotelian model may be the best way to understand virtues in general:

> Now it seems to me that the Aristotelian model is the better one for theories of epistemic normativity. This is because, it seems to me, knowledge requires both responsibility in one's cognitive conduct and reliability in achieving epistemic ends. But however this issue is decided, the main point is that virtue theories define the normative properties of beliefs in terms of the normative properties of persons, i.e. the stable dispositions or character traits that constitute their intellectual virtues, however these are to be understood. (Greco 2010: 43)

This is a crucial issue concerning the psychological underpinnings of virtues, as well as the general theoretical implications of an adequate naturalized account of epistemic virtue. Evidently, without a detailed explanation of how the normative properties of persons (their stable epistemic dispositions) are included in the causal explanatory salience that Greco endorses for knowledge attribution, one cannot determine whether such attributions comport with epistemic norms as understood above.

In the next section, we argue that no strictly causal account of the 'because of' relation is sufficient to provide the explanation needed above. This becomes a problem for any naturalized virtue-reliabilism that extends this commitment to explaining epistemic *responsibility* exclusively in terms of causal salience. To be clear, any naturalized version of epistemic virtue must appeal to causal explanation (e.g. reliable belief-forming process, stable dispositions to respond accurately given certain conditions, etc.). However, it must also explain how such explanations are compatible with a broad range of knowledge attributions that essentially include *motivational* aspects of epistemic agency, such as conscientiousness and open-mindedness.

Before proceeding, it is worth noting how explicit Greco is about the importance of responsibility for reliabilist accounts of epistemic virtue. He says that an agent S is epistemically responsible "if and only if S's believing that p is properly motivated; if and only if S's believing that p results from intellectual dispositions that S manifests when S is motivated to believe the truth" (Greco 2010: 43). He then defines epistemic virtue as follows: "S's belief that p is epistemically virtuous if and only if both (a) S's belief that p is epistemically responsible; and (b) S is *objectively reliable* in believing that p" (2010: 43, our emphasis). It seems that the upshot of these definitions is this: suppose that two agents are identical with respect to the objective reliability of their cognitive processes. Every time they form a belief, they have the same degree of objective reliability (their beliefs have an identical likelihood of being more true than false).[7] Suppose one wants to attribute knowledge to these epistemic agents. Their being reliable is a big element in their favor. But this is not enough for a reliabilist virtue epistemology. In assessing their epistemic deliverances and achievements, their abilities must be causally salient (i.e. the agents must arrive at true belief because of their abilities). This is why a reliabilist virtue epistemology is much more fine grained than standard reliabilism. According to standard reliabilism, both agents are equally justified, and if their beliefs equally comply with some safety or sensitivity constraint, then they both know. For any virtue epistemology, one also needs to show that the agent arrived at such beliefs because of their epistemic abilities, which will typically include the proper motivation to use those abilities. Thus, it is perfectly plausible to not attribute knowledge to one or both of these agents, even though their beliefs are equally reliably produced.

Now the worry is how we can include motivational states of the agent in an account of knowledge attribution that appeals exclusively to the (robust) *causal* salience of abilities. What we shall argue is that, since reliabilist virtue epistemology provides a more fine-grained theory of knowledge attribution, the semantics for such attributions must not appeal exclusively to causal salience. Rather, the semantics for such attributions must be as fine grained as virtue-theoretic achievements generally require, and will include, somehow, the motivational aspects of epistemic agents.

For a naturalized virtue epistemology of the reliabilist kind it is particularly pressing to address this issue with psychological evidence. The purpose of the next two sections is to provide the outlines of a reliabilist theory of epistemic virtue with a semantics that explicitly incorporates

---

[7] See Goldman 1992 for a classic account of the objective or scientifically constrained standards for the reliability of cognitive epistemic processes.

aims, motivations, and goals, and is based on the most recent psychological evidence.

3 Causality: folksy, metaphysical, and psychologically constrained

Greco's *explanatory salience contextualism* does not really appeal to the motivations of the agent, rather it focuses exclusively on the contextually variable "causally relevant" factors of a situation, which might or might not include motivational states of the agent being assessed. One worry here is that agents are assessed at least partly on their motivations. At a minimum, an epistemically virtuous agent will not be having motivations contrary to the aim of belief (truth, knowledge), and this is especially true in attributions of *credit-based success*. This element of epistemic assessment is clear when an agent has a defective motivation, say a desire for comforting beliefs rather than true beliefs. While this seems clear enough, properly understanding the 'desire for truth' will be an important and perhaps challenging project for naturalized virtue epistemology, and specifically for the prospects of responsibilist virtue epistemology. We can only gesture at how the epistemic-Ramsey-success account defended here can properly locate the role of desires in responsibilist virtue, but we will do so in the concluding section.

The examples offered by Greco concerning causal salience are aimed at illustrating the contextualist semantics he favors. Some of them are clearly based on practical considerations that the folk use to attribute knowledge based on abilities (such as the example of the gambler, his wife, and his friends, who have different standards and practical interests regarding his alleged abilities for choosing winning horses).[8] Other examples concerning simple causal salience, rather than knowledge attribution, appeal to practical interests, but the context seems to be framed in a more metaphysical setting and the impression one gets from these examples is that they concern causality in the strict metaphysical sense, rather than causality as understood by the folk.

For instance, Greco's example concerning the car accident is presented in terms of two different standards for salience, both based on practical interests. In describing an accident scene, the police focus on the high

---

[8] One problem with this example is that the ability to succeed in gambling may not be an epistemic virtue at all, especially if one considers what is at stake in gambling (which includes risk and luck as defining features). But we will not focus on this problem here.

speed, and for them the high speed of the car is what is causally salient (the cause of the accident), while for city planners what is causally salient is the deficient design of the road. But clearly, the limits on what is causally salient in this example are very different from the plausible metaphysical or psychological limits concerning the gambler's example. In the car accident case, the actual speed of the car is a lot more important than the interests of the police and the actual design of the road is crucial for anything the planners have to say.

What is causally salient about the accident, therefore, depends on *objective information that is preserved in the causal chain.*[9] Absent one of the facts concerning road design or speed, the accident would not have happened. This sounds like metaphysical causality, dependent on facts that remain *invariant* across different interpretations based on practical interests. For example, at some point, one can imagine a judge asking: "I know that the road in question is in very bad shape and that the speed limit was crossed. But I want to know exactly why the accident happened. Which of these two salient features was *objectively* more relevant?" This is the kind of question that forensic scientists have to answer all the time. Robust causal salience requires objective relevance and information preservation, and some form of this claim will describe what it is to properly *manifest* a disposition.[10]

One may think that forensic scientists bring new practical interests to the table. But notice that whatever interests they bring in, their assessment will be fact-involving and constitutive of a causal chain. This is in sharp contrast with the gambler example. These incompatible attributions of knowledge based on the salience of the abilities of the gambler (or lack thereof) do not seem to be constitutive of two different causal chains that preserve objective information about a situation. On the contrary, they seem to fully depend on the practical interests of the gambler's wife and his friends. The wife's concern at not having money might explain her hesitance to attribute the epistemic ability underlying the alleged 'knowledge that a horse will win' to her husband, while the other gamblers' interests in finding tips for wining bets explain their eagerness to attribute such knowledge. But this sounds just like hesitance and eagerness. More precisely, it is hard to see any causal chain being established by these practical interests that could preserve two different ways in which objective

---

[9] See Salmon 1998 for discussion on the importance of objective information-preservation in causal chains.
[10] For a nice account of the distinction between 'because of' and 'manifesting', see Turri 2011.

information is preserved. In the previous case, there are two alternative causal chains that preserve objective information. With the gambler's case there is hardly one (the alleged causal chain seems to be a feature of how different subjects interpret the situation). So this seems to be a folksy understanding of causality that is not really fact-involving, at least not in the robust counterfactually supportive way that causality generally requires, e.g. the horse could have won just by pure luck and the gambler just had a lot of consecutive lucky guesses – a very *nearby possibility* in the context of gambling, which is problematic for Greco's notion of 'practical environment'.

But even assuming that these examples are unproblematic, the abilities of *agents* need not be captured by a folk or metaphysical understanding of causality. One needs to know more about the psychology of agents and their motivations in order to determine whether they are satisfying the constraints imposed by a (reliabilist) virtue epistemology. What type of agency will be required to explain epistemic success? The psychological evidence has shown that introspective and conscious reflective constraints on epistemic processes are counterproductive.[11] People are very bad at determining their own reasons for action and decision-making, and they violate very simple rules of logic and probability when presented with irrelevant information which is, incidentally, potentially constitutive of a practical environment, as in Kahneman and Tversky's famous "Linda" case. So why would one hope that agents are any good at determining the basis for actions of other people? It seems that the best thing to do is to focus on paradigmatic reliabilist cases of cognitive dispositions: perceptual beliefs, memory, communication and testimony, language acquisition, motor control, basic forms of inductive and deductive inference, and even the proper use of heuristics. All of these involve abilities and an associated range of epistemic successes, but they also allow for a much more *minimal* sense of agency and thus avoid worries about the truth-conduciveness of reflective and epistemically costly forms of reasoning that might be required for knowledge by a (reflectively) more demanding virtue epistemology.

Even in the case of perceptual belief one must be careful. Any epistemic account of the causal salience of the abilities of agents must be informed and constrained by the relevant psychological evidence. Greco specifies two important psychological constraints on epistemic agency. He says that it need not involve conscious awareness, and also that it must allow

---

[11] See Kornblith 2013 for a full exploration of the limits of reflection in achieving knowledge.

for cognitive integration with other reliable epistemic processes, in a way that guarantees sensitivity to those processes. We will take these important constraints for granted. Epistemologists have assumed that there is only one type of agency involved in basic perceptual belief-forming processes, and reliabilists, in particular, have assumed that all perceptual belief is reliable and sensitive to accurate information from other *perceptual* cognitive processes (the qualification is important, because these processes are not in general influenced by inferential reasoning, i.e. they seem to be encapsulated, although this is not entirely uncontroversial).

However, not all the cognitive integration for perception is epistemically sensitive. Perceptual illusions illustrate this point. One consciously sees the difference in length of two lines in the Müller-Lyer illusion, even though one knows (and therefore truly believes) that they are the same length. Our conscious visual perception is, in this particular case, impervious to reliable epistemic influence. But surprisingly, motor control is epistemically sensitive to such information, even in cases of perceptual illusion. This is not because conscious belief influences motor control. On the contrary, motor control is not influenced at all by conscious belief. What is striking about this finding is that the perceptual system has a divided agent in this case. One perceptual "half" of the agent is influenced by the illusion and the other one is sensitive (in the epistemically relevant sense of the word).[12]

For instance, in the Müller-Lyer illusion, although the subjects' conscious self-report is inaccurate and reflects the illusion's cognitive influence, their motor control (specifically their unconscious manual behavior for grasping) *is accurate* and *not influenced* by the illusion. This seems to suggest that conscious perception has little influence on action. However, Stöttinger and Perner (2006) showed that although motor control is not influenced by the illusion, cognitive processes that involve agency for *action selection*, just as conscious perception, are influenced by the illusion.

In their experiment, Stöttinger and Perner presented subjects with vertical lines grouped in two sets (one with open brackets and the other with closed brackets, as in the standard Müller-Lyer illusion). When asked "which gang of lines would you fight?" subjects chose the "smaller" lines although their motor control in the absence of this question did not distinguish between the sets of lines, because it was not influenced by the

---

[12] This way of talking about divided agency is not new, and actually has become quite standard in cognitive psychology. See for instance, Kahneman 2011, who distinguishes between Systems 1 and 2 (according to Kahneman, two different forms of epistemic agency, one reliable and the other unreliable and susceptible of being influenced by irrelevant information).

illusion. This finding demonstrates the dissociation between action selection and motor control. Morsella and Bargh (2010: 7) say that this dissociation occurs because inborn or learned information from the ventral stream (which is associated with conscious urges) constrains action selection but not motor control.[13]

Conscious inclinations or urges about fighting are clearly irrelevant for reliable perception. But they are certainly constitutive of practical interests that create what Greco calls 'practical environments'. This finding strongly suggests that one should not focus on the practical environments that make a causal narrative (folksy or metaphysical) salient. In this case the salient ability of the agent is unreliable, given the fighting practical environment, while in the practical environment of grasping the object, the ability of the agent is reliable. Thus, one needs to focus on the agent's psychology to constrain causal chains based on stable epistemic dispositions, regardless of how practical environments are construed. In other words, the order of explanation should start with the agent's psychology, not with the practical environments for causal salience and practical interests. For this reason, folksy narratives seem irrelevant for epistemic responsibility, while metaphysical ones seem too broad to really explain it.

The information for action selection based on conscious inclinations may lead to good practical decisions, but not to reliably produced true belief. Accurate motor control concerning unconscious information about length, on the other hand, is a precondition for successful navigation. So it makes sense that the epistemically relevant information that allows agents to succeed, based on their knowledge of the environment, ignores, or is insensitive to, the epistemically *irrelevant* conscious information concerning who to fight, and related practical interests based on conscious urges.

Epistemic success (achieving true belief) from epistemic virtue seems to be guaranteed only at the motor-control level in this particular example, but the dissociation between motor control and action selection extends to many forms of agency. Crucially, cognitive integration for motor-control processes that lead to success in a reliable fashion is insensitive to epistemically irrelevant inclinations, or highly sophisticated theoretical or philosophical beliefs, in spite of the fact that those inclinations may underlie practical interests. However, as the example just mentioned shows, cognitive integration for conscious processes and action selection is, at least in the case of illusion, sensitive to epistemically irrelevant information.

---

[13] See also Goodale 2010.

So motor-control knowledge complies with the right kind of cognitive integration required for very *stable epistemic virtues*.

Epistemic virtues are generally described as stable dispositions attributable to an agent. The more stable the disposition, the more successful the agent. The less sensitive epistemic virtues are to practical or highly theoretical considerations, the more stable they will be, and vice versa. Epistemologists need to be selective and careful when they talk about epistemic agency. A rich sense of agency that includes all sorts of conscious and unconscious inclinations is problematic (some abilities of the same agent turn out to be unreliable in some situations, while others tend to be highly reliable, even though the perceptual stimulus is the same).

Moreover, motor-control knowledge of the type that is involved in grasping objects is firmly associated with *facts* about the environment, and the success of agents is contingent upon these facts. True beliefs about environmental features are formed reliably because of these virtues, thereby allowing agents to avoid errors and lucky guesses across a large variety of situations. So there is counterfactual dependency between the success of agents and these stable epistemic virtues that reliably form true beliefs about facts. This is the type of counterfactual dependency that is indispensable for a causal account of epistemic virtue in terms of the 'because of' relation: metaphysically plausible and psychologically informed. But this does not mean that practical reasons, conscious action selection, and introspection are epistemically irrelevant in general. As Greco says, there may be epistemic virtues of many different kinds (not necessarily associated with knowledge, but with other epistemic goals). Obviously, conscious perception is also highly reliable if not disturbed by illusions. But the point is that the same epistemic agent may manifest radically different abilities at any point, concerning the same stimulus, and, therefore, the notion of agency must be psychologically construed in order to provide a naturalized virtue epistemology.

4 Success semantics: the constraints on causality and cognitive processing

An important difficulty with respect to Greco's characterization of the 'because of' relation is that causal salience based on practical interests does not necessarily preserve objective information constitutive of causal chains. More specifically, knowledge attribution becomes problematically dependent on practical considerations concerning causal salience that assume a uniform type of agency, which does not comport adequately with the experimental evidence on action selection and motor control. This is a significant problem for the prospect of a reliabilist-naturalized virtue epistemology.

The counterfactual supporting generalizations that are characteristic of causal relations seem to demand a more direct correlation between the agent's success and the causal conditions required for their success, which should be confirmed experimentally. Practical interests may be relevant for some aspects of knowledge attribution (particularly with respect to how the term 'knowledge' is used by the folk), but they do not seem to help explain naturalized epistemic virtues. Moreover, this causal requirement is hard to square with a semantics that centers on the motivations and goals of agents.

It seems that a plausible way to address these problems is by offering a different semantics for knowledge attribution with quite unique features (e.g. causal relevance compatible with naturalistic constraints, motivational components, and abilities of agents). We shall argue that the best candidate to fulfill this role is the so-called 'success semantics,' proposed originally by Ramsey (1927). Ramsey said that knowledge is true belief that is *achieved by a reliable process* (1931). Independently of this thesis, he also proposed that the truth condition of a belief is the condition that guarantees the success of *desires* based on that belief (1927: 144).[14] These theses entail a version of reliabilism that has significant advantages because it incorporates motivational-cognitive factors into our account of epistemic abilities. The question is how Ramsey's original account of content can be tailored to accommodate the specific requirements of reliabilist-naturalized virtue epistemology.

True beliefs, according to Ramsey's proposal, can be defined as *functions* from desires (or goals) to actions that cause agents to behave in ways that succeed in satisfying their desires or goals.[15] This characterization defines belief-forming processes as functional operations or procedures that determine a mapping from an input (i.e. a desire or goal) to an output (a concrete action or the fulfillment of the goal), and it has the advantage that it does not focus *exclusively* on beliefs and their contents (propositional attitudes and possible worlds). As required by virtue epistemology, success semantics focuses on the agent and her epistemic motivations, and starts the causal order of explanation with the epistemic abilities of agents.

---

[14] This formulation of Ramsey's proposal is due to Whyte 1990.
[15] See Bermudez 2003: 66.

Moreover, this account mirrors the structure of *dispositions*, which have antecedent conditions that must be satisfied for the manifestation condition to occur, and according to a standard characterization of virtues, epistemic virtues are stable dispositions that manifest in true belief. This means that epistemic virtues, so characterized, may comply with a *safety condition* according to which, if an agent knows that something is the case, then her desires could not easily have gone unsatisfied. This is explained by the fact that the true belief could not have easily been false given that it was reliably produced. This success will also be due to the agent because the satisfaction of desire will be due to some action of the agent. It is important to emphasize that, as a general theory of content and truth, success semantics is explicitly a *causal theory*, because, as Peter Smith (2003) says:

> For certain beliefs, the content of the belief is that *p* just if, for any appropriate desire, actions caused by that belief combined with a desire will be successful in realizing the desire's object just in case that *p*. And of course, there is no magic about the relation between its being the case that p and successful action: it will be a causal condition for success. (Smith 2003: 49)

As mentioned, truth can be defined similarly, by stating that a true belief is one that causes successful actions, if combined with appropriate desires.[16] A very important feature of this definition is that it appeals to the *causal powers* of beliefs in conjunction with *motivational* states of agents, thereby allowing for a naturalistic account of epistemic motivation. The condition that must obtain for the satisfaction of desires is one that must be satisfied reliably. Success is, obviously, not guaranteed across all possible worlds. Rather, the causal powers of beliefs manifest only in conjunction with desires at a specific set of worlds, determining a contingent relation among them.

This also maps neatly with the metaphysical characteristics of dispositions, their causal bases and their manifestation conditions. Coupled with reliability, this account says that: *a belief is true if and only if, in conjunction with the right motivation, actual and possible actions caused by the belief are typically (reliably) successful.*[17] The condition that must obtain for the satisfaction of desires or motivations is called the 'utility condition'. Mellor (1991) describes it as follows:

---

[16] See Mellor 1991.
[17] See Blackburn 2011 for more advantages of success semantics as a theory of content.

[We] can't equate a belief's truth conditions with those in which every action it helps to cause succeeds. But we can if we restrict the actions to those caused just by it and some desire. Then its truth conditions are what I shall call its 'utility conditions': those in which all such actions would achieve the desired end. (Mellor 1991: 23)

This restriction is crucial because it shows that *motivational components are fundamental to constrain the range of causally relevant doxastic attitudes*, as well as the *type* of cognitive process that leads to success. These kinds of issues are also very relevant to the core project of virtue epistemology discussed in section 1 above, which centers on individuating disposition types and clarifying the causal-explanatory role of abilities in successful outcomes.

But despite its advantages, Ramsey's success semantics needs to be modified, so that one obtains not a semantics for true belief, but for knowledge attributions and our account of what it is for a true belief to be sufficiently *because of* the epistemic virtue of the believer. In other words, the beliefs in question of course must be true, what needs semantic evaluation is whether true beliefs are produced by virtuous epistemic dispositions. We claim that a success semantics for epistemology can provide valuable advances in understanding the etiological nature of knowledge by unifying the following desiderata in a straightforward action-first normative-factive principle that locates the agent right at the center of evaluation.

(1)   Provide the *right kind of causes* – reliable psychological dispositions of agents, as in the case of motor-control abilities.
(2)   These dispositions must also be attributable to the agent in a way that generates credit for any epistemic success that might be achieved because of the causal connection in (1).
(3)   Explain cognitive integration and the epistemic standings it gives rise to.
(4)   Motivational states are also included in the dispositions that manifest knowledge and sufficiently involve the agent.

This is a plausible extension of success semantics, because knowledge is a type of epistemic success. The payoff is that all the naturalistic advantages of success semantics can be used to give a virtue-theoretical account of knowledge. While the role of desires is central here, a Ramsey-success is also constrained by facts in the world outside the agent. Think of the sense in which a Ramsey-success is fact-involving this way: If you perform a complex task, like playing piano, it seems obvious that the set of beliefs that would be required to succeed in hitting the keys is larger and more varied that those you would choose based on how you want to hit the keys.

A modification of Ramsey's success semantics yields the following straightforward account of epistemic achievements, which will need further refining below: a virtuous cognitive disposition is one that causes an agent to reliably satisfy his or her epistemic desires. More specifically, the truth condition for the attribution of an epistemic achievement is the condition that guarantees the success of epistemic goals, and the action is also caused by abilities attributable to the agent. Knowledge attributions are adequate when they are based on the motivational and doxastic components of abilities that produce true belief. In the specific case of knowledge, the only relevant desire may be the desire to believe the truth and avoid falsehood (see Greco 2010). Other desires may aim for the means to truth (say the desire to have justified beliefs) or for different epistemic achievements such as understanding and intellectual creativity.

This establishes a naturalistic semantic constraint on knowledge attribution specifically, and not a constraint on propositional content in general, as Ramsey originally proposed. The variables salient for explaining success involve: (a) desires in the agent; (b) causal relations independent of these desires; (c) successful outcomes caused by (a) and (b). But this needs unpacking, because of the findings concerning motor control and action selection. A Ramsey-success cannot plausibly require the satisfaction of *a fully conscious epistemic desire* to believe the truth. Rather, we propose that it is a motivational *inclination* (which may be unconscious) that must cause the action that constitutes or causes success. Manual behavior manifests the true belief (or at least an epistemic entitlement) that the lines are equal, while the response for action selection does not. The motivational inclination in manual behavior is to succeed in accurately selecting lines because of the fact-based aspects of those lines. The abilities that underlie successful manual behavior are stable, even in the presence of illusory stimuli that trick conscious perception. Causality is specified by the facts, the abilities of the agent, and the agent's success rate, and not by narratives involving practical interests.

This may be the best way to achieve a naturalistic version of epistemic responsibility. As mentioned, Greco chooses explanatory salience contextualism for the semantic evaluation of knowledge attributions, but this semantic approach does not really appeal to the *motivations* of the agent, and rather focuses exclusively on the causally salient factors of a situation, as specified by the interests of the attributor. An advantage of the present account is that it focuses on *both* causally relevant factors and motivational components of cognitive dispositions.

5 Objections

The situationist objection to this proposal is as follows. Virtue epistemology does not need this kind of help. These divided agent findings actually have a skeptical consequence, namely, that in many circumstances, abilities are unstable and produce false belief. In particular, the findings on human rationality suggest that there are two systems, 1 and 2. System 1 is highly dependent on context, and systematically trumps the careful, though slow, epistemic processing of System 2. A divided epistemic agent is the source of worries about the stability of epistemic dispositions, and this is evidence against a reliabilist version of epistemic virtue.

A response to this objection is that the findings on Systems 1 and 2, as well as the findings on motor control and action selection, are compatible with a naturalized virtue epistemology based on very robust abilities, confirmed by experimental evidence. Motor-control abilities are remarkably sensitive and robust. Other forms of robust abilities may be found for quick inferences, across different situations, if one assumes that success rate is crucial for knowledge attribution. Notice that the difference between Systems 1 and 2 is unhelpful in the case of the illusion of length. One is squarely within System 1. But this does not open up a situationist challenge for perceptual belief. Rather, it calls for a psychological constraint on the semantics for knowledge attribution that highlights the importance of motivations, like success semantics.

Another objection is that skepticism about folksy knowledge attributions (which seem to be the relevant ones that need explaining) seems to be entailed by this proposal. If one cannot account for the person in the street attributing knowledge to her peers, then the threat of skepticism with respect to normal knowledge attribution is significant, because it seems that only experts will be able to adequately attribute knowledge to subjects.

The case of the lines is just an illustration of how epistemic agency is not a uniform and monolithic phenomenon. Rather, it comes in many varieties and involves many different abilities. But, in general, *success* is a good guide to accurate knowledge attribution, and so no skepticism about folksy knowledge attributions follows from our proposal. However, for a fully naturalized virtue epistemology, the most stable virtues must be identified, and motor-control abilities seem to be more stable than action-selection ones. In other words, motor-control abilities, because of their importance in successful navigation, seem to be a model for robust epistemic virtue. Agents have a psychology with a rich variety of these epistemic virtues, which underlie folk attributions based on the success of agents. Because of the success rate produced by these abilities, these attributions can approximate the psychological constrained ones very closely.

In order to avoid confusion, it is important to clarify that although psychological mechanisms and processing are not transparent (either introspectively or by judging the abilities of others), success is *evident* in the epistemic achievements of agents. In other words, the manifestation of these virtues is plainly in view. If agents get things right in many cases, then this by itself is evidence that they have robust epistemic dispositions to form true belief. Findings on how some epistemic stable dispositions get tricked under laboratory circumstances should not be interpreted skeptically, particularly in cases where information is ambiguously presented (e.g. set inclusion and likelihood, understood abstractly or with a concrete example concerning practical considerations).

Another objection is that unconscious motor control does not manifest in true *belief*, because beliefs have a compositional-inferential structure that epistemic abilities based on unconscious inclinations lack. A response to this objection is that if virtues had to necessarily manifest in conscious true belief, then that would place a psychologically implausible restriction on virtue theories. Another related response is that, given the psychological evidence, a naturalized epistemology should liberate the notion of what counts as a doxastic attitude. These responses have been carefully defended in the literature, so we shall not elaborate on them here.

An important source of the intuitive power behind the notion that agents are responsible only when they are in full conscious control of their actions comes from analogies with moral responsibility. How could one be morally responsible for an action if one is unconscious of producing such action? It is true that, in general, there seems to be a kind of a priori necessity to define moral responsibility in terms of fully conscious (perhaps even reflective-introspective) awareness of the action and one's own motivations to perform such action. But although analogies between moral and epistemic responsibility are sometimes useful, they are not useful in the specific case of ability attribution. Epistemic agents may succeed based on abilities to which they lack conscious access (even though conscious access is compatible with such success).

It is known that accessibilist versions of internalism may be too strong, even if one defends an internalist view of justification.[18] For reliabilist theories that are coupled with motivations in order to generate a naturalized virtue epistemology that emphasizes success, there is no reason to think that a strong reflective or conscious requirement is necessary for epistemic virtue. Greco certainly does not endorse such a requirement, and given the psychological evidence, it would be counterproductive to impose such constraints on naturalized epistemic virtues.

With the type of virtues discussed in this chapter, the epistemic agent is not in absolute, conscious reflective control of her epistemic achievements. But the agent is *sufficiently* in control to be the causal source of epistemic success, and this is all a virtue epistemology along reliabilist lines needs. With respect to the kind of motivations that epistemic virtues must have, likewise, these can be of a very minimal kind (unconscious and unreflective), such as inclinations to believe the truth about features of the environment in navigation.

A related objection is that knowledge produced by motor-control-like abilities is dumb, or animal-like. This account is, according to this objection, too minimal to explain the subtleties of traditional epistemological issues, such as skepticism, justified withheld judgment, and meta-virtues in general. It also seems to be too broad, besides being too minimal. All sorts of dumb creatures count as having knowledge (basically all creatures that can navigate have knowledge of the environment).

One response to this objection is that the account of virtue epistemology we are defending is naturalistic, and, therefore, based on the empirical evidence. The empirical evidence has shown consistently and overwhelmingly that highly reflective conscious processing is by no means required for epistemic success. On the contrary, evidence has shown that highly reflective conscious processing gets in the way of epistemic successes.[19] This is enough to respond to this objection.

With respect to the objection that this account is too broad, it is crucial to clarify that our account does not restrict epistemic virtues to navigation and animal-like behavior (although we see nothing wrong in characterizing success from ability of the animal kind as knowledge). What we are proposing is that epistemic virtues must be very robust dispositions, and, therefore, motor control-like. Knowledge of syntax is a good illustration of what we have in mind. Knowledge of syntax seems to be uniquely

---

[18] See Feldman and Conee 2001.
[19] See Kornblith 2013.

human. It is the result of unconscious abilities and cognitive processes that are extremely robust. Children can learn any language in a highly unmonitored, unconscious, and unreflective way. Thus, knowledge of syntax is an example of a highly sophisticated epistemic achievement that is motor control-like.

Finally, there are two objections that are based on the empirical evidence.[20] One objection is that motor control seems to be best understood as strictly sub-personal, and, therefore, that these abilities seem to be a collection of fragmented capacities that have little in common. If so, these abilities seem inadequate to account for knowledge that is attributable to the agent *as such*, because they are only attributable to fragmented capacities of the agent that may not be fully integrated with her motivations.

A response to this objection is that all the examples of epistemic abilities that we have used (and the only ones our account would consider as candidates for producing knowledge) involve representational capacities at the organism level (e.g. syntax processing, grasping an object based on the motor intention to do so, etc.). Moreover, as mentioned previously, we are assuming the criterion of cognitive integration, which Greco uses to respond to the odd or fleeting processes objection.

Another objection is that some experiments (e.g. Glover and Dixon 2002) seem to suggest that motor control cannot be decoupled from semantic information, in such a way that semantic information systematically affects the reliability of motor control, thus challenging the modal robustness and reliable character of these abilities. A response to this objection is that, indeed, there are multiple findings showing how semantic information decreases the accuracy of kinematic responses, such as grasping. However, the same body of research shows that this happens *only at the action-selection and planning stage*, which is conscious. Like the example we offered before, unconscious motor control is not hampered by this information. So, actually, all these findings *support* our approach.

An alternative reply to this objection is that the fact that some information interferes with the speed and accuracy of a behavioral response does not entail that the abilities involved are unreliable. In the Stroop task, the interference between inclinations (the automatic inclination to read a word vs. identifying a color) does not entail that the capacities involved are unreliable because of context sensitivity. The capacities to read and detect color are *incredibly reliable* across subjects, in many conditions. Interference only shows that having two inclinations affects processing.

[20] We are grateful to Lauren Olin for bringing these objections to our attention.

6   Conclusion

The semantics for knowledge attribution that a naturalized virtue epistemology requires must include motivation. This is important not only because of theoretical considerations, but also because the empirical evidence indicates that this is needed. While a complete naturalized virtue epistemology, based on the main tenets of reliabilism, is still a work in progress, it is important to specify the constraints and contours of such a theory. We argued that Greco's practical interests-based semantics fails with respect to the theoretical requirements of virtue epistemology and the psychological evidence. An alternative semantics must satisfy these requirements.

As Edward Craig (1990) says, subjects use knowledge attribution to flag good sources of information. Knowledge attribution based on motor-control abilities that underlie successful navigation certainly counts as a useful way of flagging good sources of information. Successful navigators need to encode information that is constantly changing by eliminating noise and unreliably formed beliefs. The evidence suggests that humans and animals have a large repertoire of these epistemic skills, and they can form the basis of a naturalized virtue epistemology, like the one Greco envisages.

Motor control-like abilities can be highly sophisticated and normative, such as those involved in unconscious syntax learning. Conscious integration may lead to knowledge too, obviously, but the integration must be such that the general constraints of success semantics are satisfied. The strong reliabilist and psychological constraints of a naturalized virtue theory require that the basic abilities that underlie knowledge be motor control-like. Thus, one can integrate motor responses with conscious information, and have more complicated inclinations, such as withholding judgment. But none of this requires strong reflective or accessibilist criteria.

However, there may be room for some strongly responsibilist epistemic virtues for agents, such as conscientiousness. One may construe such virtues in terms of meta-reliability. This connects with Craig's proposal that flagging reliable sources of information (a second-order form of reliability) is what drives knowledge attribution, which has important implications not only for virtue epistemology, but also for social and individual epistemology in general.

Appendix

Success semantics depends on aggregation (because reliability depends on rate) and sources of information. Knowledge attributions are not based just on success (blind success) or just reliability (independently of motivation). Knowledge attributions, therefore, depend on success that manifests in reliably produced true belief in the context of specific epistemic inclinations of an agent. But how does this semantics fare against the alternative proposals?

We argued that Greco's gambler's case is not a case of knowledge. Our proposal accounts for this, because there are no fact-involving aspects of the situation that could constitute a *utility condition* (i.e. luck would do). However, many cases of animal knowledge are clearly within the scope of our proposal, and qualify as knowledge from epistemic ability and inclinations. Some highly sophisticated forms of knowledge, such as knowledge of syntax, turn out to be analogous to these forms of knowledge. So our proposal has the advantages of Greco's naturalistic account, without the problems explained above.

How about other forms of contextualism, besides Greco's proposal? We shall focus on Jason Stanley's (2005) account, for the purpose of conciseness. The present proposal is contextualist in the sense that knowing information about facts and the truth-conduciveness of beliefs will not suffice for knowledge attribution. One also needs to know two extra pieces of information: whether the reliable dispositions to produce true belief are attributable to the agent, and whether the agent had the inclinations to achieve true belief with respect to a specific epistemic task. Depending on the task, the standards of evaluation change, so this is one source of contextual variance. Another source of variability concerns the modal robustness of dispositions (they do not manifest necessarily in their consequents across all possible worlds). But instead of cashing out these contextual variants in terms of interests, we propose to cash them out in terms of the more familiar metaphysical requirements for the manifestation of dispositions, which are compatible with contextualist interpretations.

Thus, we think one can obtain very similar results to the ones Stanley reports by appealing to intuitions concerning success from ability, rather than by appealing to how high or low the practical stakes are. Consider the case of Hanna and Sarah who need to deposit a check in the bank. Yes, it seems that the stakes drive the intuitions, but only insofar as we want Hanna and Sarah to *succeed* in an epistemic goal that involves a lot more than the mere fact that the bank will open. In particular, we want them to form a true belief that concerns their funds being available for a very important impending payment. This includes their abilities, inclinations, and a utility condition that includes the bank being open. This is the main example discussed by Stanley, and it seems that everything else he says about similar cases is compatible with our proposal. We think that, actually, the 'success from ability' intuition does a better job in explaining the attributions that Stanley analyzes. And, as Greco says, success from ability also captures the 'anti-luck' and 'ability' intuitions. Therefore, we believe that the success semantics approach we defend in this chapter may be the best account not only of naturalized epistemic virtue but also of the semantics of knowledge attribution.

CHAPTER 8

Re-evaluating the situationist challenge to virtue epistemology

Duncan Pritchard

1 The situationist challenge to virtue theory

The situationist challenge to virtue theory initially arose with respect to virtue ethics. In broad terms, virtue ethicists treat the character traits of the agent – specifically, her moral virtues – as fundamental to their ethical theory. The morally good person is the morally virtuous person, where this means an agent possessing the moral virtues and who thus acts appropriately across a range of different situations where morally relevant action is called for. So, for example, the good person will characteristically respond to seeing a person in need by helping them, where their good actions arise out of their recognition that the person is in need and that they ought to help them.

In this way, virtue ethicists make essential appeal to stable character traits (i.e. virtues) in setting out their view. It is precisely this element of the proposal that situationists object to, in that they claim that findings from recent studies in empirical psychology demonstrate that agents do not in general possess such character traits, and instead mostly act in response to particular features of the situation in hand. Here, for example, is Gilbert Harman's summary of the situationist thesis:

> We very confidently attribute character traits to other people in order to explain their behaviour. But our attributions tend to be wildly incorrect and, in fact, there is no evidence that people differ in their character traits. They differ in their situations and in their perceptions of their situations. They differ in their goals, strategies, neuroses, optimism, etc. But character traits do not explain what differences there are. (Harman 1999: §8)

The studies which putatively support this claim are extensive. They demonstrate that how a subject responds to a situation is in fact highly sensitive to features of the situation (or perceived features of the situation),

Thanks to Abrol Fairweather and Allan Hazlett for helpful discussions on related topics. Special thanks to Mark Alfano for detailed comments on an earlier version of this chapter.

including features of the situation of which they may be consciously unaware. Such influencing situational factors include such things as ambient odors and sounds, weather conditions, and the presence of bystanders, to list just three. Situationists therefore claim that what explains a subject's actions is not their character (where this involves stable character traits of a virtue-theoretic kind), or not normally their character anyway, but rather how they are responding to the particular situation in hand.[1]

Insofar as one grants that these studies do indeed generate this conclusion, then it follows that virtue ethicists are at the very least required to give up on the idea that their view has general application to the folk at large. That is, that while perhaps some particularly sophisticated people out there have the kind of character traits that virtue ethicists postulate, this is not true of most people. Given that virtue ethics is meant to be a proposal with general application, this would be a potentially disastrous consequence for the view.

Of course, as one would expect, virtue ethicists have disputed that these studies do have this disastrous consequence. For example, one main line of counterattack has been to claim that such studies mistakenly equate the behavior manifested by the agents concerned with the kind of character-driven behavior that virtue ethicists are concerned with.[2]

My interest here is not, however, with the challenge posed by situationism to virtue ethics, but rather a putative extension of that challenge to virtue epistemology. On the face of it, whatever challenge one makes to the former ought to straightforwardly carry over to the latter. After all, since both proposals are forms of virtue theory which hence make essential appeal to the character traits of the agent (whether they be moral or intellectual virtues), then any situationist attack on appeals to character in virtue ethics seem to be prima facie just as applicable to virtue epistemology. As we will see, on closer inspection this point is far from clear.

2 Situationism contra virtue epistemology

The clearest expression of the situationist challenge to virtue epistemology in the current literature is offered by Mark Alfano (2012; 2013: part

[1] For an excellent overview of the relevant empirical literature, see Doris 2002. See also Prinz 2009. For a comprehensive and up-to-date bibliographical survey of the literature on situationism and virtue theory (including both empirical and philosophical literature, and covering both historical and contemporary sources), see Alfano and Fairweather in press.
[2] See, for example, Merritt 2000 and Sreenivasan 2002. For an interesting variation on this kind of response to situationism, see Sosa 2009b.

II; in press), and so I will focus my attention on his presentation of the problem.[3] It is standard practice in the epistemological literature to distinguish between two main types of virtue epistemology – *responsibilist* virtue epistemology and *reliabilist* virtue epistemology – and rather than offering a generic situationist challenge to virtue epistemology, Alfano instead targets these two types of virtue epistemology separately.[4] There is a very good reason for this, since it is only responsibilist virtue epistemology which conceives of knowledge as being the product of intellectual character traits which are relevantly akin to the moral character traits employed by virtue ethics. That is, for responsibilist virtue epistemology knowledge is the product of intellectual virtues which, like moral virtues, are "motivational and reasons-responsive dispositions to act and react in characteristic ways (e.g., open-mindedness, curiosity, intellectual courage, etc.)" (Alfano 2012: 224). As such, the situationist critique of virtue ethics ought to directly carry over to responsibilist virtue epistemology. In contrast, reliabilist virtue epistemology treats knowledge as being (typically) produced by "non-motivational capacities, dispositions, or process that tend to lead their possessors to increase the balance of truths over falsehoods in their belief sets (e.g., sound deduction, good eyesight, capacious memory, etc.)" (Alfano 2012: 223–24). Given the very different way in which reliabilist virtue epistemology appeals to character traits, it is far from obvious that the situationist critique of virtue ethics should have application here, as Alfano recognizes.[5]

Let's start with Alfano's situationist attack on responsibility virtue epistemology. Alfano's strategy is to cite experiments which appear to show that situational factors have a significant bearing on agents' abilities to complete certain intellectual tasks. For example, he cites the 'Duncker candle task'.[6] This task is a test of one's intellectual flexibility and creativity, and it demonstrates a particular cognitive bias that agents are subject to, known as *functional fixedness*. The problem that subjects are asked to solve is how to fix a candle to a vertical cork board so that no wax drips.

[3] See also Doris and Olin in press for a critique of virtue epistemology which runs along the same lines as that found in Alfano (2012; 2013: part II; in press a). Although the literature on situationism as it applies to virtue epistemology is currently still nascent, there are a few useful works available. See, for example, Axtell 2010; Baehr 2011; and Hazlett 2013. See also Fairweather and Montemayor in press, which is a response to Alfano 2012, and Pritchard in press b.
[4] For an excellent overview of contemporary virtue epistemology which marks this distinction particularly well, see Axtell 1997.
[5] For an example of a reliabilist virtue-theoretic proposal, see the agent reliabilist position defended in early work by Greco (1999, 2000). For a very different neo-Aristotelian virtue-theoretic proposal which incorporates responsibilist elements, see Zagzebski 1996.
[6] See Duncker 1945, cited in Alfano 2012: 235.

The items offered to the subjects are the candle, a box of tacks, and a book of matches. The solution to the puzzle is to empty the box of tacks and use that as a candle holder, but subjects often struggle to recognize this. The problem is that they are thinking of the box as merely a container for the tacks, and not seeing that it can have other uses – that is, they are fixating on the particular function of the box as it is presented to them, and failing to see that the box can perform other functions. In contrast, if subjects are presented with the very same items for performing this task, but with the tacks already removed from the box, then they tend to very quickly recognize that the box can be used to solve the problem in hand.

The manner in which materials are presented to an agent can thus have a significant bearing on that agent's ability to perform a problem-solving task, even though this is intuitively an entirely epistemically irrelevant factor. Alfano further argues that this is not an isolated phenomenon, in that it is possible to manipulate all kinds of situational factors which are intuitively epistemically irrelevant – such as raising a subject's mood by giving them candy before asking them to perform a task – in such a way as to significantly impact on the subject's ability to perform the task.[7] The conclusion that Alfano draws is that this shows that when subjects are successful in these tasks, the success is not the product of the subject's exercise of intellectual virtue, as responsibilist virtue epistemologists suggest, but rather due to their responsiveness to these, apparently epistemically irrelevant, situational factors.

Alfano's attack on reliabilist virtue epistemology is more targeted than his critique of responsibilist virtue epistemology. Indeed, Alfano explicitly grants that reliabilist virtue epistemology is not obviously troubled by the situationist critique when it comes to specifically non-inferential knowledge, since he grants that the processes in play in this regard (perception, memory, and so on) are generally reliable.[8] Alfano's focus is thus on the reliabilist virtue epistemic account of inferential knowledge. His claim is that such an account founders for the simple reason that "our usual methods of inference ... are astonishingly unreliable" (Alfano in press a: 15–16).

The empirical case that Alfano mounts in support of this claim appeals to the well-known examples of cognitive bias developed in various studies

---

[7] See Doris and Olin in press for a fairly comprehensive overview of the relevant empirical literature in this regard.

[8] Though even that could be in dispute. As Doris and Olin (in press: §5) point out, for example, the reliability of one's vision can be dependent upon such apparently irrelevant factors as whether the visual scene in question is presented to the upper-right side of one's visual field. In order to keep the discussion manageable, in what follows I will be setting this concern to one side.

conducted since the 1970s by Amos Tversky and Daniel Kahneman.[9] Perhaps the most famous of their cases is the 'Linda' example (Tversky and Kahneman 2002), which is also employed by Alfano as part of his situationist critique of reliabilist virtue epistemology (Alfano in press a: §4). In this experiment, subjects are given some information about a person, Linda, such as that she is single and outspoken, very bright, deeply concerned about social justice, and part of the anti-nuclear movement. The subjects are then asked to rate the degree to which Linda is representative of a certain class of people, such as feminists, bank tellers, or feminist bank tellers. Subjects will typically respond by stating that Linda is more representative of feminists than she is of feminist bank tellers, and will therefore judge that it's more likely that Linda is a feminist than that she is a feminist bank teller. But, of course, it cannot be more likely that a conjunction obtains than that one of its conjuncts obtains (to think otherwise is to fall foul of the conjunction fallacy), and so it cannot be more likely that Linda is a feminist than that she is a feminist and a bank teller. The point of the example is to show that subjects are employing a particular heuristic in their reasoning – the so-called 'representativeness heuristic' – but that this causes them to engage in fallacious reasoning.

Alfano argues that since cognitive bias of this sort is widespread in our inferential judgments, so the reliabilist virtue-epistemic account of knowledge is in doubt. In particular, Alfano argues that the belief-forming processes actually employed by agents when making inferences are not the kind of reliable cognitive abilities described by reliabilist virtue theory, but in fact heuristics which are not generally reliable at all. The upshot is that reliabilist virtue epistemology is incompatible with the idea that we have the kind of widespread inferential knowledge that we ascribe to ourselves.

One way of responding to Alfano's situationist critique of virtue epistemology could be to bite the bullet and grant that we have far less knowledge than we typically suppose. When it comes to the cognitive bias cases in particular, this route strikes me as fairly plausible, in that one could imagine a reliabilist virtue epistemology simply conceding that the upshot of this empirical work is that inferential knowledge is much harder to attain across a range of cases than we hitherto imagined. For now, however, I will set this dialectical option to one side (we will return to it later).

---

[9] Alfano focuses on Tversky and Kahneman 1973, 2002.

A second way of responding to Alfano's critique of virtue epistemology might be to dispute the empirical data on which it depends, or at least argue against the particular conclusions that Alfano is deriving from this data. I have some sympathy with this style of response too, since it is not clear to me either that we should take these experimental results at face value as Alfano does, or that they pose the general challenge to virtue epistemology that Alfano imagines.[10] Nonetheless, I will not be responding to the situationist critique of virtue epistemology in this way. Instead, I will be arguing that once virtue epistemology is understood correctly, it is in fact entirely compatible with the empirical studies that Alfano cites.

3 Modest virtue epistemology and the situationist critique

In the last section we saw that Alfano offers a different version of the situationist critique of virtue epistemology depending on whether it is responsibilist or reliabilist virtue epistemology that is at issue. But there is another way of classifying virtue-theoretic proposals in epistemology which is of far more relevance to the situationist challenge, one which cuts across the responsibilist/reliabilist distinction. This is the distinction between *modest* and *robust* virtue-theoretic accounts of knowledge. According to the former, it is merely a necessary condition for knowledge that the cognitive success in question be the product of (depending on the form of virtue epistemology in play) a cognitive ability or intellectual virtue. According to the latter, in contrast, knowledge is to be exclusively defined in terms

---

[10] For example, consider again the Linda case. It has been widely noted in the psychological literature that subjects' judgments about the likelihood of an event are often best understood along counterfactual rather than probabilistic lines. (For a survey of some of the relevant psychological literature in this regard, see Pritchard and Smith 2004.) For instance, a subject might regard an event which they grant has a very low probability of occurring as being nonetheless very risky if they judge that it is the kind of event which could very easily happen to them. Conversely, if subjects judge that an event could not very easily happen to them, then they might regard it as not being risky even while simultaneously granting that it has a high probability of occurring. The relevance of this point to the Linda case is that when subjects judge it to be more likely that Linda is a feminist than that she is a feminist bank teller, they could be charitably construed as offering a (correct) counterfactual judgment. That is, given what they know about Linda, that she could more easily be a feminist than that she could be a feminist bank teller. So construed the subjects are not committing the conjunction fallacy at all. (A broadly similar line of response to the Linda case is offered by Gigerenzer 2008: 70–73 [cf. Gigerenzer 2007: ch. 6] and discussed in Fairweather and Montemayor in press: §4.) Note that I'm not suggesting that all of the cognitive bias cases can be resolved in this way. The point is rather that once we start to examine these cases more carefully, then it's far from obvious that they pose the general challenge to inferential judgments that Alfano supposes, rather than merely showing that we do not have as much inferential knowledge as we typically suppose.

of cognitive success which is appropriately related to cognitive ability/ intellectual virtue.[11]

If virtue epistemology, of either a reliabilist or responsibility variety, is construed along robust lines, then Alfano's situationist critique will have some bite. Crucially, however, virtue epistemology is only ever plausible when construed along modest lines.

In order to see this point, let us briefly consider a version of robust virtue epistemology which has been offered by John Greco (2003, 2007, 2008, 2009, 2010), and which is broadly speaking a reliabilist proposal (albeit one with some responsibilist elements to it). According to Greco, knowledge is, roughly, cognitive success (i.e. true belief) that is because of one's cognitive ability, where this means that the cognitive success in question is primarily creditable to the exercise of one's cognitive ability.[12] So, for example, the agent in a standard Gettier-style case lacks knowledge on this proposal because, while he is cognitively successful and has manifested cognitive ability in forming his true belief, his cognitive success is not primarily creditable to the exercise of his cognitive ability but rather due to the epistemic luck that is in play.

Robust virtue epistemology is certainly posed a prima facie threat by the situationist challenge. On both a responsibilist and reliabilist rendering, the worry will be that in a wide range of cases what primarily explains the agent's cognitive success is not her exercise of her cognitive abilities but rather other factors outwith her cognitive agency, such as situational factors.

The problem with robust virtue epistemology, however, is that it is independently implausible, and so the fact that it may be subject to the situationist challenge is ultimately neither here nor there. In particular, the proposal is implausible in that it is both too strong and too weak.[13] It is too strong because in epistemically friendly conditions agents can acquire knowledge even though their cognitive success is not primarily creditable to the exercise of their cognitive ability/intellectual virtue. In testimonial cases, for example, subjects can (on standard accounts of the

---

[11] I've drawn the distinction between robust and modest virtue epistemology – or 'strong' and 'weak' virtue epistemology, as I sometimes put it – in a number of works. See, for example, Pritchard 2009c: ch. 3; 2012; Pritchard *et al.* 2010: ch. 2; and Kallestrup and Pritchard 2012, 2013, in press.

[12] Broadly similar robust virtue-theoretic proposals can be found in the work of Sosa (1988, 1991, 2007, 2009a) and Zagzebski (1996, 1999). Interestingly, in earlier work – most notably Greco (1999, 2000) – Greco offered what we are here describing as a weak virtue epistemology.

[13] I develop this two-pronged critique of robust virtue epistemology in a number of places. See Pritchard (2009a; 2009b: ch. 3; 2009c; 2009d; 2012); Pritchard *et al.* 2010: chs. 2–4; and Kallestrup and Pritchard (2012, 2013, in press).

epistemology of testimony at any rate) come to acquire testimonial knowledge in epistemically friendly conditions by for the most part trusting the word of a knowledgeable informant. But we would not say in such cases that the subject's cognitive success is primarily creditable to her cognitive agency, as opposed to the cognitive agency of the informant.

Robust virtue epistemology is also too weak in that in epistemically unfriendly conditions even a cognitive success that is primarily creditable to the agent's exercise of their cognitive ability/intellectual virtue will not suffice for knowledge. In 'barn façade'-style cases, for example, an agent's cognitive success (e.g. at identifying the target barn) is no less attributable to their cognitive agency than it is in parallel cases where there are no façades in the vicinity. And yet the presence of the façades in the vicinity ensures that this is a lucky, and thus Gettierized, cognitive success, in that it is a cognitive success that could so very easily have been a failure.[14]

The point is that knowledge exhibits what I have elsewhere called an *epistemic dependence* on factors outwith the cognitive agency of the subject, where this epistemic dependency has both a positive and negative aspect.[15] It is positive when an agent exhibits a relatively low degree of cognitive agency, and yet qualifies as having knowledge nonetheless due to factors outwith her cognitive agency, such as epistemically friendly features of the environment (e.g. the kind of features that obtain in the testimonial case just considered). And it is negative when an agent exhibits a high degree of cognitive agency – such that they would ordinarily count as having knowledge – and yet they lack knowledge nonetheless due to factors outwith their cognitive agency, such as epistemically unfriendly features of the environment (e.g. the kind of features that obtain in the barn façade case just considered).

Once one recognizes the epistemic dependency of knowledge, then robust virtue epistemology ceases to be an option. Modest virtue epistemology, in contrast, is entirely compatible with the epistemic dependence

---

[14] Notice that the point in play here is not one that can be met by relativizing cognitive abilities to environments and conditions which are very narrowly conceived, as some have been tempted to do (for example, Greco 2010: ch. 5) or, approaching the issue from a slightly different angle, Fairweather and Montemayor in press: §7). For one thing, as Doris and Olin (in press: §6) point out, a virtue epistemology cast along these lines will be so far removed from the explanatory task that the viewer is meant to be engaged with as to be self-defeating. For another, and more importantly, such a tactic will not in any case work to deal with the problem posed here as one would need to make cognitive abilities narrowly relativized not just to actual environments and conditions but also to one's *modal* environment, and on no plausible conception of abilities (cognitive or otherwise) are they relativized in this way. For more on this specific point, see, for example, Kallestrup and Pritchard in press.

[15] See, especially, Kallestrup and Pritchard 2013.

of knowledge, since it merely claims that one's knowledge should be the product of cognitive ability/intellectual virtue, thereby allowing that there can be other conditions on knowledge over and above the epistemic virtue condition. Is modest virtue epistemology susceptible to the situationist critique?

In order to evaluate this issue we need to return to the situationist challenge and identify exactly what it purports to show. In particular, in order for the situationist challenge to impact even on modest virtue epistemology it needs to demonstrate in a wide range of cases not just that the agent's cognitive success, where it occurs, is not primarily creditable to her exercise of her cognitive abilities/intellectual virtues, but moreover that the agent's cognitive success is not *in any significant way* the product of her cognitive abilities/intellectual virtues. Do the cases offered by the situationist establish this stronger claim?

I suggest not. Take first the kind of case which Alfano presents against responsibilist virtue epistemology, such as the Duncker candle test. One immediate moral of such examples is that we should lower our confidence in our problem-solving abilities, given that they have been empirically shown to be less effective than we might have hitherto supposed. This is a kind of mitigated skepticism, but it is not yet the full-blown skepticism which Alfano imagines as being one route out of this problem for the responsibilist virtue epistemology. In order to get the more full-blown skepticism we need to move from considering cases where cognitive bias – in this case functional fixedness – stands in the way of cognitive success, and consider parallel cases where, due to purely situational factors, the agent is cognitive successful. That is, Alfano's claim must be that since it is just situational factors (including their absence) which often make the difference between cognitive success and cognitive failure, so even in cases of cognitive success we should not attribute this cognitive success to the subject's epistemic virtue (conceived along responsibilist lines), but to the situational factors. The skepticism thus extends out from the 'bad' cases where cognitive bias stands in the way of cognitive success, and infects even the 'good' cases where the subject is cognitive successful.

With this point in mind, imagine now that the Duncker problem is posed for the subject in a way that ensures that she does not fall foul of functional fixedness, and so easily solves the problem. That the situation has been set up to ensure success makes trouble for the idea that we should regard her cognitive success as primarily creditable to her cognitive agency, and so there is a prima facie tension between this empirical data, so described anyway, and robust virtue epistemology. That is, we should grant to Alfano that the fact that a mere change in situational factors can mark the difference between cognitive success and cognitive failure indicates that it is at least problematic to suppose that it is the subject's cognitive agency which is the overarching explanation for her cognitive success.

But once we move from robust virtue epistemology to modest virtue epistemology, even when cast along responsibilist lines, even this prima facie tension disappears. For sure, features of the situation are playing an explanatory role in the subject's cognitive success; that much is not in question. But surely the subject's cognitive abilities are also playing a significant role too (albeit one in concert with the situational factors)? If one holds that knowledge is simply a function of cognitive agency, in line with robust virtue epistemology, then there is a potential problem with situational factors having this influence on the subject's cognitive success. But if one explicitly grants, with modest virtue epistemology, that there is an epistemic dependence to knowledge acquisition, such that it isn't merely a function of cognitive agency, then one can allow that the acquisition of knowledge might well be dependent upon such extra-agential situational factors and yet be bona fide nonetheless. What counts is only that a significant degree of cognitive agency is on display. In the right circumstances – i.e. where the environment is effectively primed for success, as it is in the case where the situational circumstances are propitious – even quite a limited degree of cognitive agency can suffice for knowledge. Far from showing that modest virtue epistemology is untenable, such cases appear to offer empirical support for the view over its robust counterpart.

The same is true even if we turn to the cognitive biases that Alfano cites against reliabilist virtue epistemology. As before, we need to recognize from the outset that such cases offer by everyone's lights a basis for endorsing a mitigated skepticism about inferential knowledge. If cognitive bias is rife in our reasoning, then we should be less confident that we can gain knowledge via such reasoning. In order for this mitigated skepticism to translate into a more full-blown skepticism, however, it needs to be the case that even where agents are not subject to cognitive bias they nonetheless lack knowledge.

It is clear in the case of responsibilist virtue epistemology that Alfano thinks the move from the mitigated skepticism to the more full-blown skepticism is motivated by the fact that merely situational (and thus epistemically irrelevant) factors mark the difference between cases of cognitive failure due to cognitive bias and parallel cases of cognitive success where cognitive bias does not lead to cognitive failure. It is not so clear what the corresponding 'bridging' claim in his argument is when it comes to reliabilist virtue epistemology, but I take it the thought must be that since there is nothing in a normal agent's reasoning practices which differentiates between the reasoning which involves cognitive bias and that which is free from cognitive bias, so all inferential knowledge is called into question by the phenomenon of widespread cognitive bias.

The problem with this kind of bridging claim, however, is that it is susceptible to the very same kind of response which we just saw leveled at Alfano's critique of responsibilist virtue epistemology. If the reliability of one's reasoning is not responsive to the presence of cognitive bias, then when one's reasoning is successful one's cognitive success can hardly be primary creditable to one's cognitive agency. This much seems undeniable. But this is only a problem for a robust virtue epistemology which does not allow for the epistemic dependency of knowledge. For the modest (reliabilist) virtue epistemologist, in contrast, that one's cognitive success, while being significantly creditable to one's cognitive agency, might be in addition creditable to other factors, such as that one is presented with information in such a way as not to trigger a cognitive bias, is not in itself a problem for the view.[16]

4   Concluding remarks

Whether the situational critique extends to virtue epistemology depends, I have argued, less on whether one opts for a responsibilist or reliabilist rendering of this thesis, and more on the kind of virtue epistemology one wishes to advance. In particular, it is only if one offers a robust virtue epistemology which bravely attempts to make knowledge a function of cognitive agency that the empirical data the situationist offers against virtue epistemology present even the prima facie challenge that Alfano imagines. Once we move to a modest virtue epistemology – a dialectical shift which I have claimed is motivated on independent grounds – there is not even the prima facie tension with the situationist's empirical data. The reason for this is that a modest virtue epistemology explicitly embraces the

---

[16] I think that this point has important implications for the epistemology of education, since the dominant view in this regard is one on which the goal of education is the promotion of knowledge, where knowledge is in turn understood along broadly virtue-theoretic lines. (For a useful survey of the literature on the epistemological goals of education, see Robertson 2009.) Situationism, as applied to virtue epistemology, is thus potentially in conflict with the leading proposals in the epistemology of education. It is thus important to show that virtue epistemology, properly construed, can evade the situationist challenge. For more on the situationist challenge as it applies to the epistemology of education, see Pritchard in press b (cf. Pritchard 2013: §1).

phenomenon of the epistemic dependence of knowledge, and so can allow that factors outwith cognitive agency can have a significant role to play in the acquisition of knowledge. Indeed, it turns out that not only does the empirical data offered by situationism not pose a challenge to virtue epistemology, properly conceived, but that it effectively offers empirical support for the particular brand of virtue epistemology that most proponents of the view recognize to be the most compelling version of the thesis. Properly conceived, then, virtue epistemology has nothing to fear from the situationist critique.

CHAPTER 9

Stereotype threat and intellectual virtue

Mark Alfano

1 Prelude

I grew up with two cats. Both of them would regularly do things that cats just aren't supposed to do. They would trip while walking down the stairs, attempt to jump on to the sofa but underestimate the height, roll off the chair while enjoying belly scratches, and so on. The thing is, though, that only one of these cats was a genuinely stupid animal. He really didn't know how to put one paw in front of the other. He really couldn't estimate heights. He really didn't notice the edge of the chair until it was too late. For all I could tell, the other wasn't a particularly dumb cat; she was just highly neurotic. She was afraid of everything, and when she got scared, she lost focus and did silly things. When she tripped while walking down the stairs, it wasn't because she didn't know where her legs were, but because she would startle at a loud sound and lose her concentration. When she failed to jump onto the couch, it wasn't because she couldn't estimate heights, but because she was in a fright, fleeing an imaginary assailant. When she rolled off the chair, it wasn't because she couldn't detect the edge, but because she would panic in the middle of the belly scratches.

The point is that the same manifest behaviors can be expressions of very different dispositions. When one cat takes a tumble, it's because he's a stupid cat. When the other takes a tumble, it's because her fear distracts her and masks her feline intelligence. It would be a mistake to ignore such masking when inferring a cat's psychological dispositions from her behavior. What's needed is a nuanced accounting of how her many dispositions interact with one another and the environment to produce the behavior she manifests.

With grateful thanks for comments, discussions, and suggestions to Joshua Alexander, Steven Brence, Zhen Cheng, Andrew Conway, Abrol Fairweather, Mark Johnson, Ron Mallon, Kate Manne, Philip Mayo, Carlos Montemayor, Jesse Prinz, Brian Robinson, John Turri, and Naomi Zack.

2 The language of character

In some ways, people are more complicated than cats. We say things. We interpret what others say. We care what others think about us and expect from us. We care about how they evaluate us. We recognize ourselves in mirrors. We form long-term plans. We have desires about our own psychological dispositions. Some people want to know more in the future than they do now. Some people who don't currently enjoy opera wish they did. Some people want to be champion chess-boxers. Just as it would be a mistake to ignore the masking of dispositions when inferring a cat's psychological dispositions from her behavior, so it would be fallacious to ignore the masking of dispositions when inferring a person's psychological dispositions from her behavior.

This point is especially pertinent when the inferences we make concern what are called, for lack of a better word, virtue or character. It's intrinsically rewarding to be judged to have virtue or good character, at least by certain people. It's intrinsically punishing to be judged to have vice or bad character, at least by certain people. Moreover, when these judgments are expressed publicly, they typically have knock-on effects that radiate out through the audience of the utterance. Being judged worthy typically leads to extrinsic rewards, whereas being judged unworthy typically leads to extrinsic punishments. Get judged worthy often enough by the right people, and you might just enjoy the support you need to become worthy. Get judged unworthy often enough by the right people, and you'll probably end up flipping burgers.

Even more so, when a judgment of character is made in an official capacity, it can function more like a declaration than an assertion. Declarations are paradoxical utterances with dual direction-of-fit. Assertions have word-to-world direction-of-fit. Ordinarily, if I say, "The lights are on," I'd be making an assertion. I'd be representing the world as being a certain way, and if there is a mismatch between what I say and how the world is, it's my words that should change, not the world. Other utterances, such as imperatives, have world-to-word direction of fit. Ordinarily, if I say, "Close the window," I'd be issuing an imperative. I'd be representing the world as it ought to be, from my point of view, and if there is a mismatch between that representation and the world, it's not my words that should change, but the world. Declarations seem to have dual direction-of-fit. Ordinarily, if in my role as chair of a committee I say, "The meeting is over," I'd be making a declaration. On the one hand, I would be representing the world as being a certain way – namely, such that the meeting is over. On the other hand, by uttering those words sincerely, I would make it the case that the meeting was over. Questions that make sense in the context of assertion have no place in the context of declaration. If someone observing the meeting were to say, "The meeting is over," it would make sense to ask her how she knew. It makes no sense, however, to ask the chair of the meeting how he knows the meeting is over; the only answer he could give would be, "Because I say so."

In recent work (Alfano 2013, in press b), I've argued that virtue and vice attributions can be fruitfully compared with declarations.[1] This is especially so when the attributor holds a position of power. Easy examples are 'convicted felon' and 'sexual offender'. If the appropriate legal authority designates someone a convicted felon, then that's what he is. The labeling is a declaration: it represents him as being a certain kind of person, but the label applies partly because the declaration has been made. Such declarations enable or disable their targets in various ways. In South Carolina, a convicted felon may not serve in the state legislature. In Arkansas, convicted felons may not possess firearms, even for the purpose of hunting. In Pennsylvania, a sexual offender must register with the state police, and his name, year of birth, address, and photograph are available online for all to see.

You can see some of the ambiguity engendered by declarations like these. It's hard to imagine a convicted felon who has not been *declared* a felon. It's all too easy to imagine a sexual offender who has not been so declared. Many of our virtue and vice terms, I want to claim, exhibit this kind of ambiguity between their assertoric use and their declarative use. On a more positive note, consider the term 'genius'. When used assertorically, it refers to a person who has extraordinary cognitive, aesthetic, or creative abilities. But it can also be used declaratively, as when the MacArthur Foundation picks out its yearly list of fellows or Harold Bloom picks out a hundred people (only ten of them women) to laud. A test for whether a term t admits of both assertoric and declarative uses is to see whether it could make sense to say, "Some ts are not ts," where the first use is declarative and the second assertoric (or vice versa). For instance, some sexual offenders are not sexual offenders; that is, some people who have been declared sexual offenders never actually committed sexual offences (and

---

[1] J. L. Austin (1962) and John Searle (1969) were the first to systematically theorize speech acts. Much of what I say here, however, bears a closer affinity to work in feminist philosophy, such as Fricker (2007), who argues that disbelieving someone can strip her of knowledge, and Langton (1993), who analyzes pornography as an illocutionary act of subordination. Thanks to Kate Manne for these references.

vice versa). Likewise, some geniuses are not geniuses. For instance, Bloom declares James Boswell a genius, when in fact he was merely a toady. In contrast, it simply makes no sense to say that some even numbers are not even numbers. There's no declarative use of 'even'.

The declarative use of the language of intellectual virtue and vice, especially in official contexts, can have self-confirming effects, and the channels through which these effects flow include both the people who make the declarations (teachers, administrators, parents) and the people about whom they are made (students). Many states have special programs for "gifted and talented" youths. I couldn't tell you in any robust sense what it takes to be a genius, but I have a pretty good idea of what it means to be gifted and talented. And I can assure you that some gifted and talented youths are neither gifted nor talented. That is to say, some of the students designated in this way are unremarkable (and some who are not so designated are remarkable). Nevertheless, when they are so designated, they receive special treatment in school, their intellectual self-esteem goes up, and they often outperform otherwise comparable but unlabeled peers (Hoge and Renzulli 1993).

The contrary phenomenon also occurs. In a shocking longitudinal study, Ray Rist (1973) followed the academic careers of a cohort of students in a de facto segregated school in St. Louis from kindergarten through the end of second grade. By the end of the second week of kindergarten, these students had been assigned permanent seats at one of three tables based on what their teacher called their "qualities," which she assessed intuitively and which just so happened to be highly correlated with the students' socioeconomic status. Those at Table 1 received more and more positive attention, and unsurprisingly learned more and faster. Those at Tables 2 and 3 received increasingly less and less positive attention; unsurprisingly, their school year proceeded apace. By the end of kindergarten, the Table 1 students had an objective record of higher achievement, better behavior, and better motivation. The caste system was further cemented in first grade, and by the time second grade rolled around, the top table was now populated by "Tigers," the middle table by "Cardinals," and the last table by "Clowns." The labels fit, but that was so largely because they had been applied in the first place. When someone in a position of power, such as the kindergarten teacher, applies a label, over the course of time it can function as a self-fulfilling prophecy. The process is of course not inevitable, and students' success or failure doesn't depend solely on how they are labeled. This introduces some daylight between trait attributions and standard declarations. When a duly empowered judge declares a couple married, they are wed right there on the spot. In contrast, when a teacher labels someone an A-student, he comes to fit that description – if at all – only over time, and only through the continued signaling of expectations by the teacher and others, as well as his own self-concept.

3 Components of character

If this view is sound, it suggests certain revisions in how we conceptualize intellectual virtues.[2] Stacking the deck a bit in my own favor, I'll call a conception *naïve* if it countenances only first-order dispositions as components of virtue. Such first-order dispositions might include, among other things, dispositions to notice, think, construe, feel, want, deliberate, act, and react in characteristic ways. I call these dispositions first-order because they are dispositions to token first-order mental states (i.e. states that are not about other mental states) and to undertake first-order actions (i.e. actions that are not intentionally directed at other actions). Naïve views are understandably attractive. Without going too deep into the scholarship, I think it's fair to say that Aristotle held, or at least that most contemporary Aristotelian virtue theorists hold, a naïve conception of virtue, according to which a virtue is a disposition to do the right thing for the right reason.

In some of my recent writings on this topic, I've suggested that, in light of both empirical evidence and theoretical arguments, the naïve conception should be replaced with either a sophisticated internalist or a sophisticated externalist conception. Both conceptions countenance second-order dispositions as components of virtue, where a disposition counts as second-order if it is a disposition to token second-order mental states (i.e. states that are about other mental states) or undertake second-order actions (i.e. actions that are intentionally directed at other actions). According to the sophisticated internalist conception, for a person to possess a particular virtue is for her to have a suite of first-order dispositions as well as certain second-order dispositions to notice, construe, think, feel, and want in characteristic ways.

The distinction between first- and second-order dispositions can be illustrated with the example of open-mindedness. Somewhat roughly, on the naïve conception of open-mindedness, someone counts as open-minded

---

[2] I should clarify at this point that the account of intellectual virtue I provide here does not presuppose that knowledge is to be defined in terms of intellectual virtue. Regardless of how knowledge is defined, though, the nature and conditions for the possession of intellectual virtue seem worthy objects of philosophical investigation.

just in case she is disposed to notice when others are inclined to disagree, to construe disagreement not as a threat but as an opportunity, to think carefully about the evidence others bring to bear when a disagreement is at hand, to want to learn from others rather than merely prevail in convincing them, and so on. On the sophisticated internalist conception, she must also be disposed to think of herself as open-minded, to want to maintain her integrity in the face of disagreement, and so on. While it may be tempting to think that overlaying first-order dispositions with second-order dispositions leaves them unchanged, this layer-cake approach is conceptually and empirically dubious. Our beliefs and desires about our own beliefs and desires don't skate across the surface of the first-order mental states. They interact with them.

The sophisticated externalist conception of virtue goes a step further. In addition to countenancing the first-order and second-order dispositions of the possessor of virtue, it countenances the (signaling of) second-order dispositions of other people in the possessor's social milieu. The idea here is that your being virtuous might somehow involve other people being disposed to think that you have certain first-order dispositions, to expect you to act from those dispositions, to prefer that you have some dispositions rather than others, and so on. In fact, what's most important here is not that other people *have* these second-order dispositions, but that they *signal* them, that they convey them to you in some way. Since there is a fairly tight causal and conceptual connection between having and signaling such dispositions, however, I will sometimes elide this distinction. I call this conception externalist because it says that some of the dispositions that constitute your virtue are actually outside your skin. Your virtue, on this model, isn't a monadic property of you as a person, but rather a relation between you and other people.

There are weak and strong versions of the sophisticated externalist conception. According to the strong version, someone's possession of virtue necessarily involves (the signaling of) others' second-order dispositions. According to the weak version, someone's possession of virtue only possibly involves (the signaling of) others' second-order dispositions. Both versions of the view can be seen as the next step in the externalization of psychology. In the 1970s, Kripke (1972) and Putnam (1975) popularized the idea that mental content is external, that the meaning and reference of some words is not determined solely by what's in the heads of people who use those words. In the 1980s, Nozick (1981) and Dretske (1981) introduced the notion that one's justification for a given belief might not be determined solely by what's in one's head. In the 1990s, Clark and Chalmers

(1998) suggested that the mind itself might extend beyond the limits of the skin. The current proposal is that some psychological dispositions – namely character traits – extend beyond the limits of the skin of their possessor. On the weak version of the view, a given character trait needn't so extend, but may. On the strong version (the signaling of) others' second-order dispositions is always a component of trait possession. The strong version of the thesis is obviously more revisionary than the weak one, but it is also more parsimonious. The weak version of the thesis may seem unsatisfyingly disjunctive, since it entails that any given character trait is multiply realizable: one instance of curiosity might involve first-order and second-order dispositions contained solely within the agent, whereas another might involve those as well as second-order dispositions located outside the agent. For my current purposes, it doesn't matter whether the strong or the weak version of the sophisticated conception wins out because I want to talk about a specific family of cases in which we have good reason to think that some of the relevant dispositions are external.

4 Stereotype threat and stereotype lift

The foregoing discussion has been a somewhat roundabout way to introduce my ultimate target: stereotype threat. For decades, some ethnic minorities (African Americans, Latinos) and other marginalized groups (women, the poor) have performed worse than average on a variety of tests of ability, performance, and skill. How is this phenomenon to be understood? In a 123-page article, Arthur Jensen (1969) argued that the best interpretation attributed the differences between ethnic groups not to environmental or situational influences but to heritable traits, especially intelligence. His controversial thesis provoked a deluge of responses, from protests and rebuttals to praise and attempts to corroborate. In fact, Jensen's provocation may be the single most cited article in the entire field of intelligence research.[3]

More recently, Richard Herrnstein and Charles Murray (1996; see also Benbow and Stanley 1980, 1983; Templer and Arikawa 2006; Kanazawa 2008; and Templer 2008) in *The Bell Curve: Intelligence and Class Structure in American Life* revived a version of Jensen's argument. Among the many claims made in *The Bell Curve*, several had to do with differences between groups, including:

---

[3] As of the writing of this chapter, the Web of Knowledge registered 1,358 citations.

- East Asians are on average more intelligent than whites (272).
- Latinos are on average less intelligent than whites (275).
- African Americans are on average less intelligent than Latinos (276).

Herrnstein and Murray (1996) go on to identify what they take to be the consequences of these differences in intelligence:

- Intelligence as measured by a standardized IQ test is a stronger predictor than parental income of adult income (135).
- Intelligence as measured by a standardized IQ test is a stronger predictor than parental income of level of educational achievement (154).
- Less intelligent people are so much more accident-prone than their intelligent counterparts that they are more frequently unemployed through disability (162).
- Less intelligent people are more likely to be idle (155), i.e. to "drop out" of the labor force without a "legitimate reason" (157).
- Less intelligent people are more likely to be arrested for (246), be convicted of (247), and to serve prison time for (248) criminal behavior.

It's not hard to connect the dots. Minorities are poor because they're stupid. Their low IQs prevent them from reaching a high level of education. In fact, they're so unintelligent that they injure themselves more frequently and more severely than their high-IQ counterparts. Worse still, their low intelligence is somehow connected with laziness, and even leads them to lives of crime. Women earn less than men because they're not as bright, especially when it comes to math. Worst of all, the dumbest among us are out-breeding the rest, in part because of well-intentioned but misguided welfare policies that aim to alleviate the poverty of mothers, especially single mothers (548–49).

    Philosophers have paid scant attention to these jeremiads. To my knowledge, the only published response to *The Bell Curve* by a philosopher is Ned Block's semi-popularizing essay, "How Heritability Misleads about Race" (1996). Most philosophy of race focuses instead on the meaning of 'race' and racial predicates (e.g. 'black', 'white', 'Latino/a', 'Asian'). Various positions on these topics have been staked out in the logical space, but they do not seem particularly helpful in responding to Herrnstein and Murray and their fellow travelers. In fact, Ron Mallon (2004, 2006) persuasively argues that all prominent theories of race – from race skepticism to various forms of race constructivism to suitably chastened biological-naturalistic accounts of race – agree on the basic metaphysical facts, differing only in their semantic and normative perspectives.

Whatever the meaning of 'race' and racial predicates, the race gap in intelligence testing undeniably exists, often with depressing consequences. However races and ethnicities are individuated, then, it might seem that intellectual virtues are unevenly distributed across different groups. It would be rash, however, to draw such an inference without exploring the many ways in which differences in performance can be explained. Just as the behavior of cats results from a confluence of their various dispositions and the interaction of those dispositions with their environment, so the behavior of people in the context of intelligence testing results from a confluence of their dispositions and the interaction of those dispositions with their environment. For creatures as complex as cats, monocausal explanation is to be eschewed. Given that people are at least as complex as cats, such explanation is dubious in our case as well.

Herrnstein and Murray rush to attribute all differences in performance to differences in innate first-order dispositions. Here, I want to explore how much of the difference in performance might be attributable to situational second-order dispositions – of both the internal and the external varieties. In the same way that it is difficult, if not impossible, to be morally virtuous in a morally bad society, I want to suggest that it is difficult, if not impossible, to be intellectually virtuous in an intellectually bad society – and societies may be intellectually bad in surprising and surprisingly subtle ways.

I should clarify from the outset that in what follows I do not attempt to explain all of the observed differences situationally. There is a clear case to be made for the importance of developmental differences between groups in the United States, given the legacy of slavery, overt discrimination, structural discrimination, implicit bias, lack of opportunity, lack of role models, internalized inferiority, lack of material resources, grinding poverty, and many other factors. These all matter, and I do not want to downplay their importance, but it seems to me that, in addition to these developmental issues, there is a case to be made for the influence of situational pressures on both the internal and the external second-order dispositions that partially constitute intellectual virtue.

4.1 Stereotype threat to racial and ethnic minorities

In particular, I want to suggest that the combination of stereotype threat for minority test-takers and stereotype lift for majority test-takers may account for as much as half of the race and gender gaps in various measures of academic achievement and ability. Stereotype threat was discovered in 1995 by Claude Steele and Joshua Aronson. They began with the idea that if you're worried that others will treat your performance on a task as emblematic of your group, and your group is stigmatized as low-performing or low-ability on that task, then you will experience a level of threat that people from another group might not. In particular, since there is a stereotype in the United States that African Americans are poor students, they will experience a level of threat that white students do not experience on the same task. This experience in turn mediates performance: the more nervous you are about the inferences others might draw about your group based on your individual performance, the worse you do on the test.

To demonstrate this, Steele and Aronson (1995) conducted an experiment with African American undergraduates at Stanford University. The participants were randomly assigned to one of two groups. Only the first group was told that the test they were about to take was diagnostic of ability. Thus, their threat level was increased: if they performed poorly, it could reflect poorly on their whole group. As predicted, the students in the first group underperformed their matched peers in the second group. That is to say, merely being told that the test they were about to take was indicative of ability led to performance decrements.

Now, one might respond to this by saying that it demonstrates nothing about stereotypes in particular. After all, it could be that raising the stakes of a test would make anyone – regardless of their racial or ethnic identity – more anxious, leading to poorer performance. To rule out this possibility, Steele and Aronson (1995) conducted another experiment. As before, the participants were African American students and were randomly assigned to one of two treatments, but this time, the only thing that separated the treatments was that one group filled in a demographic survey before the test, whereas the other filled in the same survey after the test. The idea behind this experiment was that merely asking students to indicate their race before taking the test would raise their threat level and lead to worse performance, whereas asking about demographics after the test might raise their threat level but would of course leave their prior performance unaffected. As predicted, the students who were prompted to think about their group membership just prior to taking the test underperformed their matched peers who answered the same questions just after taking the same test.

Since Steele and Aronson's groundbreaking work, psychologists have begun to explore just how wide-ranging this phenomenon is. Subjecting someone to stereotype threat induces not only performance decrements, but measurable bodily changes. In one study, African Americans exhibited larger increases in mean arterial blood pressure than European Americans while taking the same high-stakes test (Blascovich *et al.* 2001).

4.2   *Stereotype threat to women*

Latinos and Latinas in the United States also suffer from stereotype threat in academic contexts (Schmader and Johns 2003), but racial and ethnic minorities are not the only groups harmed by this phenomenon. Whereas African American students appear to face stereotype threat across academic subjects, women experience it only in the science, technology, engineering and mathematics (STEM) fields, especially mathematics. Although women who endorse the negative stereotype about their sex's mathematical prowess are especially susceptible to threat (Schmader *et al.* 2004), women who reject the stereotype also experience decrements under threatening conditions (Keifer and Sekaquaptewa 2007). One of the truly insidious things about stereotype threat is that it doesn't require that anyone – the target of threat or those in contact with the target – actually believe in the accuracy of the stereotype. All that's required is that the target comes to think that her performance might be treated as emblematic or representative of her group. This thought can be triggered explicitly, by announcing at the outset that the task is a test of a stereotyped ability, or of differences between groups. But it can also be triggered subtly, for instance by administering a demographic survey that happens to ask about the relevant group identity. Danaher and Crandall (2008) estimate that roughly 5,000 more women per year would receive advanced placement credit for calculus if demographic data were collected after the test rather than before it.

Worse still, the effects of stereotype threat are quite powerful. According to a careful meta-analysis conducted by Nguyen and Ryan (2008), the average effect size for women and racial minorities is a Cohen's d between 0.2 and 0.6 depending on the group and the method of threat activation. For those unfamiliar with this statistic, I should emphasize how large it is. Cohen's d is the ratio of the difference between group means to standard deviation on the measure in question, so this basically means that stereotype threat tends to lead to a performance decrement of more than an entire standard deviation. For context, this is like finding a drug that could decrease the average American male's height by about 1.5 inches, or a geoengineering intervention that could decrease the number of rainy days per year in Eugene, Oregon, by about nineteen.

4.3   *Stereotype threat to low-SES individuals*

Other minorities also experience stereotype threat. Even controlling for race and gender, students from low socio-economic status families tend to perform worse on a variety of tests of reasoning and intelligence. One could jump to conclusions like Herrnstein and Murray, attributing their poor performance to genetic inferiority, but to do so would be to ignore the possibility that they too experience a kind of stereotype threat. And in fact this possibility has been borne out. When low-SES students are told that a test they're about to take is diagnostic of intellectual ability, they perform much worse than when they are told that the same test is not diagnostic (Croizet and Claire 1998). Similarly, when told that the purpose of the task is to determine why low SES students generally perform worse on academic tests, they do in fact perform worse, but when told that the purpose of the task it to investigate problem-solving processes, they do not (Harrison *et al.* 2006).

4.4   *Stereotype threat beyond academic contexts*

It's natural to imagine that stereotype threat must have something in particular to do with academic tests, but the phenomenon is much broader than that. Women often find negotiation threatening. Kray *et al.* (2001) showed that women perform worse in pricing negotiations when they are told that the task is diagnostic of ability than when they are not so told. Kray *et al.* (2002) upped the ante by showing that the effect of stereotype threat for sex can be flipped in the context of mixed-gender negotiations. If, prior to the negotiation, all participants are told that people who are assertive, good at problem-solving, and highly self-interested tend to succeed in the negotiation task, then the women do worse than the men, but if they are told that people who are emotional, insightful, good at listening, verbally expressive, and well prepared tend to outperform, then the men do worse than the women.[4]

Some groups are targeted by ambivalent stereotypes, or pairs of oppositely valenced stereotypes. For instance, the elderly are sometimes stigmatized as senile, but sometimes stereotyped as wise. It turns out that priming elderly participants with one of these stereotypes leads to congruent performance on a test of recall: those who are reminded of the old-is-senile stereotype recall fewer words, whereas those who are reminded of the old-is-wise stereotype recall more (Levy 1996).

Stereotype threat even arises in the context of athletics. White athletes putt most accurately when told that the experiment tests sports intelligence, less accurately when the task is framed as an investigation of sports

---

[4] The experimenters chose these lists of traits based on pre-tests of stereotype content.

psychology, and least accurately when told that it's about natural athletic ability. Exactly the opposite pattern holds for black athletes (Stone *et al.* 1999; see also Stone 2002).

Perhaps the most amusing investigation of stereotype threat is due to Yeung and von Hippel (2008), who found that Australian women are more than twice as likely to run over a jaywalker in a driving simulation when they are told that the purpose of the study is to investigate why women are bad drivers than when the negative stereotype is not primed. The increased probability of killing the jaywalker was equivalent to what happens when the driver performs a secondary task, such as talking on a cell phone.

4.5   Stereotype lift

Even more interesting is the phenomenon that's come to be known as stereotype lift. In a threatening situation, participants perform worse than controls. In some circumstances, though, being primed with one's group identity can lead participants to outperform controls. This occurs especially when the target identity is stereotyped as especially adept or skilled at the task in question. The first investigation of stereotype lift was conducted by Shih *et al.* (1999). Their subjects were East Asian American women. In the United States, East Asians are stereotyped as good at math, whereas women are stereotyped as bad at math. What Shih and her colleagues did was to prime some participants with their ethnic identity, some with their gender identity, and some not at all. Those who had been reminded of their ethnic identity correctly answered 54 percent of the questions on a difficult math test; those who had been reminded of their gender identity answered only 43 percent correctly; and those who were primed with neither group identity answered 49 percent correctly. These differences might seem small, but the average quantitative SAT score of the women in this study was 751 out of 800, and the minimum was 600, which cut down considerably on the variance in their mathematical abilities. To show that this effect was driven by the stereotype rather than by some inborn characteristic, Shih and her colleagues replicated the study in Vancouver, where pre-testing suggested that the gender stereotype persisted but the ethnic stereotype did not. In this second experiment, the participants in the control condition and those in the ethnic-priming condition were indistinguishable.

This suggests that stereotype threat and lift may sometimes be induced through comparative rather than absolute judgments about stereotyped groups. In fact, according to Walton and Cohen's (2003) meta-analysis, white men in the United States tend to experience a small but significant lift ($d = 0.24$) whenever they were primed to think of a group on whom they could look down. However, it turns out that even they can be threatened by being primed to think about a group that is stereotyped as better than them at a particular task. For instance, the Asians-are-good-at-math stereotype is so strong in the United States that white men experience stereotype threat during a math test when primed to compare themselves with Asians (Aronson *et al.* 1999).

4.6   Overcoming stereotype threat

Before proceeding, I should sound a more uplifting note. Although stereotype threat seems to be ubiquitous, and stereotype lift seems to benefit those who need it least, some ways of overcoming threat have been successfully explored. One of the most promising is the self-affirmation paradigm, in which stigmatized individuals write about why something they personally value is important to them for about fifteen minutes. This short exercise has been shown in a laboratory context to eliminate the effects of stereotype threat on women taking a math test (Martens *et al.* 2006).

Even more impressive are a pair of field studies aimed at reducing the race and gender gaps in high school and college respectively. In the first (Cohen *et al.* 2006), students in a mixed-race high school in Massachusetts were split into self-affirmation and other-affirmation groups. A couple of weeks into the semester, the self-affirmation group identified something they valued, then wrote for fifteen minutes about why they valued it, while the other-affirmation group identified something they didn't value, then wrote for fifteen minutes about why someone else might value it. The primary outcome variable for this field study was GPA in the class at the end of the semester. Whereas white students' GPAs did not differ across the two conditions, black students in the self-affirmation ended up with GPAs roughly 0.3 greater on a 4.0 scale – basically the difference between a C+ and a B–, or a B+ and an A–. This corresponded to a decrease in the racial achievement gap at that school of 40 percent. Moreover, a sentence-completion task administered several weeks after the writing exercise revealed that the concept of race had been made less accessible to the black students in the self-affirmation condition: they were least likely to fill in the gaps in the sentences with stereotypical words.

Another self-affirmation study (Miyake *et al.* 2010; see also Good *et al.* 2008) found a similar alleviation of threat for women in a college physics class. While the men in this class were pretty much unaffected by the self-affirmation vs. other-affirmation manipulation, women in the self-affirmation condition performed considerably better than their peers in the other-affirmation condition. In fact, their modal improvement was an entire letter-grade – from C to B. The effect of the self-affirmation intervention was strongest for women who had previously endorsed the women-are-bad-at-physics stereotype, but had some effect across the board. Overall, this seemingly trivial intervention closed the gender gap for women in the self-affirmation condition by 61 percent for in-class examinations and entirely for a standardized test of conceptual mastery administered at the end of the semester.[5]

5 Stereotypes and intellectual virtues

There are further studies I could cite in this context, but I hope that the rough outline of the phenomenon is now clear. Across a variety of task domains and group identities, people are susceptible to both stereotype threat and stereotype lift, often with large, measurable, real-world effects. These effects can be induced in a variety of ways, from overtly telling participants that the test is diagnostic of ability in the domain or that the purpose of the task is to investigate group differences, to much subtler primes. Merely asking for demographic information triggers stereotype threat, as does being a "solo" visible minority (Stangor *et al.* 1998; Inzlicht *et al.* 2006).

Although we now have a decent grasp on what kinds of conditions will lead to stereotype threat and stereotype lift, less is understood about their mechanisms. Among the many potential mediating variables that have been proposed are anxiety, self-efficacy, evaluation apprehension paired with a shift towards caution, divided attention, demotivation paired with effort withdrawal, and expectancy confirmation. Each of these constructs seems to partially mediate the effect, but none does the job all on its own (Spencer *et al.* 1999; Cadinu *et al.* 2003). One exception is the work of Schmader and Johns (2003), who argue that, at least in the case of women's performance on math tests, the effect of stereotype threat is fully mediated

---

[5] Another intervention that might produce similar effects would be to affirm something one found valuable about one's group (as in the black-is-beautiful movement of the 1960s). Presumably, doing so might help to change the valence of one's stereotype from negative to positive, or at least from more negative to less negative. To my knowledge, no one has tried this intervention, but it seems prima facie promising. Thanks to Steven Brence for this idea.

by decreased working memory capacity, which in turn is thought to be closely related to the fluid component of g, or general intelligence.

Even if no single variable fully mediates the effects of both stereotype threat and stereotype lift across all groups and domains, however, it should now be plausible to suppose that performance is not solely and directly a function of first-order cognitive dispositions. Second-order internal cognitive dispositions, such as thinking that you belong to a certain group, worrying that your performance on a task might be treated as representative of your group, knowing that others stereotype your group in a given way, and so on, all play a role. Moreover, these second-order internal dispositions exert top-down influence on first-order cognitive dispositions. As I mentioned in the previous paragraph, your working memory capacity – a first-order disposition if anything is – may go down in conditions of threat. It's also been shown that high self-monitoring individuals are less susceptible to stereotype threat than low self-monitoring individuals (Inzlicht *et al.* 2006). Self-monitoring is clearly a second-order internal cognitive disposition, and it moderates the effects of stereotype threat. Furthermore, even just learning about the phenomenon of stereotype threat seems to immunize against it, at least for women taking math tests (Johns *et al.* 2005). Since its content includes first-order dispositions, knowledge that you might be susceptible to stereotype threat is a second-order disposition.

These observations also help to make a case that (the signaling of) second-order external dispositions may sometimes partially constitute intellectual virtue or the lack thereof. What worries someone who experiences stereotype threat is that *other people* might treat her performance as representative of her group. In other words, other people's dispositions to judge the target's first-order dispositions can influence how those first-order dispositions get expressed – or at least, how those second-order dispositions are *perceived* can do this. Marx and Goff (2005) showed that when the test-giver belongs to the same stereotyped group as the test-takers, threat is diminished. Presumably this flows from the test-takers' assumption that a fellow target of stereotype will be less willing to find confirmation of the stereotype in their performance.

It seems to me that there are three models that might accommodate these insights: the naïve first-order model, the second-order internalist model, and the second-order externalist model. According to the first-order model, all that it takes to have good intellectual character is that you possess a cluster of first-order dispositions, as spelled out above. On this view, someone who performs poorly in the face of stereotype threat might still be intellectually virtuous, but her virtue would be masked or finked by the threatening context. Conversely, someone who performs well in the face of stereotype lift might not count as virtuous, or at least not as virtuous as he seems, since the stereotype lift could be mimicking real intellectual virtue. Worrying about how your performance might be evaluated doesn't strip you of intellectual virtue, but it does mask it. Being high self-monitoring doesn't partially constitute intellectual virtue, but it does help to prevent intellectual virtue from being masked or finked. Looking at things in this way allows us to say that many of the victims of stereotype threat really are intellectually virtuous; they just fail to express their intellectual virtue.

I find this model unappealing for several reasons. The main conceptual argument against the naïve view is simply this: if intellectual virtues are dispositions that someone who wants to believe the truth and avoid error needs or would want to have, then it's just obvious that some second-order dispositions are intellectual virtues. Part of what it takes to be a successful investigator and a worthy knower is the desire to know one's own mind, to monitor one's own first-order dispositions, to evaluate one's own intellectual responses. This might not have been obvious prior to empirical investigation, but it seems pretty certain now.

The main empirical argument against the naïve view starts from the observation that intentional states directed at other intentional states dynamically interact with their targets, whereas intentional states directed at other types of targets typically do not. Your beliefs about your own first-order cognitive dispositions shape how those dispositions are expressed. Your beliefs about the solubility of salt do not shape how that disposition is expressed. Salt dissolves in water, whether you think so or not. As Carol Dweck and her colleagues have shown, your ability to learn depends on how you conceive of that ability. Dweck distinguishes two ways of conceiving of intelligence: the *entity theory*, according to which intelligence is innate and fixed, and the *incremental theory*, according to which intelligence is acquired and susceptible to improvement with effort and practice (Dweck *et al.* 1995). In a research program that has spanned years, she has demonstrated that adolescents who endorse the entity theory get lower grades in school and are less interested in schoolwork (Dweck 1999), that girls who endorse the incremental theory tend to do just as well as boys while girls who endorse the entity theory underperform (Dweck 1999; Blackwell *et al.* 2007), that endorsement of the entity theory moderates the gender gap in university-level mathematics (Good *et al.* unpublished data) and chemistry (Grant and Dweck 2003), and that the brains of people who endorse the entity theory respond differently to mistakes: they show increased activity in the anterior frontal P3, which is associated with social comparison, and decreased activity in regions associated with the formation of new memories (Mangels *et al.* 2006). Together, these results suggest that people's conceptions of intelligence influence how their own intelligence is expressed. Furthermore, the results on the gender gap support the idea that one's theory of intelligence makes one more or less vulnerable to stereotype threat.

It might be tempting to argue that the direction of causation runs the other way. You don't express intellectual virtue because you think of intelligence in a certain way; instead, you think of intelligence in a certain way because you express intellectual virtue. The entity and incremental theories would then be symptoms of ability, not moderators of it. This argument fails, however, since it is inconsistent with the result that being taught about the malleability of the brain (which leads to a more incremental view of intelligence) induces better grades than being taught first-order skills (Blackwell *et al.* 2007).

A second empirical argument against the first-order model of intellectual virtue appeals to the intuition that if an object's disposition is *in general* masked or finked, then it ceases to be clear that the object really has the disposition. Consider a normal match, which is disposed to light when struck. Its disposition to light can of course be finked if it gets wet, but – one might argue – as soon as it dries off its underlying disposition will reassert itself. But what if the match constantly suffers dampness? It might seem that in such a case its disposition isn't just finked, but that it ceases to exist. Given how easily stereotype threat can be triggered and how strong its effect is, one might worry that the victims of stereotype threat are like the perennially dampened match: it's no longer clear that they have the intellectual virtues in question. This of course is not to say that they are somehow culpable for their lack of virtue; it's pretty clear that the perpetrators of negative stereotypes are the ones to blame. What this suggests, then, is that the right to hold responsible the perpetrators of stereotypes can be purchased at the cost of admitting the vulnerability of the victims of stereotype threat.

If the above arguments are on the right track, then the naïve first-order model should be replaced by a sophisticated model. According to the second-order internalist model, part of what it takes to be intelligent, skilled at mathematics, adept at physics, good at golf, and so on is a cluster of second-order dispositions to think about yourself in characteristic ways, to expect characteristic behavior from yourself, to want to have characteristic first-order dispositions, and so on. The right second-order dispositions immunize or at least partially immunize you to things like stereotype threat, which would otherwise mask your first-order intellectual virtues.

Of course, one can recognize the arguments for both the first-order naïve and the second-order internalist model by saying that they are simply models of different things. The first-order model might be construed, for instance, as a model of intelligence understood merely as a cognitive capacity, whereas the second-order model would be a model of intellectual virtue. The difference between them would then be that intellectual virtue is robust in a way that intelligence is not: intelligence is subject to finks, masks, and mimics that impinge on it from the second-order level. In contrast, these elements do not impinge on the second-order system; they partially constitute it. From this ecumenical point of view, then, standard *tests* of intelligence poorly operationalize the concept because they do not rule out important finks, masks, and mimics. What pass for tests of intelligence are better understood as tests of intellectual virtue, since the results they produce characterize intelligence *as modulated by* second-order elements.

On the second-order externalist model, all of this is so, but in addition part of what it takes for you to have intellectual virtue is that other people be disposed to signal certain second-order dispositions to you. This means that whether you are or become virtuous is not entirely up to you: others could strip you of virtue by failing to signal the right second-order dispositions or by signaling the wrong ones. Likewise, others could bestow virtue upon you by signaling the right second-order dispositions and not signaling the wrong ones. Although the second-order externalist model is perhaps more revisionary of the ordinary conception of intellectual virtue than the second-order internalist model, I find it more attractive. Just as your own second-order dispositions constantly interact with your first-order dispositions, so other people's second-order dispositions that target you constantly interact with your first-order dispositions. This can occur through stereotype threat and stereotype lift. It can also occur when a teacher who holds an entity theory of intelligence comforts students he takes to be low-ability with a "kind" but discouraging strategy, such as assigning less homework. Such teachers are more likely to judge students as having low ability, more likely to lend comfort at all, and more likely to lend comfort that discourages; moreover, such comfort tends to lead to lower self-reported motivation and expectations on the part of students (Rattan *et al.* 2012).

There is a longstanding prejudice in favor of the idea that character and virtue are entirely up to their bearer, but it seems to me that this prejudice may need to be abandoned. To do so would make each of us at once more vulnerable and more responsible – more vulnerable because the virtues we have or lack would be in part due to others, and more responsible because everything we do could potentially contribute to or undermine others' character.

CHAPTER 10

Acquiring epistemic virtue
Emotions, situations, and education

Heather Battaly

Knowledge is a fine thing quite capable of ruling a man … if he can
distinguish good from evil, nothing will force him to act otherwise
than as knowledge dictates.

Plato 1989: *Protagoras*, 352c

Ability to train thought is not achieved merely by knowledge of the
best forms of thought. Possession of this information is no guarantee
for ability to think well.

Dewey 1910: *How We Think*, 29

Do we acquire epistemic virtues, like open-mindedness, simply by acquiring knowledge? If not, *why* not? This chapter uses empirical work in cognitive and social psychology to argue that acquiring knowledge is not always
sufficient for acquiring epistemic virtue. It addresses two recent empirical
challenges to the acquisition of moral virtue – non-cognitive emotion and
situationism – and applies them to epistemic virtue. It argues that to possess epistemic virtues, one must perform epistemically virtuous acts. For
instance, to be open-minded, one must consider alternative perspectives
appropriately. But knowing which acts are epistemically virtuous does not
always cause one to perform those acts. A public speaker can know that it
is virtuous to consider reasonable objections to her views, and yet fail to
consider them. The factors that prevent knowledge from causing action
can be internal to one's psychology, or externally located in the environment or 'situation'. Accordingly, our public speaker can fail to do what she
knows she should because her *emotions* influence her actions, e.g. she may
be too angry to consider the objections. Alternatively, she can fail to do

I am grateful to the Spencer Foundation's Initiative on Philosophy in Educational Policy and Practice,
and to Cal State Fullerton, for providing me with grants that supported this research. Thanks to Abrol
Fairweather, Owen Flanagan, Clifford Roth, Antony Aumann, George Sher, and Kevin Raftogianis
for their terrific comments. Thanks also to the Fall 2012 Cal State Fullerton Philosophy seminar student. Special thanks to Amy Coplan for multiple discussions about emotion and virtue.

what she knows she should because features of her *situation* influence her actions, e.g. she may be in an environment in which others unanimously dismiss the objections. Philosophers and psychologists have argued that emotions and features of situations can prevent us from performing acts that we know to be *morally* virtuous. This chapter argues that emotions and features of situations can also prevent us from performing acts that we know to be *epistemically* virtuous.

Section 1 introduces virtue-responsibilism: the view that epistemic virtues are acquired character traits, for which we are partly responsible. Led by Linda Zagzebski (1996), virtue-responsibilism models its analysis of the epistemic virtues on Aristotle's analysis of the moral virtues. Like Aristotle, virtue-responsibilists reject the view that knowledge is always causally sufficient for virtue, and endorse an epistemic analog of Aristotelian *akrasia*.

Sections 2 and 3 offer different empirical explanations of epistemic *akrasia*: the former in terms of internal emotions; the latter in terms of external features of the situation. Section 2 evaluates Amy Coplan's (2010) argument that since emotions are non-cognitive, moral virtues cannot be acquired simply by acquiring knowledge. Section 2 contends that non-cognitive emotions *can* be caused by knowledge, but can also be caused by alternative routes, like emotional contagion. It concludes that non-cognitive emotions that are caused by alternative routes can prevent us from performing acts that we know to be epistemically virtuous. Section 3 argues that situational factors (e.g. group unanimity) also causally influence our epistemic actions; sometimes causing us to perform actions that we know to be epistemically wrong.

If the arguments in sections 2 and 3 are correct, then acquiring knowledge is not always enough for acquiring epistemic virtue. So, should we give up trying to get epistemic virtue? On the contrary, the final section suggests some new strategies for encouraging the development of epistemic virtues in college classrooms – strategies that embrace the challenges above. If emotions turn out to be non-cognitive, then we can use their multiple causal routes to our advantage in helping students develop epistemic virtues. We can actively use contagion to engender emotions that support epistemically virtuous acts. We can also use situational influences to our advantage. If some features of situations – e.g. group unanimity – inhibit epistemically virtuous action, then we can (at least initially) eliminate those features from our classrooms. Instead, we can design environments and engender conditions that are conducive to practicing epistemically virtuous actions. These strategies are not meant to be sufficient for producing epistemic virtues. But they suggest that we can help students develop epistemic virtues by capitalizing on what we have learned from the challenges of non-cognitive emotion and situationism.

1   Aristotle, *akrasia,* and virtue-responsibilism

Can we acquire *moral* virtues simply by acquiring knowledge? In *Protagoras*, Socrates famously argues that we can. According to Socrates, acquiring moral virtues is relatively easy – we need only acquire knowledge of which acts are virtuous. Socrates recognizes that moral virtues require dispositions of virtuous action, and that dispositions of virtuous action are *conceptually* distinct from knowledge. He argues that knowing which acts are virtuous is *causally* sufficient for producing dispositions of virtuous action. Accordingly, an agent who knows which acts are benevolent will (in the absence of external impediments) perform those benevolent acts. Arguably, Socrates also recognizes that emotions and desires are *conceptually* distinct from, and can conflict with, knowledge. But, for Socrates, emotions and desires cannot *causally* overpower knowledge. Once an agent knows which acts are virtuous, there is nothing (in her psychology) that can prevent her from performing those acts. In short, knowledge is causally sufficient for moral virtue.

Plato's *Republic* and Aristotle's *Nicomachean Ethics* (1998; henceforth NE) reject the Socratic view, opting instead for a tripartite soul in which emotion can overpower reason. As Aristotle puts the point: "arguments ... in themselves" are not enough "to make men good" (NE.X.9.1179b3–4). On his view, emotions and desires *can* causally overpower knowledge, preventing us from performing acts we know to be virtuous. Consequently, knowledge is not enough to produce the dispositions of action that moral virtue requires, and is causally insufficient for moral virtue. For Aristotle, an agent can know that it is appropriate to help others, and yet fail to help because she has competing desires that outweigh any motivational force that might be provided by her knowledge. On Aristotle's view, such agents are *akratic*, not virtuous.

Aristotle and Socrates agree that moral virtues conceptually require (a) dispositions of appropriate action, and that the virtuous person must (b) know which actions are appropriate. But, unlike Socrates, Aristotle thinks that the virtuous person must also have (c) dispositions of appropriate emotion and motivation. Some of Aristotle's reasons for this additional requirement are conceptual, others are causal. Causally, he argues that we can have knowledge, but fail to use it: Aristotle's *akratic* person "know[s] that what he does is bad," but fails to use this knowledge; performing bad acts "as a result of passion" (NE.VII.1145b12). For Aristotle, this means that we won't acquire dispositions of appropriate action unless we train our 'passions'. He thinks we must train our emotions and motivations so that they "speak, on all matters, with the same voice as reason" (NE.I.13.1102b28) – so that they are consistent with our knowledge of which acts are appropriate. How would we do that? Aristotle does not rule out the possibility that knowledge and reason can help train emotion and motivation (NE.I.13.1102b33–34). But he thinks knowledge and reason won't be enough, since "passion seems not to yield to argument but to force" (NE.X.9.1179b28–29). On his view, emotions and motivations are primarily trained via habituation, which includes repetition, guided practice, and the imitation of exemplars.[1]

What about *epistemic* virtues, like open-mindedness, epistemic courage, and epistemic humility – can we acquire them simply by acquiring knowledge? Some contemporary virtue epistemologists have already used Aristotelian reasoning to argue that we cannot. Led by Linda Zagzebski (1996), virtue-responsibilists have argued that epistemic virtues are analogous in structure to Aristotelian moral virtues.[2] Following Aristotle, responsibilists contend that, like moral virtues, epistemic virtues conceptually require (a′) dispositions of appropriate action. The epistemic virtue of open-mindedness requires the disposition to consider alternative views appropriately;[3] epistemic courage requires a disposition to defend one's beliefs against opposition appropriately;[4] and epistemic humility requires a disposition to acknowledge one's own and others' fallibility appropriately.[5] Responsibilists likewise contend that the epistemically virtuous person must (b′) know which actions are appropriate.[6]

They also argue that epistemic virtues require (c′) dispositions of appropriate emotion and motivation. Some of their reasons are conceptual; others are causal. Causally, responsibilists argue that we can know that epistemic actions are bad, but fail to activate this knowledge and can, thus, knowingly perform bad epistemic acts.[7] This occurs in cases of epistemic *akrasia*. Zagzebski's examples of epistemic *akrasia* include "knowing that the word of a certain person cannot be trusted, but believing

---

[1] See Sherman 1989.
[2] See Montmarquet 1993; Axtell 2000; Roberts and Wood 2007; and Baehr 2011.
[3] Zagzebski 1996: 177.   [4] Montmarquet 1993: 23.
[5] Roberts and Wood 2007: 250.   [6] Zagzebski 1996: 110–11.   [7] Hookway 2001: 190.

on his authority something that supports your own position" (1996: 155). Christopher Hookway's examples include: "judg[ing] that the available evidence is insufficient to support some belief I hold, or believ[ing] that the methods used to acquire it were unreliable, yet still fail[ing] to form a resolution to examine the matter further" (2001: 183). Like the Aristotelian *akratic*, the epistemic *akratic* knowingly performs bad acts – she lacks the dispositions of action required by the epistemic virtues – and does so as a result of her emotions and motivations. Those emotions and motivations include: "the feelings that accompany prejudice;" the desire to believe what is easy or comfortable; and "the desire to hold on to old beliefs."[8] Accordingly, responsibilists think that acquiring the dispositions of action that are demanded by the epistemic virtues usually requires training our emotions and motivations. Such training will typically require strengthening our delight in, and motivation for, truth, so as to overpower competing motivations.[9] How can we strengthen our delight in, and motivation for, truth? Like Aristotle, responsibilists imply that habituation will have an important role to play.[10]

2 Emotions and epistemic virtues

This section and the next offer different empirical explanations of epistemic *akrasia*. They explain how knowledge can be causally insufficient for epistemically virtuous action, and thus for epistemic virtue. This section argues that if emotions are non-cognitive, then acquiring knowledge won't always be enough for acquiring epistemic virtue. Section 2.1 examines Amy Coplan's innovative argument that non-cognitive emotion prevents knowledge from being sufficient for virtue. It identifies a shortcoming of Coplan's argument – a failure to distinguish between causal sufficiency and conceptual sufficiency. Coplan shows that non-cognitive emotion prevents knowledge from being *conceptually* sufficient for emotion, and for virtue. But she does not show that non-cognitive emotion prevents knowledge from being *causally* sufficient for emotion, or for virtue. Knowledge can cause non-cognitive emotion; even though it is not a conceptual part of non-cognitive emotion. Section 2.1 marshals evidence for non-cognitive emotion from psychological research on mere exposure and on emotional contagion. Section 2.2 argues that even if knowledge is causally sufficient for non-cognitive emotion, it is not causally sufficient

---

[8] Zagzebski 1996: 146.   [9] Zagzebski 1996: 131, 170.   [10] Zagzebski 1996: 150.

for epistemic virtue. This is because knowledge is not the only causal route to non-cognitive emotions. Non-cognitive emotions that are caused via exposure or contagion can conflict with, and overpower, non-cognitive emotions that are caused by knowledge. Hence, non-cognitive emotions, caused via these alternative routes, can prevent us from performing acts that we know to be epistemically virtuous.

2.1   Coplan on non-cognitive emotion, knowledge, and virtue

In her insightful "Feeling without Thinking" (2010), Coplan argues that different concepts of emotion generate different accounts of virtue-acquisition. She argues that if, like Socrates and contemporary theorists of cognitive emotion, we think that emotion is a species of reason, then acquiring virtue will largely be a matter of correcting our false beliefs and replacing them with knowledge. But if, like Plato and contemporary theorists of non-cognitive emotion, we think that emotion is independent from reason, then acquiring knowledge won't be enough for acquiring virtue. We will also need to train our emotions. Coplan sides with Plato and theorists of non-cognitive emotion. To sum up, she argues that: "If virtue requires appropriate emotion, and emotion cannot be made appropriate by knowledge alone, then knowledge is insufficient for virtue" (2010: 137). Specifically, she concludes that *acquiring* knowledge is insufficient for *acquiring* virtue. In her words: "moral education must include more than learning what is right and wrong. It must include the training and habituation of our emotions so that they can be conditioned, through practice and experience, to track the appropriate things" (2010: 148). If Coplan's argument succeeds, then we can apply it to epistemic virtue, and use it to explain epistemic *akrasia*.

Does it succeed? I will argue that it falls short, but only because it is too quick. In sum, Coplan argues that:

(1)   Virtue requires appropriate emotion.
(2)   Emotions are non-cognitive.
(3)   Hence, knowledge is insufficient for appropriate emotion (from 2).
       Therefore, acquiring knowledge is insufficient for acquiring virtue.

I am largely sympathetic to Coplan's conclusion. I also find her argument for non-cognitive emotion, and the current empirical evidence, compelling. The problem lies in the move from (3) to the conclusion. That move masks the ambiguity between *conceptual* insufficiency and *causal* insufficiency. The conclusion requires *causal* insufficiency.

We can solve this problem by expanding the argument:

(I)   Virtues (moral or epistemic) require appropriate action (section 1).

(II)   At least some emotions are non-cognitive (section 2.2).

(III) Knowledge is conceptually insufficient for at least some emotions (from II).

(IV)   But (at least some) non-cognitive emotions can still be caused by knowledge (section 2.1).[11]

(V)   So, knowledge is still causally sufficient for (at least some) non-cognitive emotions (from IV).

(VI)   Non-cognitive emotions can also be caused via alternative routes (e.g. contagion).

(VII) Non-cognitive emotions caused via alternative routes can (and sometimes do) conflict with non-cognitive emotions caused by knowledge, preventing us from performing acts that we know to be appropriate (section 2.3).

(VIII) So, knowledge is not always causally sufficient for virtue (from I and VII).

       Therefore, acquiring knowledge is not always sufficient for acquiring virtue (moral or epistemic).

Coplan clearly agrees with (II) and (III). But the two arguments diverge thereafter. Regarding (VII), it is *possible* to have non-cognitive emotions that support one's knowledge of which acts are appropriate (indeed, getting these is our goal!). But it is unlikely, in the absence of active intervention or sheer good luck. Section 4 suggests strategies for making it more likely – strategies for encouraging non-cognitive emotions that support, rather than undermine, our knowledge of what should be done.

What is non-cognitive emotion and why does Coplan think that knowledge is insufficient for it (see (3) above)? By and large, those who claim that emotions are 'non-cognitive' mean that beliefs are neither conceptually necessary nor sufficient for emotions. Emotions are embodied affective responses. In contrast, those who claim that emotions are 'cognitive' mean that beliefs are conceptually necessary and sufficient for emotions. Emotions are types of belief or judgment.

Briefly, cognitivists about emotion, like Martha Nussbaum, argue that evaluative beliefs are conceptually necessary and sufficient for emotions. Thus, Nussbaum thinks one has the emotion of anger when and only

---

[11] Other non-cognitive emotions may be cognitively impenetrable.

when one has a complex set of beliefs, including the beliefs that damage has been done to oneself or one's friends; the damage done is significant; the damage was done intentionally; and the perpetrator should be punished (2003: 276). Nussbaum explicitly argues that evaluative beliefs like these are conceptually sufficient for the emotion of anger; neither physiological changes in the body nor non-cognitive feelings are conceptually necessary (2003: 282–83). She also argues that such evaluative beliefs are conceptually necessary. In her words: "It is plausible to assume that each element in [the above] set of beliefs is necessary in order for anger to be present: if I should discover … that [the damage] was not serious, we could expect my anger to modify itself … or recede" (2003: 276).

In contrast, non-cognitivists about emotion, like Jesse Prinz, argue that beliefs are neither conceptually necessary nor sufficient for emotion; but physiological changes and non-cognitive feelings are. Thus, emotions are "embodied appraisals," not evaluative beliefs (2004: 243). For Prinz, one has the emotion of fear when one registers specific physiological changes in the body (e.g. increased heart rate); changes that represent danger in the environment (2004: 69). Granted, this sounds awfully cognitive! But, on Prinz's picture, physiological changes *represent* danger non-cognitively. An increased heart rate represents danger in the same way that a ringing smoke alarm represents smoke. When functioning well, heart rate reliably tracks danger in the environment, just as a properly functioning smoke alarm reliably tracks smoke. This sort of representation does not require belief, it just requires reliable tracking. Nor is our *registering* of physiological changes meant to be cognitive (though it, too, sounds cognitive) – it does not require belief. For Prinz, we register increased heart rate by feeling fear.

Of course, one's fear might fail to reliably track danger – one might be afraid of any number of things that are not dangerous (e.g. mice). Prinz suggests that we can modify non-cognitive emotions so that they reliably track what they should. How? On Prinz's view, we do so by forming new "calibration files"; i.e. we modify the causal triggers of our emotions. Roughly, a calibration file is a set of representations that consistently causes a particular emotion in a particular person. Prinz thinks that calibration files can "contain a variety of representations, ranging from explicit judgments to sensory states" (2004: 101). Thus, your calibration file for fear may include the sensory representation of mice, while my calibration file for fear may include the belief that flying is dangerous. Prinz argues that by 'recalibrating' our files, we can modify our non-cognitive emotions so that they track what they should (2004: 102). He does not explain exactly how to 'recalibrate' our files – e.g. how to get all and only the things that are dangerous to consistently cause fear in us – but he suggests we may need to start by modi-fying our beliefs and acquiring knowledge (2004: 148). To illustrate, he sug-gests that the knowledge that guns are dangerous may initially have been needed to get us to fear guns – to get us to reliably track the real danger that guns pose.[12] But he argues that once we repeatedly experience guns in con-junction with fear, the knowledge that guns are dangerous will no longer be needed to cause fear; the mere sight of a gun will be enough (2004: 74–77). In short, even if knowledge is initially needed for 'recalibration', associative learning ensures that it is not needed for long. There will be multiple repre-sentations – including the knowledge that guns are dangerous, and the sight of a gun – each of which will be sufficient for causing fear.

Coplan thinks that for non-cognitivists like Prinz, knowledge is insuf-ficient for appropriate emotion (see (3)). Coplan is entirely correct that for non-cognitivists, knowledge is *conceptually* insufficient for emotion (appropriate or otherwise). Prinz even explicitly argues that "all emotions are constituted by embodied appraisals alone"; not by their calibration files or the knowledge that those files contain, which are "causes, not con-stituents" of emotions (2004: 102). The problem is that Coplan's argument also requires the claim that knowledge is *causally* insufficient for appropri-ate emotion:

(1)   Virtue requires appropriate emotion.
(2)   Emotions are non-cognitive.
(3)   Knowledge is insufficient for appropriate emotion.
(4*)   Knowledge is causally insufficient for appropriate emotion.
        Therefore, acquiring knowledge is insufficient for acquiring virtue.

And (4*) is not entailed by non-cognitivism. Prinz explicitly argues that knowledge, and other cognitive states, are often causally sufficient for appropriate non-cognitive emotions.[13] Recall his discussion of 'recal-ibration'. There, his main point was *not* that knowledge is insufficient to cause appropriate emotion, but, rather, that knowledge is not *the only* sort of representation that is causally sufficient for appropriate emotion. In his words, "explicit, disembodied judgments are just one kind of cause among many" (2004: 77). To show that knowledge is causally insufficient for appropriate non-cognitive emotions, one would need to argue that non-cognitive emotions are cognitively impenetrable. This may be true of some non-cognitive emotions – like fear of spiders – but it is not true of non-cognitive emotions in general.

---

[12] Prinz 2004: 76.   [13] Prinz 2004: 30, 77, 148.

2.2   Evidence for non-cognitive emotion

That said, Coplan's argument for the existence of non-cognitive emotion is compelling. Here, I briefly summarize two areas of psychological research that support the existence of non-cognitive emotion: research on mere exposure and on emotional contagion. I infer a relatively modest conclusion: *at least some* of our emotions are non-cognitive (see (II) above).

First, Robert Zajonc has argued that mere exposure to symbols, like random polygons, causes an affective preference for them. In Zajonc's words: "when a particular stimulus is shown over and over again ... it gets to be better liked" (2000: 35). Zajonc's key point is that we like stimuli to which we have been previously exposed *even when those exposures are so fast that it is "impossible for [us] to become aware of [them]"* (2000: 43, my emphasis). In short, he argues that affective preference can occur without cognition. In one such study, Zajonc's subjects were exposed to a randomized series of polygons. Each exposure lasted for 1 millisecond; and each polygon was presented three times. Next, subjects were presented with two polygons – one to which they had been exposed and one to which they had not – and were asked which polygon they had been exposed to and which polygon they liked better. Subjects were unable to discriminate between polygons to which they had, and had not, been exposed. But of the polygons subjects liked better, 60 percent were polygons to which they had been exposed. In short, if Zajonc is correct, then affective preference can occur "prior to and independently of ... cognitive processes," and can be caused directly by mere exposure (2000: 32). Cognition is neither conceptually nor causally required for affective preference. Consequently, provided that we are willing to count affective preference as an emotion, Zajonc's work supports the existence of non-cognitive emotion.

Second, several psychologists have argued that we can 'catch' one another's emotions via the non-cognitive process of emotional contagion. To illustrate, one can (arguably) catch the emotion of happiness by walking through a room of happy, smiling people. In catching happiness, one undergoes physiological changes and acquires affect – the feeling of happiness. But cognition need not be conceptually or causally involved. One need not believe, or even be aware, that the people in the room are happy, or that there are any people in the room at all. Nor need one believe that life is good, that things are looking up, or anything of the sort. One might even be so stressed out and oblivious to one's surroundings (e.g. walking through a room with a looming deadline on one's mind) that, after the fact, one is surprised to find that one is happy and comes to wonder why.

Emotional contagion is thought to be a hard-wired, involuntary process that operates in multiple species – one that happens quickly and prior to cognition. How does contagion produce emotion, if *not* via cognition? Elaine Hatfield *et al.* (1994) suggest that contagion operates via the subcortical processes of facial mimicry and feedback. In short, sensory input of (e.g.) smiling people causes one to smile oneself (mimicry), and smiling causes the emotion of happiness (feedback). Several studies have argued that we tend to mimic the facial expressions of others – both Republicans and Democrats who watched news clips of Ronald Reagan were found to mimic his facial expressions.[14] What about feedback? It is ordinarily thought that emotion causes facial expression, e.g. happiness causes smiling. But multiple studies on feedback have surreptitiously manipulated the facial muscles of subjects – e.g. by placing pens in their teeth – in order to test whether facial expression causes emotion.[15] Subjects in these studies were unaware that their facial expressions mimicked those of people who were happy, sad, angry, etc. Summarizing the results of such studies, Hatfield *et al.* conclude that subjects "feel the specific emotions ... consistent with the facial expressions they adopt and have trouble experiencing emotions incompatible with those poses" (1994: 56). In short, it is thought that cognition is neither conceptually nor causally required for the emotions we catch from others. Accordingly, work on emotional contagion further supports the existence of non-cognitive emotion.

Finally, Joseph LeDoux's (1996) research on the brain may help us explain *how* contagion and exposure produce emotions without cognition. LeDoux has argued that emotions can be produced without any involvement of the neocortex, and thus without cognition. He contends that there is a direct neural pathway that links the sensory thalamus with the amygdala, the latter of which generates emotional responses. This link bypasses the neocortex. In short, he thinks our brains can produce emotional responses without slowing down to do cognitive processing.

2.3 *Non-cognitive emotion can prevent knowledge from being causally sufficient for virtue*

Thus far, section 2 has argued that some of our emotions are non-cognitive, and that knowledge is causally sufficient for at least some non-cognitive emotions. So why isn't knowledge always causally sufficient for virtue? The short answer is that there are alternative causal routes to non-cognitive

---

[14] McHugo *et al.* 1985.   [15] Strack *et al.* 1988.

emotions – knowledge is not causally necessary for non-cognitive emotion. It is possible for non-cognitive emotions that are caused via contagion and mere exposure to conflict with, and overpower, emotions that are caused by knowledge. Such emotions can prevent us from performing acts that we know to be epistemically virtuous.

To illustrate, (A) suppose that Christine has completed a study on the effects of a new drug, and has written a draft of her results. Christine is in the process of reviewing the data, and knows that she should re-check the data before submitting the draft for publication, when her colleagues burst into her lab, excited and jumping with joy. Christine catches their excitement via *contagion*. As a result, she fails to re-check the data (despite knowing that she should), and gleefully submits the draft for publication. Christine fails to do what an epistemically thorough person would have done – she fails to check evidence appropriately. (B) Suppose that Paul is repeatedly *exposed* to celebrity trivia – e.g. the whereabouts of Lindsay Lohan. As a result, he develops a preference for celebrity trivia; he likes it. Paul is currently enrolled in Intro to Philosophy, and knows that he should enjoy pursuing truths about ethics. But instead of engaging in classroom discussions about ethics, he surreptitiously reads celebrity blogs on his laptop. Paul fails to do what an epistemically temperate person would do – he fails to take pleasure in and pursue appropriate truths. (C) Suppose that Vinny presents a paper at a conference. Professor Z insults Vinny in the question and answer period. As a result, Vinny gets angry. Suppose that his anger is initially caused by his judgment that Prof. Z is deliberately insulting him. Prinz suggests that emotions that are initially caused by cognition can, via *association*, come to be caused directly via sensory input. After several similar encounters with Prof. Z, Vinny now gets angry at the mere sight of Z. At this year's conference, Z raises several good objections to Vinny's argument (and does so respectfully). Vinny knows that he should consider them, but he is so angry that he completely ignores Z. Here, Vinny fails to do what an open-minded person would do – he fails to consider alternatives appropriately.

These cases demonstrate that one can know which acts are epistemically appropriate, but fail to perform them, and thus fail to possess epistemic virtue. To possess epistemic virtues – like thoroughness, epistemic temperance, and open-mindedness – one must consistently perform appropriate acts. But non-cognitive emotions can prevent us from performing epistemically appropriate acts, just as they can prevent us from performing morally appropriate acts. This means that knowledge is not always causally sufficient for epistemic virtue. To acquire epistemic virtue, we will typically not only need to acquire knowledge, we will also need to acquire an overall set of non-cognitive emotions and other psychological motivators, which supports, rather than undermines, our knowledge of what should be done.[16]

3 Situations and epistemic virtue

'Situationists', like John Doris (2002), have argued that seemingly trivial changes in our situations or environments can influence *moral* behavior. Using the work of social psychologists, this section argues that mood and group effects can also causally influence our *epistemic* behavior, especially the behavior required for virtues like epistemic courage, epistemic autonomy, open-mindedness, and epistemic humility. In addition, this section gives us a second reason for thinking that acquiring knowledge is not always causally sufficient for acquiring the dispositions of action that are needed for epistemic virtues. We might know what we should do (e.g. stand up for our beliefs), but fail to do it because of situational influences; or know what we shouldn't do (e.g. agree with group opinion), but do it anyway.[17]

3.1 Situationism about moral action

Doris (2002) argues for three key conclusions: what I call 'weak situationism'; 'strong situationism'; and 'elimination'. Using the work of Latane and Darley (1970), Isen and Levin (1972), Darley and Batson (1973), Milgram (1974), and Zimbardo (1992), Doris argues that seemingly trivial changes in our environments or situations can causally influence whether we perform pro-social actions. Multiple studies, including Isen and Levin (1972), have found that good moods that are produced by trivial changes in the environment are correlated with pro-social behavior – actions that a virtuous person would perform. Likewise, the environmental conditions

---

[16] When one fully possesses an epistemic virtue, what happens to non-cognitive emotions? Do they all disappear, or become cognitive? Arguably, one cannot fully possess epistemic virtues unless one's actions are produced by an overall set of psychological motivators that includes cognitive motivations. But this does *not* mean that all our non-cognitive emotions disappear. Arguably, we cannot rid ourselves of non-cognitive emotions. What we can do is 'recalibrate' our non-cognitive emotions, perhaps through exposure and association, so that we arrive at a set of cognitive and non-cognitive motivators that, overall, supports our knowledge of what should be done. That set may still contain some non-cognitive emotions that, left unchecked by other motivators in the set, would prevent us from performing virtuous actions. This may have ramifications for the distinction between virtue and *enkrateia* (continence). Thanks to Abrol Fairweather for this point.

[17] See also Alfano 2012.

generated by Latane and Darley, Darley and Batson, Milgram, and Zimbardo have been found to be correlated with actions that a virtuous person would not perform: failing to report 'dangerous' smoke; failing to help confederates in distress; and 'shocking' confederates. What do these studies show?

Doris argues that these studies support three key conclusions. First, they support 'weak situationism': the view that trivial changes in one's environment can causally influence whether one performs appropriate actions. Second, Doris contends that situational influences are much better predictors of behavior than character traits are. This, in turn, leads him to support 'strong situationism': the view that the studies show that most people lack global character traits.[18] Gilbert Harman even concludes that the studies show that there may be "no such thing as character" and that "there is no empirical basis for the existence of character traits" (1999: 316). Third, Doris argues that since most people lack global character traits, notions of global character should be eliminated from ethics (2002: 108).

Briefly, I submit that such studies support weak situationism, but neither strong situationism nor elimination. To explicate, the studies succeed in showing that features of our situations can independently influence our actions. This may be revelatory for many of us working in virtue theory. It means that we do not have as much control over our actions as we might have thought. It also means that our actions are not always the products of character traits.[19] As Matthew Pamental puts the point, we have "overestimate[d] the individual's contribution to moral behavior," and underestimated the contribution of situational or environmental features (2010: 166).

But the studies fall short of showing that strong situationism is true. For starters, they are meager support for Harman's suggestion that character is a myth. Nor, relatedly, do the studies show that our actions are solely the products of situations. If they were, subjects in the studies would (nearly) all respond the same way; but they don't. More importantly, the studies do not *directly* support Doris's claim that most people lack global character traits. Granted, they do provide indirect evidence for that claim, *if* situational factors are better predictors of behavior. Direct evidence would involve longitudinal studies, which follow the same subjects from one situation to the next. Most of the studies Doris cites are not of this sort.[20]

---

[18] Doris 2002: 108. Doris endorses local, not global, traits.
[19] See also Flanagan (2009: 55–56, 64). Flanagan also endorses, what I call, 'weak situationism.'
[20] Doris 2002: 38, 121.

But we would be better off if we actually looked for global character traits in longitudinal studies, before concluding that most people lack them.[21]

Below, I suggest a middle ground of sorts: both character and situations can cause our actions. Often they work together to cause our actions, but sometimes they cause our actions independently. Specifically, I suggest that weak situationism does not prevent us from acquiring nearly global virtues – we can even use weak situationism to help us acquire those virtues. To be virtuous, we must perform appropriate actions in a wide range of situations. And to do that, we must arguably learn to recognize and overcome a wide range of situational impediments. This view assumes that virtues will be neither Doris-local, nor maximally global – they will issue appropriate actions in a variety of situations, but not in all situations. To illustrate, if I fail to help a person in distress because of group effects, or a neutral mood, then I do not have the virtue of benevolence. So virtues are not local in the way Doris suggests, since they must still issue appropriate actions in a wide variety of situations. But nor are they maximally global. This is where virtue theory should take note. Claiming that virtues must issue appropriate actions in *all* situations is tantamount to denying that situations can independently influence our actions. It is naïve to think that character-building could enable us to overcome *all* situational influences. If weak situationism is true, it can't: our actions are not always the products of character traits.

If this 'middle ground' is prima facie viable, then the real difficulty will be determining *which* situational influences we need to overcome in order to have virtues, and *why*. I won't pretend to answer this here. But it is worth considering whether responsibilist epistemic virtues should be indexed to situations in much the same way that Sosa indexes reliabilist epistemic virtues to conditions. On Sosa's view, the virtue of vision is not impugned by its failure to issue true beliefs about objects that are in the dark. Rather, its reliability is indexed to conditions in which we see nearby objects, without occlusion, in good lighting (1991: 139). Analogously, it is worth considering whether responsibilist virtues like benevolence and epistemic courage should be indexed to some situations but not others. Is the virtue of benevolence impugned by its failure to issue pro-social actions in extremely repressive societies? If not, *why* not? Is it because human beings are, in the words of Robert Adams, "adapted to live and function effectively only in a certain range of situations?" (2006: 157)

---

[21] That said, I would be surprised if most people did possess maximallly global character traits. Even nearly global virtues are difficult to acquire, especially if we are ignorant of the influence of situations on action.

In the sub-sections below, I apply studies in social psychology to *epistemic* action, arguing that situations can influence the epistemic actions required for the virtues of epistemic courage, epistemic autonomy, open-mindedness, and epistemic humility. I will also argue that situational factors can prevent us from performing epistemic acts that we *know* to be appropriate. Accordingly, acquiring knowledge will not always be enough for acquiring epistemic virtue. Situational factors can interfere.

3.2   Situations influence epistemically courageous action

Multiple studies show that situations can influence whether we perform epistemically appropriate actions; but few address whether situations can prevent us from performing acts that we *know* to be epistemically appropriate. A notable exception is the work of Solomon Asch.

In the 1950s, Asch conducted his now famous 'conformity studies'. Each subject was a member of a seven-to-nine-person group; every other member of the group was a confederate. Each group sat together, facing a board, on which four lines were drawn: a given line of a particular length, accompanied by three additional lines. The length of one of the additional lines was identical to the length of the given line; the lengths of the other two additional lines were obviously not identical to the length of the given line. Each group member was asked, in turn, which of the additional lines was the same length as the given line. Group members heard one another's answers. Every group member except the subject gave pre-arranged answers. The subject was always one of the last members of the group to answer.

Multiple trials were conducted in each group. In the first two trials, confederate group members were instructed to give the correct answers. Thereafter, confederates were instructed to unanimously give the same obviously false answer. Asch found that 33 percent of subjects gave the same (false) answer as the group (1952: 457). Asch describes the situation as one in which subjects have to make a choice and perform an action. In his words, each subject "had the choice of remaining true to the testimony of his perception and judgment, or of yielding to the majority" (1952: 465). Roughly one third yielded to the majority.

Asch's studies support two key claims. First, they support the claim that features of groups can influence whether we perform the actions required for epistemic courage. Which actions are those? James Montmarquet argues that the virtue of epistemic courage requires a disposition to "persever[e] in the face of opposition from others (until one is convinced that one is mistaken)" (1993: 23). In short, the epistemically courageous person stands up for what she believes, until it is appropriate to change her mind. Asch's studies focus on the statements of subjects: whether or not subjects verbally gave the same (false) answer as the group. Accordingly, his studies are directly relevant to the virtue of epistemic courage. They show that subjects who gave the majority answer failed to perform epistemically courageous acts, since they failed to appropriately stand up for what they believed. They yielded to group pressure. In short, Asch's studies support 'weak situationism'.[22]

Second, Asch's studies support the claim that situations can prevent us from performing acts we *know* to be epistemically appropriate, and cause us to perform acts we *know* to be epistemically inappropriate. Asch explicitly contends that many subjects who yielded to the majority opinion did not believe the majority opinion and *knew* that they should have reported what they actually believed. In his words, such subjects "kn[ew] that they [were] not acting properly, but ... [could] not change their course" (1952: 471–72). These subjects reported undergoing conflict, and feeling guilty about "acting improperly" (1952: 472). In short, they were epistemically *akratic*.

In subsequent studies, Asch found that conformity to the majority opinion was significantly reduced when the subject had a 'partner' – when one person in the group was instructed to give correct responses. This is hopeful. Overall, Asch's studies indicate that individuals are unlikely to disagree with a unanimous group about uncontroversial matters. Arguably, this means that individuals will also be unlikely to disagree with a unanimous group about controversial matters (those discussed in our classrooms). But, if Asch is correct, just one partner significantly increases the likelihood that another individual will speak his mind.

3.3 Situations influence epistemically autonomous action

Multiple studies support the claim that situations can influence whether we perform epistemically appropriate actions. In an ingenious study, Joseph Forgas and Rebekah East (2008) argue that being in a happy or sad mood can influence whether we trust or doubt the testimony of others. Their study has two stages. First, by way of set-up, it provides individual participants with the opportunity to take a movie ticket left out in the

---

[22] Asch thinks that character traits exist, and explain why subjects did not all respond the same way (1952: 497).

open. Each participant is told that whether or not she/he takes the ticket, she/he must deny taking the ticket on a subsequent videotaped interview. All participants did deny taking the ticket in their videos – some were truthful, others were lying. In the second stage of the study, those videos were shown to subjects. One group of subjects had previously watched a comedy clip; a second group had previously watched an excerpt from a nature documentary; and a third had watched a clip from a film on dying from cancer. Each subject was then asked to decide whether the participant in the video was guilty or innocent of taking the ticket; and each was asked to rate the veracity of the participant on an eight-point scale.

Forgas and East found that subjects in happy and neutral moods – those who had watched comedy or documentary clips – "failed to significantly discriminate between innocent and guilty targets" (2008: 1365). In contrast, sad subjects, who had watched the film about cancer, were significantly better at detecting deception. The authors conclude that "negative mood increased [subjects'] skepticism … and improved their accuracy in detecting deceptive communications, while [subjects] in a positive mood were more trusting and gullible" (2008: 1362).

This study supports the claim that moods can influence whether we perform epistemically autonomous actions. What actions does an epistemically autonomous person perform? According to Robert Roberts and Jay Wood, the epistemically autonomous person has a "proper ability to think for herself and not be … improperly dependent on or influenced by others" (2007: 259). The epistemically autonomous person doubts others when she should, and trusts them when she should. She also relies on her own abilities when she should. Forgas and East explicitly acknowledge that "deciding when to trust and when to be skeptical towards others" is a "cognitively demanding" task that involves action on the part of the subject (2008: 1365). Arguably, they show that being in a happy mood sometimes prevents us from doing what an epistemically autonomous person would do. Being happy can make us *too* trusting and impair our ability to detect deception. Being sad appears to improve our ability to perform epistemically autonomous actions (in environments where deception is prevalent). Further studies on the connection between sadness and epistemic autonomy can and should be conducted.

3.4   *Situations influence open-minded action*

If Forgas and East are correct, being in a good mood can make us more gullible and less epistemically autonomous. But the data on good moods isn't all bad! Alice Isen and colleagues (1987) argue that positive affect can cause us to consider alternative perspectives and solutions to problems. The disposition to consider alternatives is required for virtues like open-mindedness and creativity. In Jason Baehr's words, the open-minded person is "willing ... to transcend a default cognitive standpoint in order to ... take seriously a distinct cognitive standpoint" (2011: 152).

Isen *et al.* conducted studies using the 'candle task'. Subjects are given three objects: a candle, a book of matches, and a box of tacks. Subjects are told that they have ten minutes to affix the candle to a corkboard on the wall, and are asked to do so "in such a way that it will burn without dripping wax onto ... the floor" (1987: 1123). Isen *et al.* designed four different versions of the candle task. In version 1, subjects watched five minutes of a comedy film. Subjects in version 2 watched five minutes of a neutral film. Subjects in versions 3 and 4 saw no films. All subjects were presented with the tacks inside the box, except for subjects in version 4, who were presented with an empty box and a pile of tacks. The problem can be solved by dumping the tacks out of the box, lighting the candle, gluing it to the base of the box with wax, and then affixing the box to the wall with a tack. Isen *et al.* found that 75 percent of subjects who watched the comedy film solved the problem, compared to only 13 percent who watched no films and 20 percent who watched a neutral film. By comparison, 83 percent of subjects who were presented with an empty box (and a pile of tacks) solved the problem.

Subjects in the candle task are performing epistemic actions. They are formulating and testing hypotheses, and considering and trying out alternatives. In interpreting the results of these studies, Isen *et al.* argue that the positive affect produced by the comedy film enabled subjects to "consider alternative uses for the box" (1987: 1124). Accordingly, their study supports the claim that being in a good mood can cause one to do what an open-minded or creative person would do. In the words of Isen *et al.*: "These results indicate that creativity ... often thought of as a stable characteristic of persons, can be facilitated by a transient pleasant affective state" (1987: 1128).

3.5 *Situations influence epistemically humble action*

In contrast with an epistemically arrogant person, an epistemically humble person is disposed to recognize her own fallibility, and to recognize and value the epistemic abilities of others. According to Roberts and Wood, the virtue of epistemic humility requires a disposition to avoid "mak[ing] unwarranted intellectual entitlement claims on the basis of one's (supposed) superiority" (2007: 250). An epistemically humble person defers to the expertise of others, as appropriate. She also revises her own views, as appropriate. A recent study by Michelle Shiota and colleagues (2007) supports the thesis that feelings of awe can cause us to do what an epistemically humble person would do. Unlike Asch, Forgas and East, and Isen *et al.*, Shiota *et al.* do not explicitly argue for the causal claim of 'weak situationism', but they do contend that feelings of awe are correlated with one's "willingness to modify [one's own] mental structures" (2007: 946).

Shiota *et al.* conducted two key studies: one in which subjects self-reported their experiences of awe, joy, and pride and completed the 'need for cognitive closure scale'; and one in which subjects were first exposed to a Tyrannosaurus rex skeleton, and then generated descriptions of themselves. Shiota *et al.* found that in contrast with pride, awe was associated with a much lower need for cognitive closure, concluding that "awe-prone individuals should be especially comfortable revising their own mental structures" (2007: 958). They also found that awe was associated with a "sense of the self as part of a greater whole – a self-concept that de-emphasizes the individual self" (2007: 960). They are careful to avoid claiming that feelings of awe *cause* one's willingness to revise one's beliefs. But if awe does cause that willingness, then objects in our environment that produce awe can (via awe) trigger actions that are required for the virtue of epistemic humility. Further studies on the connections between awe and epistemic humility can and should be conducted. But if feelings of awe do engender actions that are required for epistemic humility, then we can use awe to our advantage in the classroom.

4   Acquiring epistemic virtue in the college classroom

Acquiring knowledge is not always sufficient for acquiring epistemic virtue. Non-cognitive emotions and situational factors can prevent us from performing acts that we know to be epistemically appropriate. Does this mean that we should stop trying to acquire epistemic virtues? Quite the contrary: if the above arguments are correct, they provide us with rough strategies for testing and developing potential ways to acquire epistemic virtues. Here, I suggest some strategies to test and explore in university classrooms.

Epistemic virtues require dispositions of appropriate action. We can give students opportunities to practice those actions by initially encouraging emotions and situations that are conducive to performing them.

If emotions are non-cognitive, then we can use multiple causal routes to generate emotions that will support such actions. Since knowledge can cause non-cognitive emotion, we can still use knowledge and lectures to encourage such emotions. But we can also experiment with contagion and exposure. We can monitor and discourage the contagion of emotions that are likely to prevent us from performing epistemically virtuous actions. For instance, when helping students learn whether and when to trust the media, we can experiment with discouraging happiness. The media is sometimes – arguably, often – deceptive. We can test whether discouraging happiness improves students' abilities to perform epistemically autonomous actions – to rely on media sources for their beliefs when they should and doubt media sources when they should. We can also experiment with using contagion to disseminate emotions that are conducive to performing epistemically virtuous acts. Does 'catching' happiness from us, or from other students, help a student appropriately consider alternative perspectives? We can also test whether exposure applies in the classroom. If exposure to bodies of knowledge causes us to like those bodies of knowledge, then exposure can help us generate the emotions of pleasure and delight, which are required for the virtue of epistemic temperance. And if mere exposure to bodies of knowledge is not enough to produce pleasure in them, then we can test whether rewards are also needed, and if so what kind.

In a similar vein, we can – at least initially – design our classrooms so as to eliminate situational factors that prevent students from performing epistemically virtuous acts, and include situational factors that facilitate those acts.[23] Isen *et al.* suggest something similar. In their words, teachers should make an effort "to provide the conditions that are conducive to creativity. One of those conditions is a happy feeling state ... We would suggest, for the educational context, that an atmosphere of interpersonal respect conducive to good self-esteem might be the kind of condition that would promote creativity" (1987: 1129). In short, if positive affect proves to trigger open-minded action, and awe proves to trigger epistemically humble action, then we can design our classrooms so that they allow for multiple opportunities to experience positive affect and awe.

We should also test whether the data amassed by social psychological studies can be replicated in the classroom. If students really are unlikely to disagree with a unanimous group, then we will need to establish an

---

[23] Analogously, Owen Flanagan suggests that we design our social environments so as to minimize situational factors that defeat appropriate moral actions (1991: 313–14).

atmosphere in which disagreement is encouraged. Else, we risk inhibiting students from practicing epistemically courageous acts. This can be
done at the curricular level, in one's syllabi, and in classroom discussion
itself. At the curricular level, we can encourage an atmosphere in which
disagreement is acceptable by offering courses from different traditions.
For instance, in philosophy curricula, we can offer a range of courses in
analytic, continental, and Eastern philosophy. In syllabi, we can assign
readings in which different authors provide well-reasoned arguments for
competing conclusions. In the classroom itself, we can encourage students
to advocate views that are different from their own (in assignments or
discussions). As professors, we might consider keeping our own views to
ourselves, in an effort to encourage the advocacy of multiple views.[24]

The world, however, is not a classroom; it is not neatly designed to
shield us from competing emotions and confounding situations. Students
will need to overcome many such emotions and situations, in order to
acquire nearly global traits like the epistemic virtues. Accordingly, after
we have provided students with multiple opportunities to perform epistemically virtuous actions – after they have had repeated practice – it
will also be useful to employ classroom activities that introduce competing emotions and confounding situations. Students will need to practice,
e.g., performing epistemically autonomous actions when they are glee-
ful, open-minded actions when they are bored, and epistemically courageous actions in the face of unanimous disagreement. It will not be easy
to overcome competing emotions or confounding situations. In fact, if
weak situationism is correct, there will be some confounding situations
that we cannot overcome. Empirical studies have indicated that we are
better at overcoming confounding situations when we know that they are
confounding situations.[25] So one strategy for helping students overcome
confounding situations is making them aware of the influence of those
situations on their epistemic actions.

These strategies are not enough to produce epistemic virtues. But they
suggest that we can use what we have learned from the challenges of non-
cognitive emotion and situationism to help our students make progress
toward epistemic virtues. My hope is that we will conduct further research
on strategies for acquiring epistemic virtues in university classrooms.

[24] Thanks to David Donley.   [25] Higgins 1996: 143–45, 150–51.

Virtue and the fitting culturing of the human critter

David Henderson and Terence Horgan

How does virtue epistemology relate to naturalized epistemology? Naturalized epistemology is the repudiation of first philosophy; it is epistemology enriched and informed by extant bodies of knowledge. In its meliorative aspect, naturalized epistemology aspires to a richly informed modulation of human cognitive processing, as one seeks to minimize human foibles and encourage the more reliable packages of humanly tractable processes. In its theoretical aspect, naturalized epistemology seeks to provide an understanding of normatively appropriate human belief-forming processes – including both (a) processes that humans deploy spontaneously by virtue of innate cognitive architecture, and (b) processes that humans are capable of coming to deploy, through learning and socialization. Naturalized epistemology, in both its meliorative and its theoretical aspects, draws upon achieved cultural resources – one's contemporary scientific and cultural information. What of virtue epistemology? Two classical themes from virtue epistemology are important for any epistemologist serious about the real business of understanding how best to develop systems of true beliefs. They also fit easily within naturalized epistemology. (1) What is proper and fitting in the way of forming beliefs is relative to a kind of natural cognitive and sensory creature. Human epistemology is different from and more ambitious than corvid epistemology because humans, in myriad ways, have more powerful cognitive endowments than crows or ravens. (2) What is fitting and proper to cognitive systems such as humans is a matter of a repertoire of cognitive processes many of which must be developed or learned – fostered or cultured. Notably, humans are social creatures, and this is significant in their epistemic lives. Humans jointly lay in a stock of information about themselves and their environment. This has consequences for a virtue theorist: this stock of information is doubtless significant when developing or culturing fitting human cognitive capacities. The consequence may be taken as a less familiar element of virtue theory: (3) humans, as deeply cultural creatures, must and should develop and practice their epistemic arts in a social-cultural setting. All this is consequential for the relation between virtue theory and naturalized epistemology. In drawing on extant information about humans and their environment, the virtue theorist is proceeding as a naturalized epistemologist – or should be. Epistemic virtue theory should have to do with what is natural (human cognitive capacities, including capacities for refinement of innate capacities through learning) and cultural (extant information and associated state-of-the-art norms).

Commonly, virtue epistemology incorporates a fourth theme, one that we also will discuss here: (4) rules or algorithms that purport to describe normatively appropriate modes of belief-formation really can only provide, at best, approximate characterizations; they are somehow not fitting to the best that humans can manage. Our discussion largely vindicates (4).

Virtue theorists from early on have used analogies with athletic contests and training. We will follow suit. Cultural knowledge may suggest ways of proceeding – perhaps biomechanics in a sport, perhaps cognitive skills or limits in epistemology – and one may initially implement some suggested changes in ways of thinking or doing by following certain rules. However, commonly, this stage of rule-application gives way to a more powerful cognitive stage and practice, one that is faster and more powerful. The point is familiar from cognitive scientific work on expert systems, and commonly illustrated by a story about developing expertise in chess. Apparently, with practice, one develops into a chess player for whom the learning rules would be relatively flat-footed. Similarly, by training, the expert basketball player comes to be able to respond on the court in ways that go beyond the simple drills deployed in the training. Here, the rules respected in training can somehow lead to a system that accommodates the information reflected in the rules, and yet does so in ways that are both faster and more powerful than could come from consciously rehearsing and applying articulable rules. (Increase in speed could come about merely by internalizing the rules so that their application becomes spontaneous and automatic; but increase in power comes about by developing a level of skill that outstrips what the rules themselves prescribe, thereby transcending strict conformity to them.) What is developed or cultured can be a kind of capacity. This culturing reflects (2). Fitting culturing will need to draw on information about the kinds of creature being cultured, thus (3) and (1). Point (4) has to do with the kinds of critters we humans are – about human expertise specifically, and perhaps neural nets generally. Explicating point (4), and arguing in support of it (as thus explicated), will be the principal business of the second half of this chapter. The first half will set the stage, with a discussion largely elaborating upon points (1)–(3).

1   Naturalized epistemology

To naturalize epistemology is to draw on one's best extant understanding of the world in which one undertakes epistemic investigations, and of the character and plasticity of one's human cognitive capacities, to fashion an account of tractable ways of thinking, and of structuring inquiry, that will enable humans to arrive at systematic true beliefs. This, in Quine's words, is a matter of an informed "engineering for truth-seeking" (Quine 1986: 664–65). Abandoning the aspirations of first philosophy, one seeks a more fully informed understanding of how humans can best, or at least satisfactorily, form beliefs.

There are multiple considerations that should reasonably constrain one's inquiry into the engineering for truth-seeking. Some of these have to do with the reliability of human cognitive processes in particular environments. If some processes systematically yield inaccurate beliefs in certain environments, then humans arguably should develop some sensitivity to such environments, and this sensitivity should (at least selectively) inhibit the use of those processes in those environments. Of course, there are likely costs and benefits to be weighed here. Related considerations have to do with what in particular can be managed using human cognitive and social raw materials. Human capacities are developed out of a range of rudimentary cognitive processes, including those involved in learning. There are limits to what is cognitively tractable for humans. Humans are profoundly finite cognitive systems, and, given that they want to get the most out of their cognitive resources, they reasonably look for efficient (as well as tractable) ways of managing many of their epistemic chores.

As a useful springboard for thinking about nature's epistemological engineering of innate human cognitive architecture for tractable reliability of belief-forming processes, and for thinking about humanly tractable ways that innate human capacities for reliable belief-formation can be enhanced through learning and social cooperation, one might take inspiration from the considerations weighing on the design of a vehicle for transporting people and tools about an environment.

1.1   Local reliability

One might be assigned the task of engineering a vehicle that will be deployed in some especially challenging, delimited, environment. When this challenging local environment is specified in advance, one can concentrate on engineering a vehicle that will have the capacities necessary for performing reliably just there. This is a concern for what we have termed *local reliability*.[1] A system or process is locally reliable when, relative to the specific spatiotemporally local environment that the system happens to occupy, the system/process has a strong tendency to succeed in the tasks in question.

1.2 Global reliability

One might also be assigned the task of engineering a vehicle that will be deployed in a wide range of local environments – although, effectively, never is one assigned a task of engineering a vehicle that will work in *any* local environment whatsoever. Typically those who design automobiles design them to work from the tropics to the temperate regions, in mountains (in mild seasons), in deserts, wherever roads are to be found. Those who design aircraft commonly design them to reliably transport goods and people around the globe, to wherever standard landing facilities are to be found. That said, no one supposes that they ought to perform well in extremely inhospitable local environments such as those characterized by close proximity to erupting volcanoes or thermonuclear detonations. What is sought is what we have termed *global* reliability: relative to the class of actual and potential local environments within the system's global environment the system/process in question should have the strong tendency to successfully perform the relevant tasks.

Global reliability is commonly the dominant concern – and this is commonly so given the diversity of the local environments in which vehicles or systems of the general sort will be deployed. One might also think of this as a concern in view of uncertainty regarding the local environment in which a given instance of the design may be put into service. The reasonable response to such uncertainty is a concern for global reliability. Global reliability is also a reasonable concern when one aspires to the flexible and wide deployment of the system (or such systems).

Commonly, one engineers one's system with capacities or subsystems that can be selectively called upon to meet the challenges of certain local environments. In many contexts, one begins with some existing system and re-engineers it – adding a subsystem to meet the challenges of some environments – local or global. This kind of informed re-engineering

---

[1] Henderson and Horgan 2011: chs. 3–5. The relations between the various forms of reliability are examined there. The view of naturalized epistemology sketched in the present chapter is developed at greater length in chapter 6 of that book.

seems a particularly relevant model for naturalized epistemology – as one there begins with an existing "epistemic engine" – human beings – seeking to modify ourselves as cognitive engines.

2   Local reliability and truth-seeking

2.1   Heuristics, biases, and modulational control

Apparently, humans pretty readily hit upon various ways of cutting difficult problems down to size. One way in which they do this is by substituting some easier question for a question that is more difficult – using the answer to the easier question as a proxy answer to the more difficult question. Such is the character of many cognitive heuristics (see Kahneman and Frederick 2005). Thus, when presented with character sketches of individuals and asked how likely it is that the individuals are members of particular groups, folk commonly use perceived similarity to (perhaps stereotypical) representatives of those groups to gauge the probabilities. If the described individual seems highly similar to what would be taken to be representative of fine arts majors (for example), folks judge that the individual is correspondingly likely to be a fine arts major (Kahneman and Tversky 1973). However, this representativeness heuristic can be systematically misleading in several ways. Famously, the representativeness heuristic fails to accommodate base-rate information and can lead one to judge that the probability of a conjunction is higher than the probability of each of its conjuncts independently. Such biases are characteristic of cognitive heuristics. There are less biased processes to be had, although these alternatives are more cognitively costly.

The limited, informed, selective use of cognitive heuristics allows humans to conserve their limited cognitive resources for those matters that are practically or epistemically central – where one would not want to rely wholly on heuristics.

One's use of heuristics might be modulated in an additional epistemically fitting way: reliance on a given heuristic could exhibit some sensitivity to whether the local environment is one in which that heuristic applied to the question would be locally reliable. Gigerenzer has introduced a term to characterize local reliability with respect to a limited class of questions – a process with this limited form of local reliability is said to be *ecologically rational* with respect to such matters (Gigerenzer 2007). If one is to use heuristics, and to deploy them selectively, when ecologically rational (thus locally reliable), one's use would need to be responsive to information relevant to the heuristic's reliability in the local environment in which the agent works at the time. Such a selective application of the heuristic process draws on information gotten from wider cognitive processes. Consider the recognition heuristic in which one answers a question by attending to which items one recognizes. For example, when presented with pairs of names of American cities, and asked to pick the larger city named in each pair, German students commonly choose those names that they recognize (when they recognize just one of the pair). Gigerenzer argues that the recognition heuristic is "ecologically rational" in certain conditions. Yet, obviously, this recognition heuristic is reliable only regarding matters on which there is significant correlation between the subject of the conjecture (population size, economic prospects, and the like) and the prevalence of information about the items (the cities, the corporations) in the agent's social environment.

As it turns out, there is an empirical basis for thinking that people do tend to rely on several heuristics, including the recognition heuristic, selectively. That is, they deploy the recognition heuristic largely in cases where there is correlation between recognition and the matter in question (Gigerenzer 2008: 25–27). Such selective use requires agents to be sensitive to reasonable background expectations provided by an array of background processes. To mark this generally epistemically desirable state of affairs, we will say that such processes are *under the modulational control of* wider processes. It is worth noting that such modulational control of heuristics is commonly managed with little explicit attention – it is largely unnoticed, functioning in the background.

Here is the central point at this juncture: modulational control of heuristics by wider processes enhances the "ecological rationality" of the heuristics under such control. This selective application enhances the local reliability of these cognitive processes. Suppose that a heuristic is ecologically rational only in certain environment/issue combinations. Suppose that reliable information modulates its use so that it is increasingly deployed largely in such conditions. The process, *so deployed*, is then increasingly ecologically rational, and thus increasingly locally reliable, where it is deployed.

Modulational control is a common feature of human cognition – and the reliability of human cognitive processes is greatly enhanced by the way in which human cognitive processes are yoked together so as to refine one another. We have merely illustrated a special case: the enhanced local reliability of heuristics by virtue of modulational control drawing on background information. To further appreciate the epistemological significance of such modulational control, it is necessary to refocus on global reliability.

3   Global reliability and truth-seeking

In much of the epistemological literature having to do with objective epistemic justification, global reliability has been a central concern. It is commonly noted that, in a world such as our own, and in some especially tricky local environment such as the fabled fake-barn county, one's true perceptual belief that yonder stands a barn would not count as knowledge. But one would remain objectively epistemically justified, nonetheless. Thus, global reliability has been an epistemic good with wide epistemic cachet. Clearly, global reliability of human cognitive processes is a matter of significant concern in nature's evolutionary engineering of humans as cognitive engines, and also in human-instigated practices and social institutions aimed at enhancing the reliability of belief-formation.

Generally, then, global reliability is an epistemic good, and a weighty desideratum. One wants to be using globally reliable processes such as one's standing, trained-up, perceptual processes. Lacking information to the effect that one is in a particularly inhospitable local environment that would locally compromise the reliability of the globally reliable process, its use is fitting. However, if one's wider processes have afforded information about the special inhospitable character of some local environment that one happens to occupy for a time, one's globally reliable process should not be deployed "as-is."[2] One then does better by selectively inhibiting that process.

---

[2] As a matter of fact, in a world such as the actual world, trained-up perceptual processes are not merely globally reliable. Commonly, competent human epistemic agents have each refined their perceptual processes on many matters. This refinement has been the result of perceptual feedback – either further investigation or subsequent testimony has frustrated one's perceptually engendered verdicts and expectations, or it has vindicated them. As a result, one's perceptual processes have been shaped so that they automatically avoid many pitfalls. Typically, one is pretty reliable in distinguishing dogs from other critters, for example. One suppresses judgments when the object is inopportunely occluded, or in very low light levels. Of course, there may be a few particularly tricky local environments – perhaps some in which there are many closely related critters – but, considered as a whole, perceptual dog-identification processes are globally reliable. Much the same can be said of perceptual vehicle-identification processes, or our building-type-identification processes. This would be true, even were there a few fake-barn counties. Of course, everyday perceptual processes would not be reliable in a world inhabited by deceiving demons, or were we envatted brains, but our world is comparatively epistemically hospitable. Humans have several (general and specific) globally reliable processes available to them, and they value them – typically demanding that these processes have a form of global reliability.

Two ideas stand out in the above. First, in finding out about the world, one values processes that are reliable, and whose reliability is not highly dependent upon features very specific to the local environment – one generally epistemically approves of the use of such processes. Thus, global reliability is an important desideratum. Second, when one has good information indicating that the combination of processes relied on is locally unreliable (in the environment one occupies), one ought there to forbear from there using that process, even though it might generally be globally reliable. Thus, modulational control remains an important epistemic value. The two points are not in tension. Modulational control of processes by wider processes tends to the enhancement of reliability.

Consider again the modulational control of cognitive processes that in themselves would be merely locally reliable processes (the heuristics discussed above would be instances). When a process is modulated by information that itself has been gotten in a globally reliable way, this makes for a modulated process that is *globally reliable under such modulational control*. To the extent that some process is selectively inhibited in certain local environments in which it is locally unreliable, or selectively triggered largely in those environments in which it would be reliable, that process *under that control* becomes globally reliable. Thus, modulational control that uses globally reliable sensitivity to local reliability makes for epistemically valuable global reliability, enhancing the epistemic value of processes that would otherwise be merely locally reliable.

Such modulational control can also enhance the global reliability of processes that would just in themselves have some measure of global reliability. Were such processes inhibited in specific inhospitable local environments, or triggered selectively in certain local environments in which they would be particularly reliable, the *overall global reliability* of the process would be enhanced. Accordingly, modulational control is an understandable epistemic value in connection with globally reliable processes as it is in connection with locally reliable ones. In both cases, modulational control enhances reliability.

Some clarifications will be helpful. The use or non-use of a belief-forming process P may be regulated by a wider set of processes – with or without those wider processes having yet come by information that prompts changes in, or modulations of, P. When there is such a functional relationship between processes we will say that the process P is *under the modulational control of* the wider processes. This wider set of processes may be termed *modulating processes* with respect to P. Being under the modulational control of wider processes and being a modulating process is a matter of the dispositional relationship between wider processes and some narrower processes. This does not require that the modulating processes have actually effected changes in the modulated processes, just that they are so "positioned" in the agent's cognitive system as to stand ready to do this as they, across time, tend to generate reliable information. When such modulating processes really *do* turn up information bearing on the reliability of a process *P*, and when *P* or its use thus comes to be spawned, tailored, selectively triggered or inhibited, or in some like manner refined in ways that would (provided the information is correct) make for enhanced reliability, we will say that *P* is *modulated by* those wider processes.

So a belief-forming process *P* is *under the modulational control of* a wider set of processes *S* within the agent's cognitive system, provided that *S* would tailor *P* (would trigger *P*, inhibit *P*, or the like), were *S* to come to generate or possess certain relevant information. *P is modulated by S*, provided that *S* has generated or come to possess information that prompts it to actually make some changes in how or when *P* is put in play. We have been discussing how being under the modulational control of a wider set of processes, *S*, would make for a composite process, *P + S*, that has greater reliability than *P* alone – provided that *S* itself has a significant degree of reliability. This obtains even when *P* has yet to be modulated because *S* has yet to turn up relevant information. Cognitive processes take time. One's epistemology must allow that a proper constellation of cognitive processes can yet not have issued in all the refinements that would be epistemically desirable. A humanly wonderful epistemic engine, capable of modulating itself, is never a "finished product." Nevertheless, such a cognitive system, with humanly suitable relations of modulational control obtaining between the component (somewhat plastic) processes, is well designed from the perspective of engineering for truth-seeking.

It would be easy to conclude from these paragraphs that we hold that objective epistemic justification is a matter of using processes that are globally reliable under suitable modulational control. However, this is not quite correct. The point seems not to be highly significant to what follows, but we do not want to be understood as retracting a line of argument advanced elsewhere. Elsewhere we argue that responses to various scenarios regarding highly inhospitable global environments (those involving deceiving demons or computer scientists) indicate that what is really pivotal to objective epistemic justification is a form of reliability that we term *transglobal reliability* (see Henderson and Horgan 2011, particularly chs. 3–5.) Transglobal reliability is reliability relative to a reference class comprising not just the actual global environment, but rather a certain wider range of *possible* global environments. We call these the *experientially* possible global environments; they are possible global environments in which there are epistemic agents who have experiences of roughly the character of the common, everyday experiences of human beings. Thus, transglobal reliability is characterizable this way: reliability relative to the reference class comprising the experientially possible global environments.

This is not the place to pursue details. We should, however, note this much regarding this alternative form of reliabilism. Like global reliability, transglobal reliability of cognitive processes is commonly enhanced by modulational control making use of information provided by wider reliable processes. Recall that global reliability is enhanced by modulational control in which information from wider globally reliable processes can refine the controlled process. Such refinement obtains when the workings of the controlled process are conditioned by information about the global and various local environments in which the process is put in play. In parallel ways, transglobal reliability is enhanced by modulational control in which wider processes (themselves with some measure of transglobal reliability) provide information about the global environment in which one labors. Thus, just as a global reliabilist should demand modulational control and, in effect, a concern for local reliability, so a transglobal reliabilist demands modulational control and, in effect, an epistemic concern for both global and local reliability. Modulational control enhancing reliability is a pervasive epistemic demand when engineering for truth-seeking.

4 Modulational control: synchronic and diachronic

Two aspects of modulational control can be distinguished: synchronic and diachronic. We will begin with some preliminary definitions, as a prelude to articulating the distinction explicitly. Let the *synchronic cognitive morphology*, or the *synchronic cognitive-morphological state*, of a given cognitive agent A, at a certain time t in the agent's experiential history, be the standing structure of A's cognitive architecture (at t). (If, for instance, A's cognitive architecture is subserved by a neural network whose inter-node weighted connections can be altered through learning, then A's synchronic cognitive morphology [at t] will be subserved by the standing character of the neural network [at t] – which depends not just upon those structural features of the network that persist through learning – e.g. "hardwired" inter-node connections – but also upon those structural features that can change over time – e.g. the specific weights on the inter-node connections.) A's synchronic cognitive-morphological state (at t) is to be

distinguished from A's total *occurrent* cognitive state (at t) – the latter being
a *non-structural* feature that can be different even while A's synchronic
cognitive morphology remains the same. (If A's cognitive architecture is
subserved by a neural network, then A's total occurrent cognitive state [at
t] will be subserved by a specific *activation pattern* [at t] across the nodes
of the network. Different activation patterns are possible, subserving different occurrent cognitive states, relative to a given synchronic *cognitive-
morphological* state that is subserved by a specific setting of the weights
on the inter-node connections.) Finally, let A's *diachronic cognitive morphology* be the sequence of synchronic cognitive-morphological states that A
undergoes in the course of A's lifetime.

With these notions in hand, we turn to the distinction between synchronic and diachronic modulational control, starting with the former.
Synchronic modulational control is a feature that typically operates in
a cognitive system while its synchronic cognitive-morphological state
remains unchanged.[3] When the cognitive system, at a given cognitive-
morphological stage in its history, generates a belief by deploying a fairly
isolable *subsystem*, then synchronic modulational control will be a matter
of that subsystem's being subject to external influence – e.g. inhibitory
influence, or excitatory influence – from information elsewhere in the
cognitive system. Perceptual belief-generating subsystems, which produce beliefs about features of one's ambient environment whose contents
coincide with the contents of current percepts themselves – and/or beliefs
whose contents are epistemically well warranted by the contents of current
percepts themselves – are good examples. Pertinent background information often can, and often does, modulate the operation of such subsystems. (If one knows that there are snakes hereabout that often look very
much like sticks, then that knowledge should [somewhat] *inhibit* the cognitive process whereby one's current stick-percept would generate a belief
that the object in view is a stick. If one knows that leaves with a certain
recognizable shape are poison oak, then one's current percept as-of a plant

---

[3] We say that synchronic modulational control *typically* operates this way because subtler variations
are possible. For instance, an *occurrent* cognitive state of a cognitive agent A could, while it persists,
effect a *temporary* change in A's synchronic cognitive-morphological state – a change that only lasts
as long as the occurrent cognitive state itself. This would be a form of synchronic modulational
control, albeit one in which the synchronic occurrent state exerts its control by bringing about a
temporary change in the system's synchronic cognitive-morphological state. (Such a situation can
be subserved, for instance, by two coupled connectionist networks N_1 and N_2 that are interconnected in such a way that the current activation pattern in N_1's output-layer nodes determines the
current, short-term, settings of N_2's inter-node connection weights, thereby inducing a temporary
synchronic cognitive-morphological state of N_1.)

with leaves of that shape should *trigger* the causal process whereby that percept generates the belief that the plant in view is poison oak.)

Another important kind of synchronic morphological control, prominently discussed in current cognitive science, rests on the distinction between two postulated cognitive subsystems – so-called "System 1" and "System 2." System 1 generates judgments rapidly and automatically; its outputs are present in conscious awareness, but its operation is not. System 2 operates in a consciously reflective manner – often in a way that modulates the spontaneous belief-forming tendencies of System 1, for instance by inhibiting them, or over-ruling them, or at least subjecting their deliverances to subsequent reflective scrutiny. It will be convenient to refer to such cognitive mechanisms as "System-2 synchronic modulational control."

The notion of synchronic modulational control applies most clearly and most directly in instances of belief-formation that are aptly construed as deploying reasonably well-delineated subsystems – e.g. the perceptual-belief generating subsystem insofar as under the modulational control of wider cognitive processes, or System 1 as under the modulational control of System 2. In some cases of belief-formation – for instance, abductively generated theoretical beliefs – there may not be any natural and appropriate way to construe the belief-forming process as involving a well-delineated subsystem. Rather, any pertinent information possessed by the cognitive agent that is relevant to the given belief might better be viewed as residing *within* the operative belief-generating process; and that process itself might better be viewed as deploying the *entire* belief-generating cognitive system, rather than some well-delineated cognitive subsystem. In such cases, modulational control would be better understood in terms of diachronic modulational control.

Diachronic modulational control is a matter of improvement over time in a cognitive agent's successive synchronic cognitive-morphological states. The synchronic morphological features of the cognitive system that constitute the way the system is "engineered for truth-seeking" become progressively improved as the system evolves from one synchronic cognitive-morphological state to another – so that the system becomes progressively *better* engineered for truth-seeking. Such diachronic modulation is effected by the interaction of three factors: the cognitive system's innate capacities (as subserved by its innate morphology), its current synchronic cognitive-morphological state (prior to the transition to a new synchronic cognitive-morphological state), and its current, total, occurrent cognitive state. In general, pertinent kinds of cognitive state-transitions, when diachronic modulation takes place, will involve both a change in synchronic cognitive-morphological state and a concurrent change in total occurrent cognitive state: a total morphological-cum-occurrent cognitive state, at time t, evolves to a new total morphological-cum-occurrent cognitive state at time t + Δ. In symbols: $\langle M_t, O_t \rangle \rightarrow \langle M_t + \Delta, O_t + \Delta \rangle$.

Humans exhibit very significant plasticity in their cognitive morphology; they are susceptible to substantial and significant re-engineering for truth-seeking by way of diachronic modulation. Diachronic modulational control, via experientially triggered learning processes, can and often does effect significant improvement in a human being's belief-forming cognitive processing. This fact is of key importance for the normative aspect of naturalized epistemology. From the perspective of naturalized epistemology, an account of normatively appropriate belief-formation that is applicable to human beings should take the form of a scientifically well-informed theory of human *belief-forming competence*. Such a theory, in turn, should construe belief-forming competence as something that human beings are actually capable of achieving (or at least *approximately* achieving) – which means that synchronic-morphological states subserving belief-formation that conforms (or approximately conforms) with the competence theory are reachable via one or another regiment of progressive modulational control that is a genuine psychological possibility for humans.[4]

5 Naturalized epistemology and diachronic modulational control

Diachronic modulational control is of central importance to three aspects of naturalized epistemology, and to an aspect of virtue epistemology insofar as it comports with naturalized epistemology, that we cited in the opening paragraph of this chapter. First, naturalized epistemology stresses that what is proper and fitting by way of belief-formation is relative to the kind of creature under consideration (typically, humankind); this is honored by looking to the (scientifically informed) theory of human belief-forming competence for an account of normatively proper belief-formation – and by construing such a theory as describing forms of belief-forming

---

[4] There is a lot more that could be said about a theory of epistemic competence. For instance, such a theory might be expected to characterize not merely base-line epistemic competence but also various potential forms of epistemic expertise. The theory might also be expected to characterize certain forms of social epistemic competence, and/or social epistemic expertise, that outstrip the capabilities of any single cognitive agent. For further discussion of such matters, see Henderson and Horgan 2011: ch. 6.

optimality that human beings can actually attain (or approximately attain) if they undergo certain psychologically possible regimens of diachronic modulation. Second, naturalized epistemology stresses that much of what is fitting and proper by way of belief-formation involves a repertoire of cognitive processes many of which must be developed or learned; this is honored by seeking to form a normative account aimed not merely at what nature has "hardwired" into human cognitive architecture by way of engineering for truth-seeking, but rather at how human cognition can be progressively *re*-engineered, via diachronic modulational control, for yet-better truth-seeking. Third, naturalized epistemology emphasizes the importance of the fact that humans are social creatures; this is honored by recognizing the heavy roles that cultural environment and social inter-action are apt to play in contributing to the successful ongoing diachronic modulation of any individual human's synchronic cognitive morphology. Finally, a suitably naturalized form of *virtue* epistemology emphasizes that human epistemic virtue should be construed in terms of the kind of excel-lence in belief-formation that human beings can realistically aspire to, given their inherent cognitive endowments and their cultural surround-ings; this is honored by focusing steadfastly on the kind of belief-forming competence that can be actually achieved (or approximately achieved) via psychologically possible forms of diachronic modulation in cognitive morphology.

Suitable diachronic modulational control runs the gamut from the most automatic and unreflective ways in which past successes and fail-ures may affect the synchronic cognitive morphology that subserves one's current belief-forming tendencies, to the conscious and reflective deploy-ment in one's belief-formation of the latest results from cognitive science about common psychological pitfalls in belief-formation and about how to avoid such pitfalls. We can thus understand naturalized epistemology to include diachronic modulational control as it is found in humble every-day contexts, and as it is found in sophisticated contexts. In many cases, the modulational control might be *purely* diachronic, involving inarticu-late responsiveness to extant information. In other cases it might be *indir-ectly* diachronic: diachronic modulation puts in place a new synchronic cognitive morphology under which occurrent cognitive states tend to arise which themselves then exert synchronic morphological control over cer-tain belief-forming cognitive subsystems. Here are some quick examples.

It is hard to get more humble and everyday than the training up of basic perceptual processes involved in simple matters such as applying basic color concepts, and recognizing common objects, animals, and structures

in one's environment. Children's perceptual processes undergo significant ongoing refinement. As children learn and apply their concepts, they
experience feedback, successes and failures, and something is learned in
the bargain. However, it seems clear that much of this learning is inarticulate. Doubtless, some of the changes in perceptual tendencies reflect
innate courses of maturation in humans. But it is also clear that what is
learned may go deeper than some suppose. The Müller-Lyer illusion has
commonly been thought to be the product of innate perceptual processes.
But results reported in Segall *et al.* (1966) suggest that there is significant
cultural variation in susceptibility to this illusion. Further:

> [T]hese findings suggest that visual exposure during ontogeny to factors
> such as the "carpentered corners" of modern environments may favor cer-
> tain optical calibrations and visual habits that create and perpetuate this
> illusion. That is, the visual system ontogenetically adapts to the presence of
> recurrent features in the local visual environment. (Henrich *et al.* 2010: 64;
> see also McCauley and Henrich 2006)

Put simply, children seem to inarticulately and automatically undergo a
form of diachronic modulational control in response to episodes in which
they receive information about their environment – information about
episodic successes and failures. (For a parallel example involving learning to
individuate objects, see Goldstone 2003; Mareschal and Johnson 2002.)

Of course, humble everyday cases of modulational control need not be
automatic and inarticulate. One can stand warned, and on one's guard,
against environments in which there are mimics or counterfeits that make
for difficulties for ready perceptual identification. One might, for example, be told that it is easy to mistake the scarlet king snake for the eastern
coral snake, and the reverse. One might then respond by taking note of
the distinguishing marks of the two, and modifying the care with which
one proceeds. Or perhaps one's parents tell of the deceptive appearance
as-of water (always in the distance) on hot roads. In view of this, one
may inhibit one's previous perceptual processes. Not all humble everyday
cases will involve refinements in perceptual processes. Some will involve
changes in reasoning, attention to evidence, and the like. Perhaps as a
child (or adult), when discussing a conflict with another person, your parents or teachers said to you, "What do you think that it felt like to them?"
Plausibly, this amounted to encouragement to take a more sustained, consciously reflective, look at the interaction from the perspective of the other.
(We are not concerned with the moral benefits here; the point has to do
with the epistemic benefits.) Or perhaps, when diagnosing problems with

a computer or other system, one was taught to vary one thing at a time, and to start with the most common ways in which such systems fail. This affects one's inquiry so as to make it less ambiguous in its results, and it makes it more responsive to base rates.

The examples in the previous paragraph all fall under the rubric *synchronic modulational control that is activated by diachronically modulated synchronic-cognitive morphology*. More specifically, they all can be naturally construed as cases of System-2 synchronic modulational control: System 2 is poised to deploy pertinent information in a way that can modulate the erstwhile effects on belief-formation of System 1. Hold off from believing there is water up ahead along the hot road, even though there appears to be water there; think about how your action would have felt to the other when reconstructing the interaction; first try turning off the computer and re-booting it, rather than hypothesizing some system failure of a more serious kind, etc.

Such explicit or articulate forms of everyday humble modulational control are continuous with articulate forms found in more sophisticated contexts. Think of what transpires in a methods class, where one discusses how to structure an experiment or investigation so as to avoid certain errors and to provide less ambiguous results. This can be about as articulate and sophisticated as *synchronic* modulational control ever gets. Think of graduate seminars in which one discusses papers or works – articulating weaknesses in data, structure, or reasoning. Notably, the upshot is not merely that one decides that one can or cannot rely on that study for specific points; the upshot is that one should structure one's own thinking and investigation so as to do likewise, in certain ways, and do differently in other ways. (Philip Kitcher [1993] provides one useful discussion of evolving training in scientific communities.)

What one learns in such sophisticated contexts doubtlessly is not fully articulate or articulable. Think of a philosophy seminar. From one's own and others' reactions to various pieces under discussion one may sense limitations or possibilities that one is not able to articulate. Not everything in one's positive models will be articulate or articulable to oneself. Not everything relevant to one's negative models will be articulable. So, in a way that is reminiscent of the inarticulate training up of perceptual processes, there may be an element of the training up of sophisticated reasoning processes that is responsive to successes and failures, but which is not significantly articulable. This element could well be purely morphological. That is, it might involve changes in one's cognitive morphology that turn on learned information without that information needing to be occurrently represented in the course of cognitive processing that results from such learning. In such cases, the learned information may be automatically accommodated in appropriate inferential moves, and need not be involved in the form of a morphologically generated conscious representation that then figures in System-2 synchronic modulational control. (In principle, however, it sometimes could instead involve synchronic modulation by an *unconscious* System 2 that deploys occurrent, yet unconscious, explicit representations of the pertinent background information.)

Such, as we understand it, is the range of modulational control that is aptly seen as being of key importance in naturalized epistemology. What is central here is the informed refinement of one's cognitive processes, based on extant and developing information that is attained using one's cognitive processes of related kinds. In the bargain, as a human cognitive agent one develops belief-forming capacities with enhanced reliability. Notably, in several of our examples, one is helped along by others. In some perceptual training, one relies on others for feedback regarding successes and failures. In the ongoing refinement of one's belief-forming capacities, one commonly benefits from being instructed about common ways of going wrong – and ways of avoiding them. Such instruction is found in humble everyday cases and in sophisticated cases. The information about the reliability or unreliability of ways of reasoning, or ways of inquiring, is thus commonly drawn from a social store or social stock of information. (Happily, one does not need to build for oneself a track record of all forms of cognitive frustration – and one should not.) The information may be of a simple, folksy, sort – for example, regarding mirages or the temptation for egocentric biases when reconstructing social interactions. It may be of a more cutting-edge sort – think of the issues surrounding the benefits and pitfalls associated with cognitive heuristics.[5] What is invariant here, what is invariantly epistemically fitting, is the modulation of cognitive processes beholden to what is gotten by wider cognitive processes – and to a social store of such results. What is invariant is the relevance of results regarding human cognitive capacities and associated environmental challenges. What is variable is the extant results.

As noted at the onset, naturalized epistemology thus meshes with virtue epistemology. We seek an epistemology fitting to humans as a class of cognitive systems, one that stresses the role of diachronic modulational control in fostering human epistemic excellence. This excellence is

---

[5] For one discussion of some of these debates (in which works by Tversky and Kahneman, and by Gigerenzer, feature prominently) see Samuels *et al.* 2002.

cultured – since the articulable information on which modulational control draws is largely a socially extant pool, and since some aspects of diachronic modulational control are best inculcated by socially interactive apprenticeship between expert and student. Naturalized epistemology is committed to the first three points earlier associated with virtue epistemology, and to the correlative concept of human epistemic excellence. In what remains, we will focus on a fourth point, a common substantive commitment of virtue epistemologies that is receiving significant vindication within extant developing pools of information about the character of human cognitive capacities.

6   Beyond rules and programs: one virtue-theoretic lesson from contemporary naturalized epistemology

In the second paragraph of this chapter we mentioned a commonly incorporated theme in virtue epistemology: the claim that humanly achievable epistemic excellence in belief-formation is too subtle and sophisticated to conform to rules or algorithms. In this section we will offer a proposed explication of this claim; briefly summarize some powerful looking considerations in favor of the claim (considerations that stem largely from within cognitive science); and then briefly describe a framework for cognitive science – largely inspired by connectionist modeling in cognitive science – that fits well with the virtue theorist's claim that epistemically excellent belief-formation outstrips rules.

What exactly does this claim mean? Well, it could mean various things, depending on how one construes the kinds of rules in question. So the first item of business is to offer a proposed explication of the claim – an explication that we think accords well with what virtue theorists intend (or anyway, *should* intend) by the claim, and that we think is also empirically and theoretically very plausible.

6.1   Repudiating exceptionless general rules

To fix ideas, it will be useful to describe one potential way in which, in principle at least, a complete specification could be given of all and only those cases of human belief-formation that would accord with human epistemic competence. Let a *total cognitive state* (a TCS) be a state of a cognitive agent A, at a time t, that incorporates not only all mental states occurrently tokened by A at t, but also all background information that A possesses at t. A TCS can be thought of as a pair $<Bi, Sj>$, where Bi is the full body of background information possessed by an agent at a time, and Sj is the full set of mental states occurrently tokened by A at t. Let the *epistemic competence profile* (the ECP) for a given kind of agent (e.g. the kind human) be an enormous list of completely specific cognitive transitions from one potential TCS to another:

<Bi, Sj> → <Bi+, Sj+>
<Bh, Sk> → <Bh+, Sk+>,

where t+ is a moment in time after t, and where this list embodies all the cognitive transitions that would accord with an ideally complete and correct cognitive-scientific account of cognitive competence for agents of the kind in question. The ECP abstracts away from potential "performance errors" due to tiredness, emotional distress, inattention, and the like. (And when we write as if there is a *single* ECP, we are deliberating bracketing, for simplicity, the question of whether there are multiple ECPs characterizing different versions of human epistemic competence. Generic epistemic competence surely can admit of individual differences; and there also can be various forms of epistemic expertise that transcend the generic base line for mere epistemic competence.)

Consider now the following question. Is there some compact way to *fully systematize* the human ECP? One way one might aspire to answer this question, and answer it affirmatively, is to propose that there is some set of epistemic rules – rules that (i) are universally quantified in form, and (ii) from which every entry in the ECP follows logically (by universal instantiation, essentially). These rules would be highly *general*: they would be universal quantifications with vastly many (perhaps even infinitely many) specific instantiations. And they would be *exceptionless*, rather than containing any "hedge factors" such as *ceteris paribus* clauses, for hedge factors would stand in the way of smooth logical derivation, from the rules, of all the specific entries in the ECP.

Such rules are the kind that we ourselves think virtue theorists would do well to claim do not exist. Accordingly, our proposed explication of the virtue theorists' repudiation of epistemic rules is this (with 'RR' going proxy for *Rule Repudiation*):

> (RR)   Epistemically competent human belief-formation does not conform to exceptionless general rules that would fully systematize the human ECP.

Throughout the history of philosophy, it seems fair to say, philosophers theorizing about various kinds of normativity (e.g. moral normativity and epistemic normativity) have hankered after rules or principles of exactly this sort – rules or principles that would fully systematize whatever form normativity the given philosopher seeks to illuminate. (Think of the frequent allusion, early and late, to Euclidean geometry as a guiding model.) Often it also has been supposed in addition that the sought-for rules would be *normatively authoritative*; i.e. they would be more normatively fundamental than their various specific instantiations, and hence would provide a normative-justificatory basis for specific moral-normative or epistemic-normative claims derivable by subsumption from them plus supplemental factual claims. (Roughly, one derives a specific normative claim Ought(Q), by subsumption from an exceptionless general rule plus a factual claim P, by deriving "If P then Ought(Q)" from the rule by universal instantiation, and then using modus ponens.)[6]

Suppose that one construes naturalized epistemology in the way we have recommended in the preceding sections of this chapter – so that normatively appropriate human belief-formation is to be construed as the kind of belief-formation that would be described by an accurately descriptive cognitive-scientific account of human belief-forming competence. How, then, does the virtue theorists' claim (RR) fare within this version of naturalized epistemology? That depends, of course, on what the envisioned account of epistemic competence would look like. Within recent cognitive science, one highly influential foundational framework – sometimes called the computational theory of mind (for short, the CTM) – embraces the idea that human cognitive-state transitions are all *computational*. This means that such state transitions all conform to what may be called formal *programmable representation-level rules* (for short, formal PRL rules) – roughly, rules that (i) are general, (ii) are exceptionless, (iii) operate on the formal-syntactic structure of mental representations, (iv) are tractably implementable by physical devices with physical resources roughly on the scale of those in the human brain, and (v) advert only to those formal-syntactic features of the representations that directly figure in the formal-structural encoding of the contents of those representations.[7] This

---

[6] It bears emphasizing that one could embrace (RR) without repudiating other kinds of rules, such as rules that are highly general but contain *ceteris paribus* clauses (e.g. "Lying is morally wrong, *ceteris paribus*," or exceptionless rules that are relatively limited in scope (even if universal quantificational in form) and thus fall quite short of fully systematizing a given form of normativity (e.g. "Torture is always morally wrong"). Indeed, one could not only embrace rules of one or both of these latter types, but one could also regard some such rules as normatively authoritative. Virtue theorists too could allow for such rules, while still embracing (RR) – as, indeed, we ourselves think they should.

[7] The point of clause (v) is to exclude as irrelevant any formal-syntactic structure that may belong to symbol-structures in the various sub-representational languages that figure in an "implementational

approach presupposes that human cognitive-state transitions all conform to what may be called *substantive* PRL rules – rules that (i) are general, (ii) are exceptionless, (iii) advert to intentional psychological state (types) as such (rather than to the formal-syntactic structure of mental representations), (iv) fully systematize the human ECP, and (v) are isomorphic to the posited *formal* PRL rules. (In virtue of this isomorphism, "syntax mirrors semantics": the computational *syntactic* engine effects representational-state transitions that are systematically appropriate to the contents of those representations.)

Substantive PRL rules that fully systematize human epistemic competence would qualify as rules of the kind that are repudiated by the virtue-theoretic claim (RR). So if indeed human cognition does not conform to such rules, then the CTM is a mistaken foundational framework for human cognition. (The CTM presupposes both that there are substantive PRL rules that fully systematize the ECP, and that these substantive PRL rules are isomorphic to certain *formal* PRL rules. If the posited substantive PRL rules don't exist themselves, then obviously there cannot exist formal PRL rules that are isomorphic to those non-existent substantive PRL rules.) Thus if human belief-formation conforms to the CTM, then the virtue theorists' claim (RR) cannot be embraced and accommodated by the form of naturalized epistemology we advocated in preceding sections.

But the CTM faces daunting, in-principle-looking, problems that strongly suggest that belief-forming cognition does not conform to PRL rules. We will turn to those in the next subsection.

Before doing so, however, let us highlight two negative claims that are entailed by claim (RR), and hence will be embraced by any virtue theorist who embraces claim (RR) itself. (The main point we want to stress is that (RR) is logically *stronger* than either of these entailed claims – which means that it would be a mistake to construe either of them as the *principal* negative claim of the virtue theorist.) We will formulate the claims using the expression 'actual competent human belief-formation', by which we mean actual human belief-formation that is either fully competent or at least approximates full human epistemic competence reasonably well. The two claims, both consequences of (RR), are these:

---

hierarchy" whereby the high-level symbol-structures that directly encode representational content are successively implemented by successively lower-level symbol-structures in the successively lower-level programming languages. (In computers, such implementational hierarchies ultimately bottom out with "machine language" symbol-structures that get directly implemented in physical states of the computer.)

First consequence: Actual competent human belief-formation often fails to be a process of *conscious* subsumption of a concrete evidential situation under a PRL rule.

Second consequence: Actual competent human belief-formation often fails to be a subsumption process (either conscious or unconscious) deploying an explicit representation (either conscious or unconscious) of a PRL rule.

The first consequence seems obvious on independent introspective grounds: one can tell just by introspection that often – indeed, virtually always – one's belief-formation occurs without the *conscious* deployment of PRL rules. The virtue theorist should be happy to embrace this consequence, but also should embrace the stronger claim (RR) as well. After all, the first consequence is consistent with this contention: although competent human belief-formation is always a process of subsumption under a PRL rule, normally this happens *unconsciously*.

The second consequence transcends the capacity of introspection – and is therefore more interesting. It too is a claim that the virtue theorist should be happy to embrace. But it too is weaker than the claim (RR) – a fact that is important to appreciate. For this second consequence is consistent with the following contention: although competent human belief fixation is always a process (often unconscious) of subsumption under a PRL rule, often this process operates by *automatically* generating a belief that is warranted by a given PRL rule in specific evidential circumstances – rather than by first producing an *explicit representation* (either conscious or unconscious) of the rule. As long as such automatic PRL-rule conformity is a feature of the cognitive system's "engineering design for truth-seeking," it doesn't matter whether the belief-forming process deploys an explicit representation of the rule. The CTM could perfectly well be true of human belief-formation even if PRL-rule conforming belief-formation normally operates in this purely automatic way – just as special-purpose hand-held calculators sometimes automatically execute PRL rules for performing mathematical calculations, rather than deploying explicit representations of the rules they execute.

Principle (RR) precludes not only PRL-rule subsumption via explicit representation of a PRL rule, but also the kind of automatic PRL-rule subsumption just described. It is because (RR) precludes this possibility too – and only because it does so – that (RR) is indeed incompatible with the CTM.

6.2   Morals of the frame problem

The challenge to the CTM we have in mind arises from a nest of interconnected issues concerning how to tractably manage all available relevant information via tractable computation, when undertaking certain cognitive tasks like belief fixation (i.e. the generation of new beliefs and the ongoing maintenance of retention-worthy beliefs) and action planning. The depth and difficulty of such issues first came to light in cognitive science under the rubric 'the frame problem' – roughly, the problem of how to delimit (i.e. "put a frame around") the range of available information that might need to be consulted or updated in the course of accomplishing a given cognitive task. That rubric has come to be used in a fairly generic way (a practice we will follow here); the family of issues we will here call the frame problem is also sometimes called the *relevance* problem.

A canonical early formulation of this challenge to the CTM was given by Jerry Fodor, in the final chapter of Fodor 1983. There it is argued that the CTM confronts what look to be in-principle problems, and hence that the prospects for understanding human cognitive processes like belief fixation within the framework of the CTM are very bleak indeed. These problems continue to plague the computational approach to the mind, and suggest the need for a radically different approach.

The main claim of Fodor 1983 is that the human cognitive system possesses a number of important subsystems that are *modular*: domain-specific, mandatory, limited in their access to other parts of the larger cognitive system, fast, and informationally encapsulated. Where classicism has gotten somewhere, Fodor says, is in understanding such modular subsystems, which by their nature delimit the class of relevant information.

Work within the CTM framework has made very little progress in understanding *central* processes, however. Belief fixation – the generation of new beliefs on the basis of current input together with other beliefs – is a paradigmatic example. Updating of the overall belief system in light of currently available new information is a closely related example. Fodor argues convincingly that these processes are non-modular: they need to have access to a wide range of cognitive subsystems, and to information on an indefinitely wide range of topics. And the very considerations that point to non-modularity, he maintains, also constitute grounds for extreme pessimism about the prospects of explaining central processes within the CTM framework.

Fodor argues that central processes possess two crucial features (features that are clearly exhibited in scientific confirmation which amounts to a special case of belief fixation). Central processes of belief fixation are, in Fodor's terminology, *isotropic* and *Quinean*. To say that they are isotropic is to say that any bit of actual or potential information from any portion of one's belief system might, in some circumstances, be evidentially relevant to any other (1983: 105). To say that these processes are Quinean is to say that belief fixation is holistic in that it turns on "such considerations as 'simplicity, plausibility, and conservatism'," which are determined by the global *structure* of the whole of the current belief system and of potential successor systems (1983: 108). Fodor argues that these features pose deep problems for CTM. "The problem in both cases is to get the structure of the entire belief system to bear on individual occasions of belief fixation. We have, to put it bluntly, no computational formalisms that show us how to do this, and we have no idea how such formalisms might be developed" (Fodor 1983: 128–29). Fodor, in the passages bemoaning the lack of an available computational formalism, is telling us that human central processing evidently does not operate via any kinds of computation we currently know about or can even contemplate. And he has rightly and emphatically reiterated this same message more recently – for instance, in Fodor 2000. There, he argues, concerning recent enthusiasm in cognitive science for the idea that central processes like belief fixation are "massively modular" – i.e. are the product of many interacting, special-purpose, informationally encapsulated, modules – that massive modularity is massively implausible, precisely because it has no realistic hope of coping with the isotropic and Quinean features of central processing. Something else is needed in place of the CTM.

The case for the conclusion that cognitive processes like human belief-formation largely fail to conform to the CTM – drawing largely upon the holistic, Quinean-isotropic, features of belief fixation that generate the frame problem – is further elaborated by Horgan and Tienson (1996). Horgan and Tienson also describe an alternative, non-computational, foundational framework for cognitive science – a framework that promises to accommodate the virtue theorists' claim (RR). We have discussed these ideas and their epistemological significance in Henderson and Horgan 2011. The reader may want to consult these works for a more sustained presentation of the argument against CTM, and for articulation and defense of the alternative framework. We now offer a *very* brief sketch of the framework.

The *dynamical cognition* framework (or DC framework), as Horgan and Tienson call it, is inspired partially by connectionism and partially by the persistence of the frame problem within classical computational cognitive science. The DC framework treats cognition in terms of the mathematics of dynamical systems: total occurrent cognitive states are mathematically/structurally realized as points in a high-dimensional dynamical system, and these mathematical points are physically realized by total-activation states of a neural network with specific connection weights. The framework repudiates the CTM's assumption that cognitive-state transitions conform to a tractably computable transition function over cognitive states. The framework also makes conceptual space for the possibility of systematically content-sensitive cognitive-state transitions that (i) automatically accommodate lots of relevant information without explicitly representing it during cognitive processing, and (ii) are too subtle to conform to any tractably computable cognitive transition function.

The DC framework suggests a way around the frame problem, involving two key ideas. First, holistic, Quinean/isotropic background information is implicitly embodied in the standing physical structure of a neural network ("in the weights" of the inter-node connections, as connectionists like to say). This implicit holistic information does not need to be found, fetched, explicitly represented, or computationally manipulated during belief-updating; rather, it gets accommodated automatically. Second, even if the transitions from one total *neural-network* state to another are tractably computable (as they are in standard connectionist models, which allow these models to be simulated on digital computers), nevertheless the inter-level realization relation from total *cognitive* states (TCSs) to total *neural-network* states may well be so subtle and complex that the feature of tractable computability fails to "transfer upward" from total-neural-network-state transitions to TCS transitions.[8]

---

[8] A crucial point here is that rules governing total-network-state transitions do not advert to the structural features of the dynamical system that *subserve the contents* of the TCSs; hence, total-network-state-update-rules are *subrepresentational*, rather than being PRL rules. We also recognize that, to some extent, the CTM can allow background information to get automatically accommodated during processing without becoming explicitly accommodated. This can be accomplished by means of *special-purpose* rules that are custom designed to effect transitions over TCSs in such a way as to be appropriate relative to the unrepresented background information. (As it is sometimes put, that information is *proceduralized* in the computational system, rather than explicitly represented; the rules specify procedures for converting one TCS to another that automatically accommodate the unrepresented background information.) But the frame problem arises all over again if one tries to handle the holistic, Quinean-isotropic, aspects of belief fixation via proceduralized rules: one quickly encounters an exponential explosion of such rules. Thus in addressing the frame problem it is not enough to posit massive implicit content. Rather, one also needs to envision TCS transitions that do not constitute *computations* – i.e. do not conform to PRL rules, either substantive or formal.

At the present stage of intellectual history, it is probably fair to say that the DC framework for cognitive science constitutes a "just-so" story about how the human mind solves the frame problem. By this we mean that the story is fairly speculative, with few details filled in and without a strong base of empirical support. (Extant connectionist models do not provide strong empirical support, in our view, because arguably they do not yet come anywhere close to scaling up from simple toy problems to genuine human-like cognition.) But even a "just-so" story is something to be valued and appreciated, given the current state of cognitive science, for at least it provides the broad outlines of one possible answer to the extremely daunting question, "How could human cognition possibly exhibit the holistic, Quinean-isotropic, features that appear to be required for doing epistemically appropriate belief fixation?"

Furthermore, although the DC framework is perhaps little more right now than a just-so story, there already does appear to be a fairly strong abductive case for two key ideas embraced by the DC framework, namely: (1) that much human belief fixation relies essentially upon the automatic accommodation of massive amounts of holistic, Quinean-isotropic, background information in the form of morphological content; and (2) that much human belief fixation is too subtle, in its accommodation of both explicit, occurrent information and implicit, morphological information, to conform to exceptionless general rules. Thus currently there is a fairly strong abductive case in favor of the virtue epistemologists' claim (RR) – their repudiation of exceptionless general rules for belief-formation.

7   Conclusion

The fitting culturing of the human creature – in particular, the inculcation of the virtuous capacity that constitutes epistemic belief-forming competence – should draw upon pertinent information from cognitive science about human cognitive endowments and limitations, and also upon socially mediated forms of melioration. Moreover, humanly achievable epistemic belief-forming competence quite probably is too subtle and too informationally holistic to obey exceptionless general rules or algorithms. In these important respects, virtue epistemology and naturalized epistemology are smoothly complementary.

CHAPTER 12

Expressivism and convention-relativism about epistemic discourse

Allan Hazlett

Consider the claim that open-mindedness is an epistemic virtue, the claim that true belief is epistemically valuable, and the claim that one epistemically ought to cleave to one's evidence. These are examples of what I'll call "epistemic discourse." Here I'll propose and defend a view called "convention-relativism about epistemic discourse." In particular, I'll argue that convention-relativism is superior to its main rival, expressivism about epistemic discourse. Expressivism and convention-relativism both jibe with anti-realism about epistemic normativity, which is motivated by appeal to philosophical naturalism (section 1). Convention-relativism says that epistemic discourse describes how things stands relative to a conventional set of "epistemic" values; such discourse is akin to criticism relative to the conventional rules of a club (section 2). I defend convention-relativism by appeal to a "reverse open question argument," which says, pace expressivism, that epistemic discourse leaves normative questions open (section 3).

My three examples of epistemic discourse (above) represent three species of *epistemic*: (i) attributions of the property of being an epistemic virtue, or "epistemic virtue attributions," for short; (ii) attributions of the property of having epistemic value, or "epistemic value attributions," for short; and (iii) attributions of epistemic obligation.[1] Epistemic virtue attributions and epistemic value attributions are species of *epistemic evaluation*; epistemic obligation attributions can be understood as non-evaluative.

Thanks to Matthew Chrisman and Guy Fletcher for comments on an earlier draft of this chapter.

[1] I have left attributions of knowledge off the list, as they raise some complex issues that are orthogonal to our main topic. First, some knowledge attributions do not even appear to be normative. Second, the thesis of "pragmatic encroachment" threatens the idea that knowledge attributions are a species of *epistemic* discourse. I have also left attributions of epistemic reasons off the list. It seems to me that either (i) epistemic reasons entail epistemic obligations, in which case what I say about epistemic obligation attributions can be said about epistemic reasons attributions, or (ii) epistemic reasons derive from epistemic values, in which case what I say about epistemic value attributions can be said about epistemic reasons attributions.

Epistemic discourse seems normative. I'll appeal to a more precise criterion of the normativity of discourse, below (section 3.1), but the following will suffice to motivate the idea that epistemic discourse seems normative. To say that open-mindedness is an epistemic virtue seems to be to say that open-mindedness really is a virtue, i.e. that it is good or desirable or admirable to be open-minded; to say that true belief is epistemically valuable seems to be to say that true belief really is valuable, i.e. that true belief is good or worthy of pursuit or approbation; to say that one epistemically ought to cleave to one's evidence seems to be to say that one really ought to cleave to one's evidence, i.e. that one would (or at least could) deserve blame or censure or sanction for not so cleaving. As Christine Korsgaard (1996) puts it, "[c]oncepts like knowledge, beauty, and meaning, as well as virtue and justice, all have a normative dimension, for they tell us what to think, what to like, what to say, what to do, and what to be" (9). Epistemic discourse seems normative in (at least something like) the same way.

1   Naturalism and anti-realism about epistemic discourse

Employing epistemic discourse also seems to commit one to the existence of epistemic virtue, epistemic value, and epistemic obligations. Do these things really exist? This is the question of realism and anti-realism about *epistemic normativity*. There are a number of ways to articulate the realism/anti-realism distinction (alternatively: a number of realism/anti-realism distinctions); here we shall understand realism about *x* as a thesis about the explanatory connection between *x* and the appropriateness of a certain species of discourse. We shall understand realism about epistemic normativity as follows:

> *Realism about epistemic normativity:* The appropriateness of epistemic discourse is explained by the existence of epistemic virtue, epistemic value, and epistemic obligations.

The negation of realism about epistemic normativity is *anti-realism about epistemic normativity*.

Realism and anti-realism are metaphysical views, about the explanatory relationship (if there is one) between epistemic value (for example) and the appropriateness of epistemic value attributions. If you think that there is no such thing as epistemic value, then you are an anti-realist of the most straightforward kind. But if you think that epistemic value exists *because* it is appropriate for us to engage in the attribution of epistemic value, perhaps because you think that *what it is* for something to be valuable is for people to consistently value it (e.g. Williams 2002: 91–92), then you are also an anti-realist, although of a less straightforward kind. Distinct from this metaphysical question are related questions about the semantics and pragmatics of epistemic discourse. The realist is in a position to give a descriptivist account of the semantics of epistemic discourse, which jibes with her view about the explanatory relationship between (again, for example) epistemic value and the appropriateness of epistemic value attributions. The appropriateness of uttering "True belief is epistemically valuable," when it is appropriate, will be explained, in part, by the fact that the sentence is true, and the truth of the sentence will be explained by the epistemic value of true belief. The anti-realist will need to offer an alternative account.

Although our focus will be on epistemic *discourse*, a semantics for epistemic discourse will naturally apply, *mutatis mutandis*, to its analog in *thought*. If we can explain (again, for example) what sentences of the form <*x* is epistemically valuable> mean, i.e. if we can give an account of the content of such sentences, then we should be in a position to explain the content of people's thoughts when they think that something is epistemically valuable.

The basic argument for anti-realism about epistemic discourse (cf. Hazlett 2013: part II) appeals to philosophical naturalism, and is based on three premises:

(1) Given philosophical naturalism, we have pro tanto reason to avoid positing categorical normativity (cf. Kelly 2003: 614–18; see also Papineau 1999: 17–18, Drier 2001: 29–30; Owens 2003: 283–84; Steglich-Petersen 2006: 500).

(2) Teleological accounts of epistemic normativity, on which epistemic normativity is a species of (naturalistically kosher) instrumental normativity, fail (Kelly 2003; Owens 2003; Grimm 2008, 2009).

(3) Epistemic normativity is either categorical or instrumental.

Given these three premises, and some natural assumptions (including that the naturalist's pro tanto reason to avoid positing categorical normativity isn't trumped in this case), anti-realism can be defended. Premise (1) speaks against realist accounts of epistemic normativity that explain the existence of epistemic virtue, value, or obligations by appeal to the normativity of belief (Wedgwood 2002; Boghossian 2003b, 2005; Shah 2003; Shah and Velleman 2005; Lynch 2009a, 2009b). (The normativity in question is called "categorical" because it applies regardless of the desires or intentions of the believer.) Premise (2) rules out realist versions of the familiar epistemological idea that the existence of epistemic virtue, values, or obligations can be understood by appeal to a "truth goal" (Foley 1987, 1993; Goldman 1999; Sosa 2003, 2007, 2009a; Steglich-Petersen 2006, 2009, 2011; Greco 2010). Premise (3) says that these are the only realist games in town. The anti-realist concludes that realism is false. There is obviously much to be said about this argument, but here I will assume anti-realism about epistemic normativity, since this is common ground between me (section 2.2) and my expressivist interlocutors (section 2.1)

2   Articulating convention-relativism

In recent years, anti-realists about epistemic normativity have defended expressivist accounts of epistemic discourse (Gibbard 1990, 2003: 227–29; Chrisman 2007; Field 2009; Kappel 2010), on which epistemic discourse is understood as expressive of non-cognitive attitudes of endorsement, acceptance, approval, or valuation. Their critics have been realists about epistemic normativity (Cuneo 2007; Lynch 2009a, 2009b; Shah 2010). I will articulate and defend an alternative to both expressivism about epistemic discourse and realism about epistemic normativity. My proposed view is consistent with anti-realism about epistemic normativity, but maintains that epistemic discourse is not (always) expressive of non-cognitive attitudes (cf. Fumerton 2001; Sosa 2007). In this section I'll describe expressivism about epistemic discourse (section 2.1) and then articulate my proposed alternative, "convention-relativism about epistemic discourse" (section 2.2).

2.1   Expressivism about epistemic discourse

The leading idea behind *expressivism about epistemic discourse* is that epistemic discourse is essentially (though not necessarily exclusively) expressive of certain non-cognitive attitudes of endorsement, acceptance, approval, or valuation.[2] Allan Gibbard (1990) defends and elaborates the view that "to call something rational is not ... to attribute a property to it," but rather "to express a state of mind" (9). In particular, "to think something rational is to accept norms that permit it" (46). The relevant non-cognitive attitude here is accepting a norm. Gibbard's account applies equally to actions, feelings, and beliefs, so to think a belief is

---

[2] We should avoid, if we can, any attempt to define the "cognitive" and the "non-cognitive." Empirical beliefs are paradigm cognitive attitudes; desires are paradigm non-cognitive attitudes.

rational is (among other things) to accept norms that permit it, and to say that a belief is rational is (among other things) to express such acceptance. Gibbard (2003: 227–29) has also argued that to think that S knows that p is to plan to rely on S's judgment about whether p, and thus to say that S knows that p is to express such planning. The relevant non-cognitive attitude in this case is planning. "Coherence and agreement on the plain facts doesn't guarantee agreement on whether" someone knows, for whether we attribute knowledge to someone will depend on our plans; the concept of knowledge is thus "plan-laden" (228). Along similar lines, Matthew Chrisman (2007) articulates a "norm-expressivist" account of knowledge attributions, on which the attribution of knowledge to S expresses a complex state of mind consisting of both (i) the belief that S is entitled by norms *e* to her true belief that p *and* (ii) the acceptance of those norms (241).

This is compatible with a plurality of accounts of the semantics of epistemic discourse. It is compatible with the view that the sentences involved in epistemic discourse are not "truth apt." But contemporary expressivists reject this view, in favor of the view that the relevant utterances are "truth apt" (Chrisman 2007: 237; Field 2009: 267). They propose an account on which utterances of such sentences express both beliefs (and so are often true) and non-cognitive attitudes; for example, see Chrisman's (i) and (ii), above.[3] Alternatively, as Hartry Field (2009: 262–64, 272–78) argues, an expressivist account of epistemic discourse could be articulated by appeal to John MacFarlane's (2005a, 2005b) notion of "assessment sensitivity," with differences in assessor's accepted epistemic norms making for differences in relative truth, such that the proposition that open-mindedness is an epistemic virtue might be true as assessed relative to my preferred epistemic norms, but not true as assessed relative to your preferred epistemic norms. Finally, the "truth aptness" of epistemic evaluation could be secured by embracing a "quasi-realist" approach to truth (Gibbard 2003: 18–20, 180–84).

There are also various ways for the expressivist to explain the existence of disagreement in epistemic discourse. On Chrisman's (2007) view, for example, to attribute knowledge to S is to express your belief in the proposition that S is entitled by norms *e* to her true belief that p, so disagreement about whether someone knows something might just come down to

---

[3] Note that the belief and non-cognitive attitude expressed need not be understood as distinct mental states; they could be understood as aspects of one complex mental state (cf. Chrisman 2007).

old-fashioned cognitive disagreement about the truth of that proposition. However, this isn't the end of the story:

> [T]he norm-expressivist can also recognize that different utterances can express the acceptance of opposing or concurring norms. Thus ... two [normative] claims can express genuine opposition or agreement even if they do not express logically contradictory or identical propositions. (239)

We may agree that norms *e* entitle someone to believe that p, but since I accept, and you do not accept, those norms, we disagree about whether she knows that p. Alternatively, if we follow Field (2009) in articulating expressivism in terms of assessment sensitivity, then you and I might disagree about the proposition that S knows that p – since this proposition is true, relative to the norms that I accept, but not true, relative the norms that you accept.

Expressivism jibes with (although it does not entail) anti-realism about epistemic normativity (section 1). Gibbard (1990) writes that his "analysis is not directly of what it is for something to *be* rational, but of what it is for someone to *judge* that something is rational" (8, cf. 46) and that on his view "apparent normative facts" are "no real facts at all; instead there [are] facts of what we are doing when we make normative judgments" (23).[4] This is why the expressivist can be said to "change the question" from that of the nature of goodness and of the definition of 'good', to the question of "what *states of mind* ethical statements express" (Gibbard 2003: 6). This is why Gibbard can "weasel" (2003: 182) about the existence of normative properties, facts, and truths: because his account of normative thought and talk is free of commitment to the existence of normative properties, facts, and truths. As Chrisman (in press) explains, expressivism about epistemic discourse is a "metaepistemological" view about "what it means to claim that a belief is justified, rational, known, etc.," rather than a "normative epistemological" view about what it is for a belief to be justified, rational, known, etc. This is all good news, from the perspective of anti-realism.

How should the expressivist explain the appropriateness of epistemic discourse, in a way that is consistent with philosophical naturalism (cf. section 1)? Gibbard (1990) suggests an evolutionary account: "Humanity evolved in groups" (24), he writes; "we are, in effect, designed for social life," and "[o]ur normative capacities are part of the design" (26). The crucial idea here is that of "the need for complex coordination" (26)

---

4 Although compare his "quasi-realism" (Gibbard 2003: 18–20, 180–84).

among human beings. But natural history might only take us so far: it might explain why we engage in epistemic discourse, without explaining why epistemic discourse is appropriate. Some naturalists might want to stop there. But we can, if we are comfortable, go further, by adopting a social-functional account of the value of epistemic discourse (Craig 1990; Williams 2002; Dogramaci 2012). "Knowledge attributions," Chrisman (2007) writes, "could be seen as playing a crucial role in keeping track of who can be trusted about which kinds of information" (242–43). For these (and other) reasons, "treating a belief as a known belief is beneficial in the right sort of circumstances" (Kappel 2010: 184), and in connection with this we might "debate norms by debating whether they are likely to lead to desirable results – in particular, truth-oriented results of various sorts" (Field 2009: 278). But we must be careful here: the anti-realist about epistemic normativity can say that epistemic discourse is good because engaging in this practice is beneficial or useful or socially desirable; but she must be careful not to appeal to the *epistemic* value of true belief, for example, in her account of the appropriateness of epistemic evaluation. The anti-realist can say that not adopting these policies would lead to "things that we ... dislike" (Field 2009: 256); she can't say that not adopting these policies would be epistemically bad in virtue of the epistemic value of truth (cf. Field 2009: 260).[5]

2.2   Convention-relativism about epistemic discourse

That's expressivism about epistemic discourse (section 2.1). But there's an (anti-realist) alternative to expressivism.[6] Consider Ernie Sosa's (2007) idea of an "insulated critical domain," which is "a set of interrelated entities evaluable through correspondingly interrelated values" (73). Sosa asks us to:

---

[5] Consider also an inferentialist semantics for epistemic discourse (Chrisman 2011), which appeals to "the distinctively practical kinds of inferential relations in which ... normative [epistemic] concepts are caught up" (123). On such a view, for example, we might say that <S knows that p> has the following "practical implications": "I shall act as if p is true" and "I shall stop enquiring as to whether p" (123). This jibes with a social-functional vindication of epistemic evaluation, on which there are "good pragmatic reasons to explain why it is better to use concepts embodying these inferential roles rather than some other concepts," thus establishing "our unconditional right to use [these] concepts" (128).

[6] And surely more than one. Error theory about epistemic discourse has attracted a few detractors (Cuneo 2007: ch. 4; Lynch 2009a: 232) but no explicit defenders (although Olson 2011 offers a critique of the detractors).

Consider the world of coffee – of its production, elaboration, and consump-
tion. One central value organizes the critical assessment distinctive of that
domain. I mean the value of liquid coffee that is delicious and aromatic.
Think of the assessment of coffee beans, fields, coffee machines, baristas,
ways of making liquid coffee, plantations, harvests, etc. What organizes all
such evaluation, the value at the center of it all, from which the other relevant values are derivative, is the value of good coffee, of liquid coffee that is
delicious and aromatic. (Sosa 2007: 73)

Various things – cups of coffee, fields of coffee beans, methods of making
coffee – can be evaluated relative to the central organizing value of delicious and aromatic liquid coffee. And, as Sosa argues, we might understand epistemology as a critical domain of this kind, organized around
the central organizing value of true belief (73). To say that x is epistemically good, or good from the epistemic point of view, on Sosa's view, is
to say that x does well vis-à-vis the central organizing value of the critical
domain of the epistemic, namely, true belief, just as to say that x is good
from the perspective of the world of coffee is to say that x does well vis-
à-vis the central organizing value of the critical domain of the world of
coffee, namely, delicious and aromatic liquid coffee.

So far this is consistent with expressivism about epistemic discourse:
we could understand an utterance of <x is epistemically valuable> (for
example) as expressing both (i) the belief that x does well vis-à-vis the
central organizing value of the critical domain of the epistemic and (ii)
endorsement, acceptance, approval, or valuation of that central organizing value (namely, true belief). However, Sosa rejects such an account,
since critical evaluation does not require the recognition of any "domain-
transcendent value":

> [S]omeone knowledgeable about guns and their use for hunting, for mili-
> tary ends, and so on, may undergo a conversion that makes the use of guns
> abhorrent. The good shot is thus drained of any real value that he can dis-
> cern. Nevertheless, his critical judgment within that domain may outstrip
> anyone else's, whether gun lover or not. Critical domains can be viewed as
> thus *insulated*. (Sosa 2007: 73–74)

The critic of guns can describe the Smith and Wesson .44 Magnum as "an
excellent gun," without expressing her endorsement, acceptance, approval,
or valuation of the central organizing value of the world of guns – namely,
as Harry Callahan articulates it, that of blowing people's heads clean off.
Gun evaluation does not necessarily express any non-cognitive attitude
towards the central organizing value of the world of guns. Likewise, for
Sosa, epistemic evaluation does not necessarily express any non-cognitive

attitude towards the central organizing value of the critical domain of the epistemic. The central organizing value, relative to which evaluation within a critical domain operates, is not necessarily something that the evaluator values.

What then makes true belief the central organizing value of the critical domain of the epistemic? What explains the fact that true belief is the central organizing value of this domain? On Sosa's view, not the value of true belief:

> Our present worry abstracts from such Platonic issues of epistemic normativity. Truth may or may not be intrinsically valuable absolutely, who knows? Our worry requires only that we consider truth the *epistemically fundamental* value. (Sosa 2007: 72)

But if it is not the value of true belief that explains its status, as the central organizing value of the critical domain of the epistemic, what explains its status?

"Convention-relativism about epistemic discourse" (more on which below) says: convention. What makes one thing, rather than another, the central organizing value of the critical domain of the epistemic is a matter of what we mean by "epistemic." Because "epistemic" is a term of art, employed by academic theorists rather than ordinary speakers (contrast "moral" and "aesthetic"), the relevant conventions supervene on the historical and contemporary practices of the relevant theorists – the ones who use the term "epistemic."[7] True belief, on Sosa's view, is *the* central organizing value of the critical domain of the epistemic. The convention-relativist need not make this assumption. The convention-relativist should define "epistemic" so as to capture, as best as possible, the use of this term by the relevant theorists. Given this criterion of adequacy, we should adopt a broader conception of the epistemic: the central organizing value of the critical domain of the epistemic is "cognitive contact with reality" (Zagzebski 1996: 167) or **accuracy** (Grimm and Ahlstrom 2013). True belief is a paradigm species of this, but the present formulation leaves open other possible species of accuracy, such as understanding (Zagzebski 2001; Grimm and Ahlstrom 2013), "carving nature at the joints" (Sider 2009, 2011; Treanor 2013; Hazlett unpublished manuscript), having fitting or

---

[7] The *Oxford English Dictionary*, noting that it is a philosophical term, defines "epistemic" as follows: "Of or relating to knowledge or degree of acceptance." The three listed uses are from academic philosophy: from a book on logic, from an issue of *Mind*, and from a book on Mill. The earliest use listed is from 1922. Compare "moral" (not marked as philosophical, first listed use 1387) and "aesthetic" (non-philosophical meanings given, first listed use 1764).

appropriate emotions (Nussbaum 2001; Price 2006), perceptual acquaint-
ance with the intrinsic properties of external things (Johnston 1996), or
knowledge of intrinsic properties (Langton 1998; Lewis 2008).[8] But nothing here will ride on the assumption of accuracy as the central organizing
value of the epistemic.

Although Sosa suggests the individuation of critical domains in terms
of "values," we could just as easily describe a critical domain by articulating a set of rules (e.g. principles of evidence), where following the rules
is understood as the central organizing "value" of that domain. And we
need not understand critical domains as defined by *one* central organizing
value; a critical domain might be defined by a plurality of central organizing values. Finally, although Sosa speaks of *evaluation* relative to a central organizing value, nothing stands in the way of speaking of normative
discourse more broadly, including "ought" claims: we can say that, from
the perspective of the world of coffee, one ought not use a sock as a filter;
and we can say that, from the epistemic perspective, one ought to cleave
to one's evidence.

According to *convention-relativism about epistemic discourse*, then, the
utterances of the sentences involved in epistemic discourse express beliefs
about how things stand relative to the central organizing value (or values)
of the critical domain of the epistemic, and, moreover, the utterance
of such sentences does not necessarily express non-cognitive attitudes
(towards the central organizing value [or values] of the critical domain
of the epistemic). Such expression is no part of the conventional meaning of the relevant sentences, although this doesn't mean that epistemic
discourse doesn't, in some cases, express non-cognitive attitudes (section
3.2); it only means that such expression isn't built into the meaning of the
sentences uttered in epistemic discourse. This distinguishes convention-
relativism from expressivism about epistemic discourse (section 2.1). On
Chrisman's (2007) view, to say that S knows that p is to express the belief
that S is entitled by norms *e* to her true belief that p (241), and on Field's
(2009) view, to evaluate something positively in epistemic evaluation is
to think or say that that it does well vis-à-vis some set of norms (258–61).
But expressivists will insist that this does not yet capture the essence of
epistemic discourse: we must add that employing epistemic discourse

---

[8] A further wrinkle will be required to distinguish the epistemic from the moral or ethical (Hazlett
2012; Hazlett 2013: §9.3): we shall have to individuate critical domains in terms of what they take to
have final and *intrinsic* value. Accuracy is taken, from the epistemic point of view, to have final and
intrinsic value; this is compatible with the idea that accuracy has final *constitutive* value (Zagzebski
2004; Baril 2010; Greco 2010), from the moral or ethical point of view.

involves expressing non-cognitive attitudes as well. For Chrisman, to say that S knows that p is also to express acceptance of the relevant norms (2007), and for Field, in epistemic evaluation, the set of norms in question must be preferences that the speaker has or policies that she endorses (2009: 274). What distinguishes convention-relativism from expressivism is that the convention-relativist rejects the view that a non-cognitive attitude is necessarily expressed in epistemic discourse.

This also distinguishes convention-relativism from what Paul Boghossian (2006) calls "epistemic relativism" (84–85, see also Kalderon 2009), on which judgments of justification commit one to accepting a particular "epistemic system." On convention-relativism, employing epistemic discourse involves no such commitment.

Convention-relativism is a metaepistemological view (cf. section 2.1) about epistemic discourse. Issues of metaepistemology are orthogonal to issues in first-order normative epistemology, e.g. about the nature of epistemic justification or the status of various character traits as epistemic virtues. Consider, for another example, what Roger White (2007) calls "epistemic subjectivism": the view that "what I (epistemically) ought to believe depends on which epistemic rules *I* happen to adopt" (117). Convention-relativism is orthogonal to this.

My formulation of convention-relativism is intentionally vague in referring to beliefs "about how things stand relative to" some value or values. (Above we spoke of "doing well vis-à-vis" some value.) This is compatible with a plurality of more specific ways of spelling out the content of the beliefs expressed in the various species of epistemic discourse. For example, you might opt for an *individualistic teleological account* of attributions of epistemic virtue, on which <x is an epistemic virtue> is true iff having x tends to promote one's share of accuracy. This might be adopted for other species of epistemic discourse, e.g. attributions of epistemic obligation: <S ought to believe that p> is true iff believing that p will promote S's share of accuracy. These formulations are rough and surely would need refinement. And there are myriad alternatives to these, even given the assumption that accuracy is the central organizing value of the critical domain of the epistemic. For example, we might adopt a *social teleological account* on which e.g. <x is an epistemic virtue> is true iff having x tends to promote people's shares, in general, of accuracy. Or we might adopt an *intentional account* on which e.g. <x is an epistemic virtue> is true iff having x essentially requires desiring accuracy. If we drop our assumption that accuracy is the central organizing value of the critical domain of the epistemic, even more options are available. Suppose that central organizing value of the critical domain of the epistemic is the following "evidentialist rule": "It is wrong to believe on insufficient evidence." We could then adopt a *rule-following account* on which e.g. <S ought to believe that p> is true iff S's believing that p is an instance of following the evidentialist rule.

We can compare epistemic discourse, on convention-relativism, with another case of normative discourse relative to a set of conventions: criticism relative to the rules of a club. Suppose that Plantation Club rules strictly forbid the eating of peas with a spoon. The prohibition of eating peas with a spoon makes it possible to criticize people's behavior, relative to that rule. The sentence "It's wrong to eat peas with a spoon, relative to the rules of the Plantation Club" is true iff eating peas with a spoon is forbidden by the rules of the Plantation Club. The truth of this sentence is determined entirely by the conventional rules of the Plantation Club. The convention-relativist says the same, *mutatis mutandis*, about epistemic discourse. The truth of the sentence "True belief is epistemically valuable," for example, is determined entirely by the conventional meaning of "epistemic." Saying that true belief is epistemically valuable, on the convention-relativist view, is in this respect akin to saying that it's wrong to eat peas with a spoon, relative to the rules of the Plantation Club.

For this reason, convention-relativism about epistemic discourse jibes with anti-realism about epistemic normativity (section 1). Critical domains are "insulated" and free from commitment to the "real" existence of the relevant values. To say that true belief is epistemically valuable is not to say anything about the worth of the central organizing value of the critical domain of the epistemic, just as to say that it's wrong to eat peas with a spoon, relative to the rules of the Plantation Club, is not to say anything about the worth of the Plantation Club's rule against eating peas with a spoon. However, convention-relativism about epistemic discourse is consistent with, and can explain, the fact that epistemic normativity is *inescapable*, in Philippa Foot's (1972) sense: both morality and etiquette "are inescapable in that behavior does not cease to offend against either morality or etiquette because the agent is indifferent to their purposes and to the disapproval he will incur by flouting them" (311). Just as someone's eating peas with a spoon violates the rules of the Plantation Club, regardless of her interests or desires, so someone can violate her "epistemic obligations" (for example), regardless of her interests or desires.[9]

---

[9] This is the reason that teleological accounts of epistemic normativity fail (section 1).

As well, convention-relativism can explain the existence of disagreement in epistemic discourse. We might disagree, for example, about whether some character trait really does promote one's share of accuracy. Convention-relativism is not equivalent to a form of *speaker* relativism on which to say that some belief is epistemically justified is to say that it does well relative to the *speaker's* standards or values (or relative to what the *speaker* takes the central epistemic value[s] to be). Such a view would have trouble making sense of disagreement in epistemic discourse (cf. Chrisman 2007: 234). Convention-relativism posits an absolute, non-speaker-relative meaning of "epistemic," thus allowing for the possibility of disagreement. (This makes for another difference between convention-relativism and Boghossian's "epistemic relativism.") As well, it might be unclear what the rules of the Plantation Club are; we might disagree about that. Likewise, it might be unclear what the central organizing value or values of the critical domain of the epistemic are, and we might disagree about that – about the meaning of "epistemic." It might also be unclear how the central organizing values of a critical domain are to be weighted, and we might disagree about that. Finally, we might debate whether the rules of the Plantation Club ought to be changed, or whether we ought to adopt a new set of rules. Likewise for the meaning of "epistemic." But once we have established what the rules of the Plantation Club are, there is no further question of whether those are "really" the rules of the Plantation Club. Likewise, once we have established what the central organizing value (or values) of the critical domain of the epistemic are, there is no further question of whether those are "really" the epistemic values.

The comparison to club rules may suggest that epistemic discourse is capricious or arbitrary, and thus might suggest that epistemic discourse is somehow groundless and unjustified. But the comparison shouldn't put us off: the Plantation Club might have good reasons for adopting the rules that it does, including rules that may, in some important sense, be arbitrary. The convention-relativist, in other words, is in no worse a position than any other anti-realist about epistemic normativity, when it comes to explaining the appropriateness of epistemic discourse (cf. section 2.1). Alternatively, she might offer something more modest. Consider, again, the rules of the Plantation Club. Why follow these rules? One might appeal to the benefits of membership and to the fact that following these rules is necessary to remain a member. But one might also simply say that these are the rules that we members of the Plantation Club choose to follow. Why not eat peas with a spoon? Because it disgusts us, or offends us, or pains us, to see peas eaten with a spoon – or because we simply don't like it. The same might explain the appropriateness of epistemic evalua-tion, as Fred Dretske argues:

> The only *fault* with fallacious reasoning, the only thing *wrong* or *bad* about mistaken judgments, is that, generally speaking, we don't like them ... This ... leaves the normativity of false belief and fallacious reasoning in the same place as the normativity of foul weather and bad table manners – in the attitudes, purposes, and beliefs of the people who make judgments about the weather and table behavior. (2000: 248)

So much for the articulation of convention-relativism about epistemic discourse. Why adopt the view?

3 In defense of convention-relativism

In this section I present an argument for convention-relativism (section 3.1), offer an account of the apparent normativity of epistemic discourse (section 3.2), and discuss two objections to my argument (section 3.3 and section 3.4).

3.1 *The reverse open question argument*

You might think that epistemic discourse not only seems normative, as I said above, but *is* normative. As Hartry Field (2009) argues:

> In an evaluative claim ... one doesn't intend to be making a claim about a specific norm ... [A] claim about what is *justified according to a specific norm* would be straightforwardly factual, with no evaluative force. (It would encourage the Moore-like response "Sure that's justified *according to that norm*; but is it justified?") (251–52; cf. Blackburn 1998: 69–70 and Gibbard 2003: 33)

And you might go on to argue that convention-relativism entails that epi-stemic discourse is *not* normative. Convention-relativism (section 2.2) seems to treat epistemic discourse as involving the utterance of "straight-forwardly factual" sentences[10] about how things stand relative to a con-ventional value (or set of values). To say that it's wrong to eat peas with a spoon, relative to the rules of the Plantation Club, isn't to say that it really is wrong to eat peas with a spoon, and, for the convention-relativist, to say

---

[10] That is to say, it treats epistemic discourse as involving the utterance of sentences that are "straight-forwardly factual" according to the correct semantic account of them, the truth of which account may not be straightforward.

that true belief is epistemically valuable (for example) isn't to say that true belief really is valuable.[11]

Field (2009) suggests that the claim that *x* is justified according to a specific norm is *not* normative if it invites – allows the coherent articulation of – the question of whether *x* really is justified. There is a *normative question* – whether *x* really is justified – associated with the would-be normative claim – that *x* is justified according to a specific norm – such that the claim is a genuine *normative claim* only if it does not allow the coherent articulation of the corresponding normative question. We can adapt this criterion of normativity (for claims) to our three species of epistemic discourse:

(i)   The claim that *x* is an epistemic virtue is normative only if it does not allow the coherent articulation of the question of whether *x* really is a virtue.

(ii) The claim that *x* is epistemically valuable is normative only if it does not allow the coherent articulation of the question of whether *x* really is valuable.

(iii) The claim that S epistemically ought to believe that p is normative only if it does not allow the coherent articulation of the question of whether S really ought to believe that p.

And let's assume that epistemic discourse is *normative* only if these three types of claim are normative. We now must consider two questions: First, does convention-relativism imply that epistemic discourse is not normative? And, second, is epistemic discourse normative?

As I have suggested, it seems that the answer to the first question is Yes. It is perfectly coherent to say that it is wrong to eat peas with a spoon, relative to the rules of the Plantation Club, and go on to ask whether it really is wrong. If epistemic discourse is akin to criticism relative to the rules of the Plantation Club, then epistemic discourse is not normative.

What about the second question? Is epistemic discourse normative? I think not (cf. Fumerton 2001). The reason is that instances of our three species of epistemic discourse *do* allow the coherent articulation of the corresponding normative question – epistemic discourse leaves the relevant normative questions open. For example: we can grant that open-mindedness is an *epistemic* virtue, and still coherently ask whether open-mindedness really is a virtue; we can grant that true belief is *epistemically* valuable,

---

[11] Convention-relativism has this in common with the view suggested by Mike Ridge (2011) on which epistemic evaluation involves attributive uses of "good" and cognate expressions.

and still coherently ask whether true belief really is valuable; and we can grant that one *epistemically* ought to cleave to one's evidence, and still coherently ask whether one really ought to cleave to one's evidence.

There are two kinds of situations in which these questions can coherently be asked. The first kind of situation is one in which we question the value of accuracy in general. Consider Gary, who is an "anti-epistemologist" (cf. Railton 1997: 54–59): he is completely indifferent to accuracy – he does not care about true belief, knowledge, understanding, etc. He admits that accuracy is what epistemologists treat as a central organizing value. But he is completely indifferent to accuracy. He admits that open-mindedness is an epistemic virtue, that true belief is epistemically valuable, and that one epistemically ought to cleave to one's evidence. But he still wonders: is open-mindedness really a virtue? Is true belief really valuable? Is it really the case that one ought to cleave to one's evidence? (Alternatively, we might appeal to the fact that I can ask whether epistemic rules or norms are legitimate rules or norms, whether they are rules or norms that are worthy of my allegiance, whether I ought to conform my conduct to these rules or norms, etc.)[12]

The second kind of situation is one in which we question the value of accuracy in particular cases. Imagine that it is true that the number of grains of sand on the beach at Coney Island is even. Assuming that you find the question of the evenness of the number of grains of sand on the beach at Coney Island utterly uninteresting, you might wonder whether believing this true proposition would have any value, even though you concede that it would have some *epistemic* value, in virtue of being an instance of accuracy. Situations of this kind can also arise when believing as you epistemically ought would be disvaluable. Imagine that Andy has acquired strong, undefeated evidence that he will lose his upcoming tennis match with Roger Federer. He epistemically ought to believe that he will lose, but believing this seems disvaluable, given the fact that Andy needs confidence and self-belief to even stand a chance against Federer. It is coherent to wonder whether it is really the case that Andy ought, even pro tanto, to believe this proposition.

The upshot of all this is that sometimes accuracy seems, or seems like it may very well be, worthless. In such situations, it becomes coherent to ask the relevant normative question, even having conceded the corresponding claim of epistemic discourse. Therefore, epistemic discourse is not normative. Call this the *reverse open question argument*.

---

[12] Note that the argument here assumes that epistemic normativity is inescapable (section 2.2).

Is it coherent to see accuracy as worthless? For our purposes we need only show that it is coherent to ask whether accuracy is valuable. But this question can coherently be asked, by asking: Should I really care about accuracy? Is this really worthy of my pursuit? Is it, in other words, really good?

Compare Gibbard's (1990) critique of the "irrationalist," who thinks that in many cases the rational thing is not what is to be done. But "[t]he irrationalist cannot be what he thinks himself to be, for whatever he endorses he thereby thinks rational" (48–49). Given this, "what is rational to believe settles what to believe" (49). But this is not true of *epistemic* rationality: the question of what to believe is left open by a conclusion about the requirements of *epistemic* rationality. And this is because we can refrain from endorsing *epistemic* value (or *epistemic* rules or norms). We might put our point this way: we can coherently question the normative force of *epistemic* value (or of *epistemic* rules or norms).[13] "Epistemically good" and "epistemically ought" are different from words like "good" and "ought," *sans* qualification. There is an obvious sense in which it is incoherent to ask whether the good really is good, or whether one really ought to do what one ought to do. This provides at least one sense in which good-talk and ought-talk is normative. But this doesn't apply, *mutatis mutandis*, to epistemic discourse. Words like "good" and "ought" have normative and non-normative uses. Consider the *good assassin* (cf. Sosa 2007; Ridge 2011): I can grant that someone is a good assassin, while coherently questioning whether she is good. To say that someone is a good assassin is just to say that she is a dispassionate and effective killer; we can coherently question the value of being a dispassionate and effective killer. Consider *legal obligation*: I can grant that Φing is required by law, while coherently questioning whether I ought to Φ. To say that something is legally obligatory is just to say that it is what the statues require; we can legitimacy challenge those requirements.[14]

---

[13] What about moral normativity? Can we coherently question the normative force of moral value, or of moral rules or norms? I leave this question open, but I think there is an important difference between "epistemic" and "moral": the former is a piece of philosophical jargon, while the latter is part of ordinary language (cf. section 2.2).

[14] Consider popular theories of epistemic justification, like reliabilism, evidentialism, and coherentism. We can coherently ask whether reliably formed beliefs, or evidentially well-founded beliefs, or beliefs that cohere with a large body of other beliefs, really are justified. These theories of justification leave the corresponding normative question open. You might argue, following Moore's "open question argument," that this reveals the inadequacy of these theories. It seems to me that the opposite conclusion should be drawn: these are perfectly good epistemological theories; what we should conclude is that epistemic discourse isn't normative.

3.2   Explaining the apparent normativity of epistemic discourse

Gibbard (1990) argues that there is a "special element that makes normative thought and language normative," namely, the fact that such thought
and language "involves a kind of endorsement – and endorsement that
any descriptivistic analysis treats inadequately" (33; cf. Blackburn 1998;
69–70). I have just argued that epistemic discourse is not normative (section 3.1), but I said that it appears normative. What explains the appearance? On my view, epistemic discourse sometimes, but not always, involves
endorsement – it sometimes, but not always, involves the expression of
non-cognitive attitudes. That it does explains why epistemic discourse
seems normative: we mistake a common feature of epistemic discourse
for an essential property. The convention-relativist account is therefore
incomplete until I can explain how, and in what way, epistemic discourse
sometimes involves the expression of non-cognitive attitudes.

   On my view, the expression of non-cognitive attitudes in epistemic
discourse is down to pragmatic features of some uses of the sentences
involved in epistemic discourse. This contrasts with the expressivist view
(section 2.1) that such expression is down to semantic features of those
sentences, i.e. their conventional meanings. For the expressivist, the normativity of epistemic discourse is down to facts about the conventional
meaning of the relevant *sentences*; on my view it is down to (pragmatic)
facts about some *uses* of those sentences. Utterances are normative, on my
view, not in virtue of the meaning of the words or sentences uttered, as on
expressivism, but in virtue of pragmatic facts about the use of those words
or sentences.

   Consider utterances of <S epistemically ought not believe that p>. On
my proposal, utterances of this sentence will sometimes express criticism
of S's belief. When they do, this will be a matter of *conversational implicature*. Suppose it is common ground in our conversational context that we
endorse, or value, or are simply interested in accuracy (e.g. true belief),
and you sincerely utter <S epistemically ought not believe that p>. On
the (mutual) assumption that you are being cooperative, and in particular
on the (mutual) assumption that you are trying to make your contribution to our conversation relevant, I can infer that you intend to express
criticism of S's belief – because the claim that S epistemically ought not
believe that p is a claim about how S's belief stands relative to accuracy
(section 2.2). Your utterance therefore expresses criticism of S's belief (cf.
Fumerton 2001: 57). Compare now two conversations about Andy's belief
that he will beat Federer:

Gamblers: A pair of gamblers are discussing whether to bet against Federer. They are interested in, and only in, the truth about the question of whether Federer will lose. They wonder what tennis experts predict the outcome of the match will be. One notes: "Well, Andy believes that he will win. But he epistemically ought not believe that he'll win. So we shouldn't take his belief into account."

Commentators: A pair of tennis commentators are discussing the underdog's psychology. They assume Federer will win, and are only interested in the phenomenon of confidence and self-belief. One argues: "Sure, Andy epistemically ought not believe that he will win. But that's no mark against a belief in this situation. It's exactly the belief he should have, going into a match like this."

The gambler's utterance of "Andy epistemically ought not believe that he will win" expresses criticism of Andy's belief, but the commentator's utterance expresses no such criticism. Whenever it is common ground that the speakers endorse, or value, or are simply interested in accuracy, utterance of the sentences involved in epistemic discourse can involve expression of criticism. But when that is not common ground, no such criticism will be expressed.

This implication passes the so-called "tests" for conversational implicature. First, it is calculable: the second gambler can figure out that the first gambler's utterance expresses criticism of Andy's belief based on his knowledge of their shared purpose (finding out the truth about the outcome of the match) and tacit understanding of the cooperative principle. Second, it is non-detachable: the gambler could just as easily have criticized Andy's belief by saying that it was formed in an unreliable way or by saying that it goes against the evidence. Third, it is cancellable. That was the upshot of the reverse open question argument (section 3.1).

Compare the debate over whether the expressive implications of moral discourse are a matter of conversational implicature. Stephen Finlay (2004, 2005) argues that attributions of moral goodness sometimes, but not always, express non-cognitive attitudes of approval. When they do, it is down to conversational implicature (2004: 217–22; 2005). The all-important "test" of cancellability is passed by appeal to the amoralist, who indifferently attributes moral goodness (2004: 209; 2005: 15). The view I have proposed is the analog of Finlay's view, transposed to the epistemic domain. Subjectivists, cognitivist realists, and expressivists about moral discourse, however, will all reject Finlay's account on the grounds that the normativity of moral discourse is down to (semantic) facts about the conventional meaning of the relevant sentences. In this connection, some argue that the expression of non-cognitive attitudes in moral discourse is down to *conventional implicature* (Barker 2000, Copp 2001). The convention-relativist about epistemic discourse can leave these questions about moral discourse open (cf. section 3.1).

It is worth pointing out that this account of the expressive implications of epistemic discourse could be applied, *mutatis mutandis*, to the expressive implications of other species of conventional evaluation, such as criticism relative to the rules of the Plantation Club (section 2.2). Compare two conversations:

> *Caught in the act*:   The President of the Plantation Club looms over an offending diner and says, gravely, "Club rules forbid eating peas with a spoon."

> *Rebellion*:   Wooster tells the diner: "Club rules forbid eating peas with a spoon, but damn the rules, do it anyway!"

The President expresses disapproval of the diner's behavior; Wooster expresses no such disapproval. The President is criticizing the diner, while Wooster is encouraging her. The difference is down to conversational implicature: I know that the President loathes violations of the rules of the Plantation Club, and so can deduce that she is trying to admonish the diner, while Wooster's utterance amounts to an explicit cancellation of any such implication. All this, despite the fact that "Club rules forbid eating peas with a spoon" is uncontroversially non-normative.

3.3   Objection: the epistemic as the doxastic

My argument assumes what we can call an *axial conception* of the epistemic, where the epistemic is characterized in terms of a certain value or values – above (section 2.2), I suggested accuracy. The assumption of such a conception seems needed to advance the reverse open question argument (section 3.1) – it is what allows the coherent articulation, for example, of the question of whether what one epistemically ought to believe is what one really ought to believe. This conception jibes with epistemologists' use of such expressions as "epistemic justification," where this is standardly contrasted with "prudential justification."[15] On the axial conception, the epistemic essentially contrasts with the prudential, the moral, and the aesthetic. You might object that this conception of the epistemic is

---

[15] Characterizing the epistemic in terms of accuracy also has an etymological virtue: "ἐπιστήμη" is best translated with "knowledge" or "understanding."

illegitimate, and offer a *doxastic conception* of the epistemic, where "epistemic" is understood as synonymous with "doxastic" (meaning "of or concerning belief"), "intellectual," or "theoretical." This conception jibes with certain uses of "epistemic" in philosophy, such as "epistemic agency," and with the idea that the epistemic essentially contrasts with practical. The doxastic conception of the epistemic is a natural assumption for those realists about epistemic normativity who appeal to the normativity of belief. For them, epistemic norms and values can be understood as norms and values that flow from the essential nature of belief. Above I set that view aside by appeal to philosophical naturalism (section 1).[16]

It seems to me that, if we adopt the doxastic conception of the epistemic, then the reverse open question argument is unsound. Consider the thought (cf. section 3.1): "Andy epistemically ought to believe that p. But is it really the case that he ought to believe that p?" If "epistemic" means the same as "doxastic," then it seems that there can be no distinction between what someone epistemically ought to believe and what she ought to believe. When we are considering what someone ought to *believe*, we are already considering matters "of or concerning belief," and so the addition of "epistemically" would be redundant, if "epistemic" means the same as "doxastic." The same, *mutatis mutandis*, when it comes to the distinction between what is epistemically valuable and what is valuable – or, at least, when it comes to the distinction between a *belief's* being epistemically valuable and that belief's being valuable. The matter is a bit more complex when it comes to the notion of an epistemic virtue. We do, I think, have a notion of an "intellectual virtue" where this means, roughly, a "virtue of the mind." *Intellectual virtues*, in this sense, are to be contrasted with practical virtues: the former are character traits having essentially to do with how one *thinks*; the latter are character traits having essentially to do with how one *acts*. Now it seems to me that this distinction is problematic: paradigm practical virtues involve thought (e.g. the courageous person is aware of the dangers she faces), and paradigm intellectual virtues involve action (e.g. the open-minded person will allow other people to have their say in conversation). But we can set that issue

---

[16] There is a way to make the normativity of belief jibe with philosophical naturalism: by adopting an anti-realist account of belief attribution (Dennett 1989; Shah and Velleman 2005: 510). Naturalism loathes categorical normativity, and the normativity of belief, we assumed, implies the existence of categorical normativity, wherever belief is to be found. But if belief is not to be found anywhere, then no categorical normativity is implied. And an anti-realist account of belief attribution implies that belief is not to be found anywhere: whether something is to be called a "belief" is not ultimately a factual matter, but a matter of the attitude one adopts towards it. I have tacitly assumed realism about belief here.

aside: the doxastic conception of the epistemic yields a coherent notion of the epistemic virtues as "virtues of the mind." But this is not the same notion of the epistemic virtues that we would get were we to assume an axial conception of the epistemic, e.g. on which the epistemic is characterized in terms of accuracy. That would yield a notion of the *epistemic virtues* as (say) those character traits conducive to accuracy (cf. section 2.2). And to assume a priori that "virtues of the mind" are necessarily character traits conducive to cognitive contact with reality is to illegitimately conflate two different conceptions of the epistemic. In any event, we can see that the assumption of the doxastic conception of the epistemic undermines the distinction between an epistemic virtue, i.e. a "virtue of the mind," and a virtue: for a virtue of the mind is ipso facto a virtue. And so the reverse open question argument is unsound, if we adopt the doxastic conception.

There is no disagreement between the doxastic conception of the epistemic and an axial conception – these are just two different sense of "epistemic." But the doxastic conception has some curious consequences. Imagine that Andy believes, against his evidence, that he will beat Federer, providing him with much-needed confidence. Intuitively, there is some sense in which this is a good belief. But it seems that the doxastic conception implies that this belief is therefore *epistemically* good – since we are talking about the goodness of a *belief.* But this is counterintuitive: a belief formed in the face of strong, undefeated contrary evidence is not *epistemically* good, even if it is (say) prudentially good. Beliefs can be good without being *epistemically* good. This suggests that there is a coherent distinction between an epistemically valuable belief and a valuable belief, and between what one epistemically ought to believe and what one ought to believe, and between an epistemic virtue and a virtue. An axial conception of the epistemic can capture these distinctions; it seems to me that the doxastic conception cannot.[17]

3.4   Objection: epistemic discourse and the reactive attitudes

Epistemic discourse (section 1) seems sometimes to involve reactive attitudes. Epistemologists sometimes speak of "epistemic praise" and "epistemic blame." The careful reasoner and the honest inquirer sometimes inspire our praise and admiration, while the sloppy reasoner and the wishful thinker sometimes inspire our blame and contempt. If epistemic

---

[17] My argument here is (especially) controversial. For more on these issues, see Hieronymi 2005; Shah 2006; Reisner 2008, 2009.

discourse is akin to evaluation relative to the conventional rules of the Plantation Club (section 3.1), how can these reactive attitudes be justified? This is unproblematic when the subject of our reactive attitudes is someone who endorses or values accuracy: we praise her for getting what she wanted, and blame her for failing to get what she wanted. But what about the case in which the subject of our reactive attitudes does not endorse or value accuracy?

As Bernard Williams (1995) notes, an internalist about practical reasons faces a similar challenge. To blame S for Φing seems to require thinking that S had reason to Φ (41). But consider now a man who is a "very hard case": he treats his wife badly, and in response to our criticism ("you ought to be nicer to your wife," "you have a reason to be nicer to her, namely, that she's your wife") he responds with indifference ("Don't you understand? I really do not care"). He has no internal reason to be nicer to his wife, and if all reasons are internal reasons (as the internalist claims), then he has no reason to be nicer to his wife. Blaming him for his cruelty, therefore, seems inappropriate, given our assumption connecting blame and reasons for action. Williams articulates two possible lines of response for the internalist. The first appeals to the idea that blame is a "proleptic mechanism" (44), such that hard cases may have "a motivation to avoid the disapproval of other people," as part of "a general desire to be ethically well related to people they respect." In virtue of this: "[T]he expression of blame serves to indicate the fact that in virtue of this, they have a reason to avoid those things they did not have enough reason to avoid up to now" (41). In blaming the hard case: "Our thought may ... be this: if he were to deliberate again and take into consideration all the reasons that might now come more vividly before him, we hope he would come to a different conclusion" (42). And among his reasons for coming to this different conclusion might be "this very blame and the concerns expressed in it" (42). The convention-relativist about epistemic discourse can say something similar about those cases in which epistemic evaluation involves reactive attitudes. When I blame David for believing that there were weapons of mass destruction in Iraq, I express my hope that he will proceed with more intellectual caution in the future, and aim ideally to bring this about, in part, through David's recognition of my disapprobation. Epistemic blame, I propose, can be understood as a "proleptic mechanism": the expression of disapprobation aimed at epistemically improving the offender, through her recognition of said disapprobation. Epistemic blame could serve this proleptic function even when it comes to an *epistemic* "hard case" – i.e. Gary, the anti-epistemologist (section

3.1). Although he is indifferent to accuracy, he might not be indifferent to ethical recognition and approval, and might be brought into the epistemic fold, so to speak, in response to our blame.

But what if the anti-epistemologist is indifferent not only to accuracy, but to ethical recognition and approval as well? What if she lacks "any general disposition to respect the reactions of others" (Williams 1995: 43)? In this case, and this is Williams's second line of response, blame is once again problematic for the internalist. But this is as it should be: such people we "regard as hopeless or dangerous characters rather than thinking that blame is appropriate to them" (43). And this applies for "epistemic blame" as well. The sociopathic anti-epistemologist is not a suitable object for the reactive attitudes; she deserves pity, perhaps, but not blame. Nonetheless, if she fails to cleave to the evidence, then she violates her epistemic obligations. The reactive attitudes are not required for epistemic discourse – this is predicted by convention-relativism, and that convention-relativism predicts this speaks in its favor.[18]

4 Conclusion

I have motivated anti-realism about epistemic normativity by appeal to philosophical naturalism (section 1), articulated convention-relativism about epistemic discourse (section 2), and defended convention-relativism (section 3). The upshot of my argument is that we can concede (for example) that open-mindedness is an epistemic virtue, that true belief is epistemically valuable, and that one epistemically ought to cleave to one's evidence, while leaving the following normative questions open:

(i)   Is open-mindedness a virtue?
(ii)   Is true belief valuable?
(iii)   Ought one cleave to one's evidence?

These are difficult normative questions. If convention-relativism about epistemic discourse is correct, then we are ill-served by focusing on the "epistemic" analogs of these questions, at least until we have an adequate answer to the question of the value of accuracy.

---

[18] Cf. Fumerton (2001): there is no "*conceptual* connection between judging of a belief that it is epistemically irrational and criticizing the belief," for we can "imagine societies in which one values a kind of irrationality" (57).

Bibliography

Adams, R. M. (2006). *A Theory of Virtue*. Oxford University Press.

Alfano, M. (2012). Expanding the situationist challenge to responsibilist virtue epistemology. *Philosophical Quarterly*, 62(247), 223–49.

(2013). *Character as Moral Fiction*. Cambridge University Press.

(In press a). Extending the situationist challenge to reliabilism about inference. In A. Fairweather (ed.) *Virtue Scientia: Bridges between Philosophy of Science and Virtue Epistemology*. Dordrecht, the Netherlands: Springer.

(In press b). What are the bearers of virtues? In H. Sarkissian and J. Wright (eds.) *Advances in Moral Psychology*. New York: Continuum.

Alfano, M. and Fairweather, A. (In press). Situationism and virtue theory. *Oxford Bibliographies: Philosophy*.

Allport, G. and Odbert, H. (1936). *Trait Names: A Psycho-Lexical Study*. Psychological Monographs 47. Washington, DC: American Psychological Association.

Anscombe, G. E. M. (1958). Modern moral philosophy. *Philosophy*, 33(124), 1–19.

Aristotle. (1998). *The Nicomachean Ethics*, trans. D. Ross. Oxford University Press.

Aronson, J., Lustina, M., Good, C., Keough, K., Steele, C., and Brown, J. (1999). When white men can't do math: necessary and sufficient factors in stereotype threat. *Journal of Experimental Social Psychology*, 35, 29–46.

Asch, S. E. (1952). *Social Psychology*. Englewood Cliffs, NJ: Prentice-Hall.

Ashton, M. and Lee, K. (2001). A theoretical basis for the major dimensions of personality. *European Journal of Personality*, 15, 327–53.

(2005). Honesty-humility, the Big Five, and the Five-Factor model. *Journal of Personality*, 73, 1321–53.

Austin, J. L. (1962). *How to Do Things with Words*. London: Oxford University Press.

Axtell, G. (1997). Recent work in virtue epistemology. *American Philosophical Quarterly*, 34, 410–30.

(2000). *Knowledge, Belief, and Character*. Lanham, MD: Rowman & Littlefield.

(2010). Agency ascriptions in ethics and epistemology: or, navigating intersections, narrow and broad. *Metaphilosophy*, 41, 73–94.

Baehr, J. (2011). *The Inquiring Mind: On Intellectual Virtues and Virtue Epistemology*. Oxford University Press.

Baril, A. (2010). A eudaimonist approach to the problem of significance. *Acta Analytica*, 25(2), 215–41.

Barker, S. (2000). Is value content a component of conventional implicature? *Analysis*, 60(3), 268–79.

Battaly, H. (2008). Virtue epistemology. *Philosophy Compass*, 3(4), 639–63.

   (2010). Epistemic self-indulgence. In H. Battaly (ed.) *Virtue and Vice*, pp. 215–35. Malden, MA: Wiley-Blackwell.

Bedau, M. (1991). Can biological teleology be naturalized? *Journal of Philosophy*, 88, 647–55.

Benbow, C. and Stanley, J. (1980). Sex differences in mathematical ability: fact or artifact? *Science*, 210, 1262–64.

   (1983). Sex differences in mathematical reasoning ability: more facts. *Science*, 222, 1029–31.

Berker, S. (2013). Epistemic teleology and the separateness of propositions. *Philosophical Review*, 122, 337–93.

   (Unpublished manuscript). The rejection of epistemic consequentialism.

Bermudez, J. L. (2003). *Thinking without Words*. Oxford University Press.

Bishop, M. and Trout, J. D. (2005). *Epistemology and the Psychology of Human Judgment*. Oxford University Press.

Blackburn, S. (1998). *Ruling Passions: A Theory of Practical Reasoning*. Oxford University Press.

   (2011). *Practical Tortoise Raising and Other Philosophical Essays*. Oxford University Press.

Blackwell, L., Trzesniewski, K., and Dweck, C. (2007). Implicit theories of intelligence predict achievement across an adolescent transition: a longitudinal study and an intervention. *Child Development*, 78(1), 246–63.

Blascovich, J., Spencer, S., Quinn, D., and Steele, C. (2001). African-Americans and high blood pressure: the role of stereotype threat. *Psychological Science*, 12, 225–29.

Block, J. (1995). A contrarian view of the Five-Factor approach to personality description. *Psychological Bulletin*, 117, 187–215.

Block, N. (1996). How heritability misleads about race. *Boston Review*, 20(6), 30–35.

Bloomfield, P. (2000). Virtue epistemology and the epistemology of virtue. *Philosophy and Phenomenological Research*, 60(1), 23–43.

Boag, S. (2011). Explanation in personality psychology: "verbal magic" and the Five-Factor model. *Philosophical Psychology*, 24, 223–43.

Bogg, T. and Roberts, B. (2004). Conscientiousness and health-related behaviors: a meta-analysis of the leading behavioral contributors to mortality. *Psychological Bulletin*, 130, 887–919.

Boghossian, P. (1996). Analyticity reconsidered. *Noûs*, 30, 360–91.

   (1997). Analyticity. In B. Hale and C. Wright (eds.) *Companion to the Philosophy of Language*, pp. 331–68. Oxford: Blackwell.

   (2003a). Epistemic analyticity: a defense. *Grazer Philosophische Studien*, 66, 15–35.

(2003b). The normativity of content. *Philosophical Issues*, 13, 31–45.

(2005). Is meaning normative? In C. Nimtz and A. Beckermann (eds.) *Philosophy – Science – Scientific Philosophy*, pp. 205–18. Paderborn: Mentis.

(2006). *Fear of Knowledge: Against Relativism and Constructivism*. Oxford University Press.

(In press). What is inference? *Philosophical Studies*.

BonJour, L. (1998). *In Defense of Pure Reason: A Rationalist Account of A Priori Justification*. Cambridge University Press.

(2005). In defense of the a priori. In M. Steup and E. Sosa (eds.) *Contemporary Debates in Epistemology*, pp. 98–105. Oxford: Blackwell.

Boyd, R. (1988). How to be a moral realist. In G. Sayre-McCord (ed.) *Essays on Moral Realism*, pp. 181–228. Ithaca, NY: Cornell University Press.

Brink, D. O. (1989). *Moral Realism and the Foundations of Ethics*. Cambridge University Press.

Burge, T. (2003). Perceptual entitlement. *Philosophy and Phenomenological Research*, 67(3), 503–48.

(2010). *Origins of Objectivity*. Oxford University Press.

Buss, D. (1996). Social adaptation and five major factors of personality. In J. Wiggins (ed.) *The Five-Factor Model of Personality: Theoretical Perspectives*, pp. 180–207. New York: The Guilford Press.

Cadinu, M., Maass, A., Frigerio, S., Impagliazzo, L., and Latinotti, S. (2003). Stereotype threat: the effect of expectancy on performance. *European Journal of Social Psychology*, 33, 267–85.

Caprara, G. and Cervone, D. (2000). *Personality: Determinants, Dynamics, and Potentials*. Cambridge University Press.

Carroll, L. (1895). What the tortoise said to Achilles. *Mind*, 14, 278–80.

Caspi, A., Roberts, B., and Shiner, R. (2005). Personality development: stability and change. *Annual Review of Psychology*, 56, 453–84.

Cervone, D. (1999). Bottom-up explanation in personality psychology: the case of cross-situational coherence. In D. Cervone and Y. Shoda (eds.) *The Coherence of Personality: Social-Cognitive Bases of Consistency, Variability, and Organization*, pp. 303–41. New York: The Guilford Press.

Cervone, D., Shoda, Y., and Downey, G. (2007). Construing persons in context: on building a science of the individual. In Y. Shoda, D. Cervone, and G. Downey (eds.) *Persons in Context: Building a Science of the Individual*, pp. 3–15. New York: The Guilford Press.

Chrisman, M. (2007). From epistemic contextualism to epistemic expressivism. *Philosophical Studies*, 135, 225–54.

(2011). From epistemic expressivism to epistemic inferentialism. In A. Haddock, A. Millar, and D. Pritchard (eds.) *Social Epistemology*, pp. 112–28. Oxford University Press.

(In press). Epistemic expressivism. *Philosophy Compass*.

Clark, A. and Chalmers, D. (1998). The extended mind. *Analysis*, 58(1), 7–19.

Cohen, G., Garcia, J., Apfel, N., and Master, A. (2006). Reducing the racial achievement gap: a social-psychological intervention. *Science*, 313, 1307–10.

Cohen, S. (2002). Basic knowledge and the problem of easy knowledge. *Philosophy and Phenomenological Research*, 65, 309–29.

Conee, E. and Feldman, R. (1998). The generality problem for reliabilism. *Philosophical Studies*, 89, 1–29.

Coplan, A. (2010). Feeling without thinking. In H. Battaly (ed.) *Virtue and Vice*, pp. 133–51. Malden, MA: Wiley-Blackwell.

Copp, D. (1995). *Morality, Normativity, and Society*. Oxford University Press.

(2001). Realist-expressivism: a neglected option for moral realism. *Social Philosophy and Policy*, 1(8), 21–43.

(2007). *Morality in a Natural World*. Cambridge University Press.

(2009). Toward a pluralist and teleological theory of normativity. *Philosophical Issues*, 19, 21–37.

Cosmides, L. and Tooby, J. (1992). Cognitive adaptations for social exchange. In J. Barkow, L. Cosmides, and J. Tooby (eds.) *The Adapted Mind: Evolutionary Psychology and the Generation of Culture*, pp. 163–228. Oxford University Press.

Costa, P. and McCrae, R. (1992). *Revised NEO Personality Inventory (NEO-PI-R) and NEO Five-Factor Inventory (NEO-FFI) Professional Manual*. Odessa, TX: Psychological Assessment Resources.

(1994). "Set like plaster"? Evidence for the stability of adult personality. In T. Heatherton and J. Weinberger (eds.) *Can Personality Change?*, pp. 21–40. Washington, DC: American Psychological Association.

(1995). Domains and facets: hierarchical personality assessment using the revised NEO personality inventory. *Journal of Personality Assessment*, 64, 21–50.

Craig, E. (1990). *Knowledge and the State of Nature*. Oxford University Press.

Croizet, J. and Claire, T. (1998). Extending the concept of stereotype threat to social class: the intellectual underperformance of students from low socio-economic backgrounds. *Personality and Social Psychology Bulletin*, 24, 588–94.

Cruz, J. and Pollock, J. (2004). The chimerical appeal of epistemic externalism. In R. Schantz (ed.) *The Externalist Challenge*, pp. 125–42. Berlin: De Gruyter.

Cuneo, T. (2007). *The Normative Web*. Oxford University Press.

Danaher, K. and Crandall, C. (2008). Stereotype threat in applied settings re-examined. *Journal of Applied Social Psychology*, 38, 1639–55.

Darley, J. M. and Batson, C. D. (1973). From Jerusalem to Jericho. *Journal of Personality and Social Psychology*, 27, 100–8.

Dennett, D. (1984). *Elbow Room: The Varieties of Free Will Worth Wanting*. Cambridge, MA: MIT Press.

(1989). *The Intentional Stance*. Cambridge, MA: MIT Press.

Dewey, J. (1910). *How We Think*. New York: D. C. Heath & Co.

DeYoung, C., Quilty, L., and Peterson, J. (2007). Between facets and domains: 10 aspects of the Big Five. *Journal of Personality and Social Psychology*, 93, 880–96.

Digman, J. (1990). Personality structure: emergence of the Five-Factor model. *Annual Review of Psychology*, 41, 417–40.

Dogramaci, S. (2012). Reverse engineering epistemic evaluations. *Philosophy and Phenomenological Research* 84(3), pp. 513–530.

Doris, J. M. (1998). Persons, situations, and virtue ethics. *Noûs*, 32, 504–30.

  (2002). *Lack of Character: Personality and Moral Behavior*. Cambridge University Press.

Doris, J. and Olin, L. (In press). Vicious minds: virtue, cognition, and skepticism. *Philosophical Studies*.

Dretske, F. I. (1981). *Knowledge and the Flow of Information*. Cambridge, MA: MIT Press.

  (2000). Norms, history, and the constitution of the mental. In *Perception, Knowledge, and Belief: Selected Essays*, pp. 242–58. Cambridge University Press.

Drier, J. (2001). Humean doubts about categorical imperatives. In E. Millgram (ed.) *Varieties of Practical Reasoning*, pp. 27–47. Boston: MIT Press.

Duncker, K. (1945). *On Problem Solving*, trans. L. S. Lees. Psychological Monographs 58. Washington, DC: American Psychological Association.

Dweck, C. (1999). *Self-Theories: Their Role in Motivation, Personality, and Development*. Philadelphia: Taylor and Francis/Psychology Press.

Dweck, C., Chiu, C., and Hong, Y. (1995). Implicit theories and their role in judgments and reactions: a world from two perspectives. *Psychological Inquiry*, 6(4), 267–85.

Epstein, S. (1994). Trait theory as personality theory: can a part be as great as the whole? *Psychological Inquiry*, 5(2), 120–22.

Evans, I. and Smith, N. D. (2012). *Knowledge*. Cambridge: Polity.

Fairweather, A. (2001). Epistemic motivation. In A. Fairweather and L. Zagzebski (eds.) *Virtue Epistemology: Essays on Epistemic Virtue and Responsibility*, pp. 63–81. Oxford University Press.

Fairweather, A. and Montemayor, C. (In press). The meeting of the twain: Alfano on situationism and virtue epistemology. *Philosophical Quarterly*.

Feldman, R. (2001). Voluntary belief and epistemic evaluation. In M. Steup (ed.) *Knowledge, Truth, and Duty: Essays on Epistemic Justification, Responsibility, and Virtue*, pp. 77–92. Oxford University Press.

Feldman, R. and Conee, E. (2001). Internalism defended. In H. Kornblith (ed.) *Epistemology: Internalism and Externalism*, pp. 231–60. Oxford: Blackwell.

Feldman, R. and Cullison, A. (2012). Evidentialism. In A. Cullison (ed.) *The Continuum Companion to Epistemology*, pp. 92–105. New York: Continuum.

Field, H. (2006). Recent debates about the a priori. In T. Gendler and J. Hawthorne (eds.) *Oxford Studies in Epistemology*, vol. 1, pp. 69–88. Oxford University Press.

  (2009). Epistemology without metaphysics. *Philosophical Studies*, 143, 249–90.

Finlay, S. (2004). The conversational practicality of value judgement. *Journal of Ethics*, 8(3), 205–23.

  (2005). Value and implicature. *Philosophers' Imprint*, 5(4), 1–20.

Firth, R. (1981). Epistemic merit, intrinsic and instrumental. *Proceedings and Addresses of the American Philosophical Association*, 55, 5–23.

Flanagan, O. J. (1991). *Varieties of Moral Personality: Ethics and Psychological Realism*. Cambridge, MA: Harvard University Press.

(2006). Varieties of naturalism. In P. Clayton and Z. Simpson (eds.) *The Oxford Companion to Religion and Science*, pp. 430–52. Oxford University Press.

(2009). Moral science? Still metaphysical after all these years. In D. Narvaez and D. Lapsley (eds.) *Personality, Identity, and Character: Explorations in Moral Psychology*, pp. 54–65. Cambridge University Press.

Fodor, J. A. (1983). *The Modularity of Mind: An Essay on Faculty Psychology*. Cambridge, MA: MIT Press.

(2000). *The Mind Doesn't Work That Way: The Scope and Limits of Computational Psychology*. Cambridge, MA: MIT Press.

Foley, R. (1987). *The Theory of Epistemic Rationality*. Cambridge, MA: Harvard University Press.

(1993). *Working without a Net*. Oxford University Press.

Foot, P. (1972). Morality as a system of hypothetical imperatives. *Philosophical Review*, 81(3), 305–16.

(1978). *Virtues and Vices*. Oxford: Blackwell.

(2001). *Natural Goodness*. Oxford: Clarendon Press.

(2010). Exemplarist virtue theory. *Metaphilosophy*, 41(1/2), 41–57.

Forgas, J.-P. and East, R. (2008). On being happy and gullible: mood effects on skepticism and the detection of deception. *Journal of Experimental Social Psychology*, 4(4), 1362–67.

Fricker, M. (2007). *Epistemic Injustice: Power and the Ethics of Knowing*. Oxford University Press.

Frieman, J. (2002). *Learning and Adaptive Behavior*. South Melbourne, Australia: Wadsworth.

Fumerton, R. (2001). Epistemic justification and normativity. In M. Steup (ed.) *Knowledge, Truth, and Duty: Essays on Epistemic Justification, Responsibility, and Virtue*, pp. 49–60. Oxford University Press.

(2008). Externalism and skepticism. In E. Sosa, J. Kim, J. Fantl, and M. McGrath (eds.) *Epistemology: An Anthology*, pp. 394–406. Oxford: Blackwell.

Gibbard, A. (1990). *Wise Choices, Apt Feelings: A Theory of Normative Judgment*. Oxford University Press.

(2003). *Thinking How to Live*. Cambridge, MA: Harvard University Press.

Gigerenzer, G. (2007). *Gut Feelings: The Intelligence of the Unconscious*. New York: Viking.

(2008). *Rationality for Mortals: How People Cope with Uncertainty*. Oxford University Press.

Glover, S. and Dixon, P. (2002). Semantics affect the planning but not control of grasping. *Experimental Brain Research*, 146(3), 383–87.

Goldberg, L. (1981). Language and individual differences: the search for universals in personality lexicons. In L. Wheeler (ed.) *Review of Personality and Social Psychology*, vol. II, pp. 141–65. Beverly Hills: Sage.

(1992). The development of markers for the Big-Five factor structure. *Psychological Assessment*, 4, 26–42.

(1993). The structure of phenotypic personality traits. *American Psychologist*, 48, 26–34.

Goldberg, L. and Saucier, G. (1995). So what do you propose we use instead? A reply to Block. *Psychological Bulletin*, 117, 221–25.

Goldberg, S. (2012). Reliabilism. In A. Cullison (ed.) *The Continuum Companion to Epistemology*, pp. 106–23. New York: Continuum.

Goldman, A. I. (1988). Strong and weak justification. *Philosophical Perspectives*, 13, 51–69.

(1992). Epistemic folkways and scientific epistemology. In A. I. Goldman (ed.) *Liaisons: Philosophy Meets the Cognitive and Social Sciences*, pp. 155–75. Cambridge, MA: MIT Press.

(1994). Naturalistic epistemology and reliabilism. *Midwest Studies in philosophy*, 19(1), 301–20.

(1999). *Knowledge in a Social World*. Oxford University Press.

(2001). The internalist conception of justification. In H. Kornblith (ed.) *Epistemology: Internalism and Externalism*, pp. 36–67. Oxford: Blackwell.

(2011). Reliabilism. In *The Stanford Encyclopedia of Philosophy* (Spring 2011 edition), ed. E. N. Zalta, http://plato.stanford.edu/archives/spr2011/entries/reliabilism.

Goldstone, R. L. (2003). Learning to perceive while perceiving to learn. In M. Kimchi, M. Behrmann, and C. Olson (eds.) *Perceptual Organization in Vision: Behavioral and Neural Perspectives*, pp. 233–78. Englewood Cliffs, NJ: Lawrence Erlbaum Associates.

Good, C., Aronson, J., and Harder, J. A. (2008). Problems in the pipeline: stereotype threat and women's achievement in high-level math courses. *Journal of Applied Developmental Psychology*, 29, 17–28.

Good, C., Dweck, C., and Rattan, A. (Unpublished data). An incremental theory decreases vulnerability to stereotypes about math ability in college females. Columbia University, 2005.

Goodale, M. A. (2010). Transforming vision into action. *Vision Research*, 10(1016), 7–27.

Graham, P. J. (2010). Testimonial entitlement and the function of comprehension. In A. Haddock, A. Millar, and D. Pritchard (eds.) *Social Epistemology*, pp. 148–75. Oxford University Press.

(2011a). Psychological capacity and positive epistemic status. In J. G. Hernandez (ed.) *The New Intuitionism*, pp. 128–51. London: Continuum.

(2011b). Does justification aim at truth? *Canadian Journal of Philosophy*, 41, 51–72.

(2011c). Perceptual entitlement and basic beliefs. *Philosophical Studies*, 153, 467–75.

(2012a). Epistemic entitlement. *Noûs*, 46, 449–82.

(2012b). Epistemic value and proper function. Paper presented to the 2012 meeting of the Pacific Division of the American Philosophical Association, Seattle, WA.

(In press a). Perceptual entitlement and natural norms. In P. Graham and N. J. Pedersen (eds.) *Epistemic Entitlement: Warrant without Reason*. Oxford University Press.

(In press b). The function of perception. In A. Fairweather (ed.) *Virtue Scientia: Bridges between Philosophy of Science and Virtue Epistemology*. Dordrecht, the Netherlands: Springer.

(In press c). Epistemic evaluation and social norms. In J. Greco and D. Henderson (eds.) *Epistemic Evaluations*. Oxford University Press.

(Unpublished manuscript a). Epistemic normativity as performance normativity.

(Unpublished manuscript b). Two conceptions of warrant.

Grant, H. and Dweck, C. (2003). Clarifying achievement goals and their impact. *Journal of Personality and Social Psychology*, 85, 541–53.

Greco, J. (1993). Virtues and vices of virtue epistemology. *Canadian Journal of Philosophy*, 23(3), 413–32.

(1999). Agent reliabilism. *Noûs*, 33(s13), 273–96.

(2000). *Putting Skeptics in Their Place: The Nature of Skeptical Arguments and Their Role in Philosophical Inquiry*. Cambridge University Press.

(2003). Knowledge as credit for true belief. In M. DePaul and L. Zagzebski (eds.) *Intellectual Virtue: Perspectives from Ethics and Epistemology*, pp. 111–34. Oxford: Clarendon Press.

(2007). The nature of ability and the purpose of knowledge. *Philosophical Issues*, 17, 57–69.

(2008). What's wrong with contextualism? *Philosophical Quarterly*, 58, 416–36.

(2009). Knowledge and success from ability. *Philosophical Studies*, 142, 17–26.

(2010). *Achieving Knowledge: A Virtue-Theoretic Account of Epistemic Normativity*. Cambridge University Press.

Greco, J. and Groff, R. eds. (2013). *Powers and Capacities in Philosophy: The New Aristotelianism*. Abingdon: Routledge.

Greco, J. and Turri, J. (2011). Virtue epistemology. In *The Stanford Encyclopedia of Philosophy* (Spring 2011 edition), ed. E. N. Zalta, http://plato.stanford.edu/archives/win2011/entries/epistemology-virtue/.

Grimm, S. R. (2006). Is understanding a species of knowledge? *British Journal for the Philosophy of Science*, 57(3), 515–35.

(2008). Epistemic goals and epistemic values. *Philosophy and Phenomenological Research*, 77(3), 725–44.

(2009). Epistemic normativity. In A. Haddock, A. Millar, and D. Pritchard (eds.) *Epistemic Value*, pp. 243–64. Oxford University Press.

Grimm, S. R. and Ahlstrom, K. (2013). Getting it right. *Philosophical Studies*, 166(2), 329–47.

Harman, G. (1999). Moral philosophy meets social psychology: virtue ethics and the fundamental attribution error. *Proceedings of the Aristotelian Society*, 99, 315–31.

(2000). The nonexistence of character traits. *Proceedings of the Aristotelian Society*, 100, 223–26.

Harrison, L., Stevens, C., Monty, A., and Coakley, C. (2006). The consequences of stereotype threat on the academic performance of white and non-white lower income college students. *Social Psychology of Education*, 9, 341–57.

Hatfield, E., Cacioppo, J., and Rapson, R. (1994). *Emotional Contagion.* Cambridge University Press.

Hazlett, A. (2012). Non-moral evil. *Midwest Studies in Philosophy*, 36, 18–34.

(2013). *A Luxury of the Understanding: On the Value of True Belief.* Oxford University Press.

(Unpublished manuscript). Limning structure as an epistemic goal.

Hempel, Carl (1959). The logic of functional analysis. In L. Gross (ed.) *Symposium on Sociological Theory*, pp. 271–307. New York: Harper & Row.

Henderson, D. and Horgan, T. (2001). Practicing safe epistemology. *Philosophical Studies*, 102, 227–58.

(2011). *The Epistemological Spectrum: At the Interface of Cognitive Science and Conceptual Analysis.* Oxford University Press.

Henrich, J., Heine, S. J., and Norenzayan, A. (2010). The weirdest people in the world? *Behavioral and Brain Sciences*, 33(2–3), 61–83. doi: 10.1017/s0140525x0999152x.

Herrnstein, R. and Murray, C. (1996). *The Bell Curve: Intelligence and Class Structure in American Life.* New York: Simon & Schuster.

Hieronymi, P. (2005). The wrong kind of reason. *Journal of Philosophy*, 102(9), 437–57.

Higgins, E. Tory. (1996). Knowledge activation: accessibility, applicability, and salience. In E. T. Higgins and A. W. Kruglanski (eds.) *Social Psychology*, pp. 133–68. New York: The Guilford Press.

Hogan, R. (1996). A socioanalytic perspective on the Five-Factor model. In J. Wiggins (ed.) *The Five-Factor Model of Personality: Theoretical Perspectives*, pp. 163–79. New York: The Guilford Press.

Hoge, R. and Renzulli, J. (1993). Exploring the link between giftedness and self-concept. *Review of Educational Research*, 63(4), 499–65.

Hookway, C. (2001). Epistemic akrasia and epistemic virtue. In A. Fairweather and L. Zagzebski (eds.) *Virtue Epistemology: Essays on Epistemic Virtue and Responsibility*, pp. 178–99. Oxford University Press.

(2003). Affective states and epistemic immediacy. *Metaphilosophy*, 34(1–2), 78–96.

Horgan, T. and Tienson, J. (1996). *Connectionism and the Philosophy of Psychology.* Cambridge, MA: MIT Press.

Inan, I. (2012). *The Philosophy of Curiosity.* Abingdon: Routledge.

Inzlicht, M., Aronson, J., Good, C., and McKay, L. (2006). A particular resiliency to threatening environments. *Journal of Experimental Social Psychology*, 42, 323–36.

Isen, A. M. and Levin, P. F. (1972). Effect of feeling good on helping. *Journal of Personality and Social Psychology*, 21, 384–88.

Isen, A. M., Daubman K., and Nowicki, G. (1987). Positive affect facilitates creative problem solving. *Journal of Personality and Social Psychology*, 52(6), 1122–31.

Jenkins, C. S. (2007a). Entitlement and epistemic rationality. *Synthese*, 157, 25–45.

(2007b). Epistemic norms and natural facts. *American Philosophical Quarterly*, 44, 259–72.

(2008a). *Grounding Concepts: An Empirical Basis for Arithmetical Knowledge*. Oxford University Press.

(2008b). Boghossian and epistemic analyticity. *Croatian Journal of Philosophy*, 8, 113–27.

(2013). Naturalistic challenges to the a priori. In A. Casullo and J. Thurow (eds.) *The A Priori in Philosophy*. Oxford University Press.

Jensen, A. (1969). How much can we boost IQ and scholastic achievement? *Harvard Educational Review*, 39, 1–123.

John, O. and Robins, R. (1994). Traits and types, dynamics and development: no doors should be closed in the study of personality. *Psychological Inquiry*, 5, 137–42.

John, O., Naumann, L., and Soto, C. (2008). Paradigm shift to the integrative Big Five trait taxonomy: history, measurement, and conceptual issues. In O. John, R. Robins, and L. Pervin (eds.) *Handbook of Personality, Theory and Research*, 3rd edn., pp. 114–58. New York: The Guilford Press.

Johns, M., Schmader, T., and Martens, A. (2005). Knowing is half the battle: teaching stereotype threat as a means of improving women's math performance. *Psychological Science*, 16, 175–79.

Johnston, M. (1996). Is the external world invisible? *Philosophical Issues*, 7, 185–98.

Kahneman, D. (2011). *Thinking Fast and Slow*. New York: Farrar, Straus and Giroux.

Kahneman, D. and Frederick, S. (2005). A model of heuristic judgment. In K. Holyoak and R. Morrison (eds.) *The Cambridge Handbook of Thinking and Reasoning*, pp. 267–93. Cambridge University Press.

Kahneman, D. and Tversky, A. (1973). On the psychology of prediction. *Psychological Review*, 80(4), 237–51.

Kalderon, M. E. (2009). Epistemic relativism. *Philosophical Review*, 118(2), 225–40.

Kallestrup, J. and Pritchard, D. H. (2012). Robust virtue epistemology and epistemic anti-individualism. *Pacific Philosophical Quarterly*, 93, 84–103.

(2013). Robust virtue epistemology and epistemic dependence. In T. Henning and D. Schweikard (eds.) *Knowledge, Virtue and Action: Putting Epistemic Virtues to Work*, pp. 209–26. Abingdon: Routledge.

(In press). Virtue epistemology and epistemic twin earth. *European Journal of Philosophy*.

Kamtekar, Rachel. (2004). "Situationism and Virtue Ethics on the Content of Our Character." *Ethics*, 114 (April 2004): 458–491.

Kanazawa, S. (2008). Temperature and evolutionary novelty as forces behind the evolution of general intelligence. *Intelligence*, 36, 99–108.

Kappel, K. (2010). Expressivism about knowledge and the value of knowledge. *Acta Analytica*, 25, 175–94.

Keifer, A. and Sekaquaptewa, D. (2007). Implicit stereotypes and women's math performance: how implicit gender-math stereotypes influence women's susceptibility to stereotype threat. *Journal of Experimental Social Psychology*, 43, 825–32.

Kelly, T. (2003). Epistemic rationality as instrumental rationality: a critique. *Philosophy and Phenomenological Research*, 66, 612–40.

Kim, J. (1988). What is "naturalized epistemology"? *Philosophical Perspectives*, 2, 381–405.

Kitcher, P. (1993). *The Advancement of Science: Science without Legend, Objectivity without Illusions*. Oxford University Press.

Kornblith, H. (1993). Epistemic normativity. *Synthese*, 94, 357–76.

(2001). Epistemic obligation and the possibility of internalism. In A. Fairweather and L. Zagzebski (eds.) *Virtue Epistemology: Essays on Epistemic Virtue and Responsibility*, pp. 231–48. Oxford University Press.

(2002). *Knowledge and its Place in Nature*. Oxford University Press.

(2010). What reflective endorsement cannot do. *Philosophy and Phenomenological Research*, 80, 1–18.

(2013). *On Reflection*. Oxford University Press.

Korsgaard, C. M. (1983). Two distinctions in goodness. *Philosophical Review*, 2, 169–95.

(1996). *The Sources of Normativity*. Cambridge University Press.

(2008). Aristotle's function argument. In *The Constitution of Agency: Essays on Practical Reason and Moral Psychology*, pp. 129–50. Oxford University Press.

Kray, L., Thompson, L., and Galinsky, A. (2001). Battle of the sexes: gender stereotype confirmation and reactance in negotiations. *Journal of Personality and Social Psychology*, 80, 942–58.

Kray, L., Galinsky, A., and Thompson, L. (2002). Reversing the gender gap in negotiations: an exploration of stereotype regeneration. *Organizational Behavior and Human Decision Processes*, 87, 386–409.

Kripke, S. (1972). *Naming and Necessity*. Oxford: Blackwell.

Kvanvig, J. L. (2003). *The Value of Knowledge and the Pursuit of Understanding*. Cambridge University Press.

Langton, R. (1993). Speech acts and unspeakable acts. *Philosophy and Public Affairs*, 22(4), 293–330.

(1998). *Kantian Humility: Our Ignorance of Things in Themselves*. Oxford University Press.

Latane, B. and J. M. Darley. (1970). *The Unresponsive Bystander*. New York: Appleton, Century, Crofts.

Leary, M. (2004). *Introduction to Behavioral Research Methods*, 4th edn. Boston: Pearson.

LeDoux, J. (1996). *The Emotional Brain*. New York: Simon & Schuster.

Lehrer, K. (1990). *Theory of Knowledge*. Boulder, CO: Westview.

Levy, B. (1996). Improving memory in old age through implicit self stereotyping. *Journal of Personality and Social Psychology*, 71, 1092–107.

Lewis, D. (2008). Ramseyan humility. In D. Braddon-Mitchell and R. Nola (eds.) *Conceptual Analysis and Philosophical Naturalism*, pp. 203–21. Boston: MIT Press.

Lynch, M. P. (2009a). The values of truth and the truth of values. In A. Haddock, A. Millar, and D. Pritchard (eds.) *Epistemic Value*, pp. 225–42. Oxford University Press.

(2009b). Truth, value, and epistemic expressivism. *Philosophy and Phenomenological Research*, 79(1), 76–97.

Lyons, J. (2011). Response to critics. *Philosophical Studies*, 153, 477–88.

McAdams, D. (1992). The Five-Factor model in personality: a critical appraisal. *Journal of Personality*, 60, 329–61.

(1994). A psychology of the stranger. *Psychological Inquiry*, 5, 145–48.

McCauley, R. N. and Henrich, J. (2006). Susceptibility to the Müller-Lyer illusion, theory-neutral observation, and the diachronic penetrability of the visual input system. *Philosophical Psychology*, 19(1), 79–101. doi: 10.1080/09515080500462347.

McCrae, R. (1994). New goals for trait psychology. *Psychological Inquiry*, 5, 148–53.

McCrae, R. and Costa, P. (1987). Validation of the Five-Factor model of personality across instruments and observers. *Journal of Personality and Social Psychology*, 52, 81–90.

(1995). Trait explanations in personality psychology. *European Journal of Personality*, 9, 231–52.

(1996). Toward a new generation of personality theories: theoretical contexts for the Five-Factor model. In J. Wiggins (ed.) *The Five-Factor Model of Personality: Theoretical Perspectives*, pp. 51–87. New York: The Guilford Press.

(1997). Personality trait structure as a human universal. *American Psychologist*, 52, 509–16.

(2003). *Personality in Adulthood: A Five-Factor Theory Perspective*, 2nd edn. New York: The Guilford Press.

(2008). The Five-Factor theory of personality. In O. John, R. Robins, and L. Pervin (eds.) *Handbook of Personality: Theory and Research*, 3rd edn., pp. 159–81. New York: The Guilford Press.

McCrae, R. and John, O. (1992). An introduction to the Five-Factor model and its applications. *Journal of Personality*, 60, 175–215.

McCrae, R., Costa, P., Ostenfdorf, F., Angleitner, A., Hřebíčková, M., Avia, Sanz, J., Sánchez-Bernardos, M. L., Kusdil, M. E., Woodfield, R., Saunders, P. R., and Smith, P. B. (2000). Nature over nurture: temperament, personality, and life span development. *Journal of Personal and Social Psychology*, 78(1), 173–86.

MacFarlane, J. (2005a). Making sense of relative truth. *Proceedings of the Aristotelian Society*, 105(1), 205–23.

(2005b). The assessment sensitivity of knowledge attributions. *Oxford Studies in Epistemology*, 1, 197–233.

McHugo, G. L., Lanzetta, J. T., Sullivan, D. G., Masters, R. D., and Englis, B. G. (1985). Emotional reactions to a political leader's expressive displays. *Journal of Personality and Social Psychology*, 49, 1513–29.

Mackie, J. L. (1977). *Morality: Inventing Right and Wrong*. Harmondsworth, UK: Penguin Books.

McLaughlin, P. (2001). *What Functions Explain: Functional Explanation and Self-Reproducing Systems*. Cambridge University Press.

Mallon, R. (2004). Passing, traveling and reality: social constructionism and the metaphysics of race. *Noûs*, 38,4, 644–73.

(2006). "Race": normative, not metaphysical or semantic. *Ethics*, 116(3), 525–51.

Mangels, J., Butterfield, B., Lamb, J., Good, C., and Dweck, C. (2006). Why do beliefs about intelligence influence learning success? A social cognitive neuroscience model. *Social Cognition and Affective Neuroscience*, 1(2), 75–86.

Mareschal, D. and Johnson, S. P. (2002). Learning to perceive object unity: a connectionist account. *Developmental Science*, 5(2), 151–85.

Martens, A., Johns, M., Greenberg, J., and Schimel, J. (2006). Combating stereotype threat: the effect of self-affirmation on women's intellectual performance. *Journal of Experimental Social Psychology*, 42, 236–43.

Marx, D. and Goff, P. (2005). Clearing the air: the effect of experimenter race on target's test performance and subjective experience. *British Journal of Social Psychology*, 44, 645–57.

Mellor, D. H. (1991). I and now. In *Matters of Metaphysics*, pp. 17–30. Cambridge University Press.

Merritt, M. (2000). Virtue ethics and situationist personality psychology. *Ethical Theory and Moral Practice*, 3(4), 365–83.

Milgram, S. (1974). *Obedience to Authority*. New York: Harper & Row Publishers.

Millar, A. (2008). Perceptual-recognitional abilities and perceptual knowledge. In A. Haddock and F. Macpherson (eds.) *Disjunctivism: Perception, Action, Knowledge*, pp. 330–47. Oxford University Press.

Miller, C. (2003). Social psychology and virtue ethics. *Journal of Ethics*, 7(4), 365–92.

(2013). *Moral Character: An Empirical Theory*. Oxford University Press.

(2014). *Character and Moral Psychology*. Oxford University Press.

Millikan, R. G. (1984). *Language, Thought, and Other Biological Categories: New Foundations for Realism*. Cambridge, MA: MIT Press.

Mischel, W. (1968). *Personality and Assessment*. New York: John Wiley and Sons.

(2009). From *Personality and Assessment* (1968) to personality science, 2009. *Journal of Research in Personality*, 43, 282–90.

Mischel, W. and Shoda, Y. (1994). Personality psychology has two goals: must it be two fields? *Psychological Inquiry*, 5, 156–58.

(1998). Reconciling processing dynamics and personality dispositions. *Annual Review of Psychology*, 49, 229–58.

Miyake, A., Kost-Smith, L., Finkelstein, N., Pollock, S., Cohen, G., and Ito, T. (2010). Reducing the gender achievement gap in college science: a classroom study of values affirmation. *Science*, 330, 1234–37.

Montmarquet, J. (1993). *Epistemic Virtue and Doxastic Responsibility*. Lanham, MD: Rowman and Littlefield.

Moore, G. E. (1993). *Principia ethica*, ed. T. Baldwin. Cambridge University Press (first published 1903).

Morsella, E. and Bargh, J. A. (2010). What is an output? *Psychological Inquiry*, 21, 354–70.

Mount, M. and Barrick, M. (1998). Five reasons why the "Big Five" article has been frequently cited. *Personnel Psychology*, 51, 849–57.

Nanay, B. (2012). Success semantics: the sequel. *Philosophical Studies*, 1(15), 151–65.

Neta, R. (2007). How to naturalize epistemology. In V. F. Hendricks and D. Pritchard (eds.) *New Waves in Epistemology*, pp. 324–53. Basingstoke, UK: Palgrave Macmillan.

Nettle, D. (2007). *Personality: What Makes You the Way You Are*. Oxford University Press.

Nguyen, H.-H. D. and Ryan, A. M. (2008). Does stereotype threat affect test performance of minorities and women? A meta-analysis of experimental evidence. *Journal of Applied Psychology*, 93, 1314–34.

Nozick, R. (1981). *Philosophical Explanations*. Cambridge, MA: Belknap Press.

Nussbaum, M. (1986). *The Fragility of Goodness*. Cambridge University Press.

(2001). *Upheavals of Thought: The Intelligence of the Emotions*. Cambridge University Press.

(2003). Emotions as judgments of value and importance. In R. C. Solomon (ed.) *What Is an Emotion?*, pp. 271–83. Oxford University Press.

Olson, J. (2011). Error theory and reasons for belief. In A. Reisner and A. Seglich-Petersen (eds.) *Reasons for Belief*, pp. 75–93. Cambridge University Press.

Owens, D. (2003). Does belief have an aim? *Philosophical Studies*, 115, 283–305.

Ozer, D. and Benet-Martínez, V. (2006). Personality and the prediction of consequential outcome. *Annual Review of Psychology*, 57, 401–21.

Ozer, D. and Reise, S. (1994). Personality assessment. In L. Porter and M. Rosenzweig (eds.) *Annual Review of Psychology*, vol. XLV, pp. 357–88. Palo Alto, CA: Annual Reviews.

Pamental, M. (2010). Dewey, situationism, and moral education. *Educational Theory*, 60(2), 147–66.

Papineau, D. (1999). Normativity and judgment. *Proceedings of the Aristotelian Society*, 73, 16–43.

Paunonen, S. and Jackson, D. (2000). What is beyond the Big Five? *Journal of Personality*, 68, 821–35.

Pervin, L. (1994). A critical analysis of current trait theory. *Psychological Inquiry*, 5, 103–13.

Piedmont, R. (1998). *The Revised NEO Personality Inventory: Clinical and Research Applications*. New York: Plenum Press.

Pinker, S. (1997). *How the Mind Works*. New York: Norton.

Plato (1989). *Protagoras*. In *Collected Dialogues*, ed. E. Hamilton. Princeton University Press.

Price, C. (2006). Fearing Fluffy: the content of an emotional appraisal. In G. Macdonald and D. Papineau (eds.) *Teleosemantics*, pp. 208–28. Oxford University Press.

Prinz, J. (2004). *Gut Reactions*. Oxford University Press.

(2009). The normativity challenge: cultural psychology provides the real threat to virtue ethics. *Journal of Ethics*, 13, 117–44.

Pritchard, D. H. (2007). Recent work on epistemic value. *American Philosophical Quarterly*, 44, 85–110.

(2009a). Apt performance and epistemic value. *Philosophical Studies*, 143, 407–16.

(2009b). Knowledge, understanding and epistemic value. In A. O'Hear (ed.) *Epistemology*, pp. 19–43. Royal Institute of Philosophy Supplement 64. Cambridge University Press.

(2009c). *Knowledge*. Basingstoke, UK: Palgrave Macmillan.

(2009d). The value of knowledge. *Harvard Review of Philosophy*, 16, 2–19.

(2012). Anti-luck virtue epistemology. *Journal of Philosophy*, 109(3), 247–79.

(2013). Epistemic virtue and the epistemology of education. *Journal of Philosophy of Education*, 47 (2013), 236–47.

(In press b). The situationist challenge, epistemic dependence, and the epistemology of education. In A. Fairweather and A. Alfano (eds.) *Epistemic Situationism*. Oxford University Press.

Pritchard, D. H. and Smith, M. (2004). The psychology and philosophy of luck. *New Ideas in Psychology*, 22, 1–28.

Pritchard, D. H., Millar, A., and Haddock, A. (2010). *The Nature and Value of Knowledge: Three Investigations*. Oxford University Press.

Putnam, H. (1975). The meaning of "meaning." In *Philosophical Papers*, vol. II, *Mind, Language, and Reality*, pp. 215–72. Cambridge University Press.

Pytlik Zillig, L., Hemenover, S., and Dienstbier, R. (2002). What do we assess when we assess a Big 5 trait? A content analysis of the affective, behavioral, and cognitive processes represented in Big 5 personality inventories. *Personality and Social Psychology Bulletin*, 28, 847–58.

Quine, W. V. O. (1969). Epistemology naturalized. In *Ontological Relativity and Other Essays*, pp. 69–90. New York: Columbia University Press.

(1986). Reply to Morton White. In L. Hahn and P. Schlipp (eds.) *The Philosophy of W. V. O. Quine*, pp. 663–65. La Salle, IL: Open Court.

Railton, P. (1986). Moral realism. *Philosophical Review*, 95, 163–207.

(1997). On the hypothetical and non-hypothetical in reasoning about belief and action. In G. Cullity and B. Gaut (eds.) *Ethics and Practical Reason*, pp. 53–79. Oxford University Press.

Ramsey, F. P. (1927). Facts and propositions. *Aristotelian Society Supplementary Volumes*, 7, 153–70.

(1931). Knowledge. In *The Foundations of Mathematics and Other Logical Essays*, ed. R. B. Braithwaite, pp. 258–59. New York: Harcourt Brace.

Rattan, A., Good, C., and Dweck, C. (2012). "It's OK – not everyone can be good at math": instructors with an entity theory comfort (and demotivate) students. *Journal of Experimental Social Psychology*, 48, 731–37.

Reisner, A. (2008). Weighing pragmatic and evidential reasons for belief. *Philosophical Studies*, 138, 17–27.

(2009). The possibility of pragmatic reasons for belief and the wrong kind of reason problem. *Philosophical Studies*, 145(2), 257–72.

Ridge, M. (2011). Getting lost on the road to Larissa. *Noûs*, 47(1), 181–201.

Riggs, W. (2007). The value turn in epistemology. In V. F. Hendricks and D. Pritchard (eds.) *New Waves in Epistemology*, pp. 300–23. Basingstoke, UK: Palgrave Macmillan.

(2009). Understanding, knowledge, and the *Meno* requirement. In A. Haddock, A. Millar, and D. H. Pritchard (eds.) *Epistemic Value*, pp. 331–38. Oxford University Press.

Rist, R. (1973). *The Urban School: A Factory for Failure*. Cambridge, MA: MIT Press.

Roberts, B. (2009). Back to the future: *Personality and Assessment* and personality development. *Journal of Research in Personality*, 43, 137–45.

Roberts, R. and Wood, W. J. (2007). *Intellectual Virtues: An Essay in Regulative Epistemology*. Oxford: Clarendon Press.

Robertson, E. (2009). The epistemic aims of education. In H. Siegel (ed.) *The Oxford Handbook of Philosophy of Education*, pp. 11–34. Oxford University Press.

Rosenthal, H., Crisp, R., and Suen, M.-W. (2007). Improving performance expectancies in stereotypic domains: task relevance and the reduction of stereotype threat. *European Journal of Social Psychology*, 37, 586–97.

Ruse, M. (1971). Functional statements in biology. *Philosophy of Science*, 38, 87–95.

Russell, D. C. (2009). *Practical Intelligence and the Virtues*. Oxford University Press.

Ryan, S. (1999). What is wisdom? *Philosophical Studies*, 93, 119–39.

Salmon, W. C. (1998). *Causality and Explanation*. Oxford University Press.

Samuels, R., Stich, S., and Bishop, M. (2002). Ending the rationality wars: how to make disputes about human rationality disappear. In R. Elio (ed.) *Common Sense, Reasoning, and Rationality*, pp. 236–68. Oxford University Press.

Sánchez-Bernardos, M. (2000). Nature over nurture: temperament, personality, and life span development. *Journal of Personality and Social Psychology*, 7(8), 173–86.

Schimel, J., Arndt, J., Banko, K., and Cook, A. (2004). Not all self-affirmations were created equal: the cognitive and social benefits of affirming the intrinsic (vs. extrinsic) self. *Social Cognition*, 22, 75–99.

Schmader, T. and Johns, M. (2003). Converging evidence that stereotype threat reduces working memory capacity. *Journal of Personality and Social Psychology*, 85(3), 440–52.

Schmader, T., Johns, M., and Barquissau, M. (2004). The costs of accepting gender differences: the role of stereotype endorsement in women's experience in the math domain. *Sex Roles*, 50, 835–50.

Schueler, G. F. (1995). *Desire: Its Role in Practical Reason and the Explanation of Action*. Cambridge, MA: MIT Press.

Searle, J. (1969). *Speech Acts*. Cambridge University Press.

Segall, M. H., Campbell, D. T., and Herskovits, M. J. (1966). *The Influence of Culture on Visual Perception*. Indianapolis: Bobbs-Merrill Co.

Shah, N. (2003). How truth governs belief. *Philosophical Review*, 112, 447–82.

(2006). A new argument for evidentialism. *Philosophical Quarterly*, 56, 481–98.

(2011). Can reasons for belief be debunked? In A. Reisner and A. Steglich-Petersen (eds.) *Reasons for Belief*, pp. 94–107. Cambridge University Press.

Shah, N. and Velleman, J. D. (2005). Doxastic deliberation. *Philosophical Review*, 114, 497–534.

Sherman, N. (1989). *The Fabric of Character*. New York: Clarendon Press.

Shih, M., Pittinsky, T. L., and Ambady, N. (1999). Stereotype susceptibility: identity salience and shifts in quantitative performance. *Psychological Science*, 10, 80–83.

Shiota, M., Keltner, D., and Mossman, A. (2007). The nature of awe: elicitors, appraisals, and effects on self-concept. *Cognition and Emotion*, 21(5), 944–63.

Sider, T. (2009). Ontological realism. In D. Chalmers, D. Manley, and R. Wasserman (eds.) *Metametaphysics: New Essays on the Foundations of Ontology*, pp. 384–423. Oxford University Press.

(2011). *Writing the Book of the World*. Oxford: Clarendon Press.

Slingerland, E. (2011). The situationist critique and early Confucian virtue ethics. *Ethics*, 121(2), 390–419.

Smith, P. (2003). Deflationism: the facts. In H. Lillehammer and G. Rodriguez-Pereyra (eds.) *Real Metaphysics*, pp. 43–52. New York: Routledge.

Snow, N. E. (2010). *Virtue as Social Intelligence: An Empirically Grounded Theory*. Abingdon: Routledge.

Sosa, E. (1988). Beyond skepticism, to the best of our knowledge. *Mind*, 97, 153–89.

(1991). *Knowledge in Perspective: Selected Essays in Epistemology*. Cambridge University Press.

(1993). Proper functionalism and virtue epistemology. *Noûs*, 27(1), 51–65.

(2003). The place of truth in epistemology. In M. DePaul and L. Zagzebski (eds.) *Intellectual Virtue: Perspectives from Ethics and Epistemology*, pp. 155–79. Oxford University Press.

(2007). *A Virtue Epistemology: Apt Belief and Reflective Knowledge*, vol. I. Oxford University Press.

(2009a). Knowing full well: the normativity of beliefs as performances. *Philosophical Studies*, 142, 5–15.

(2009b). *Reflective Knowledge: Apt Belief and Reflective Knowledge*, vol. II. Oxford: Clarendon Press.

(2009c). Situations against virtues: the situationist attack on virtue theory. In C. Mantzavinos (ed.) *Philosophy of the Social Sciences: Philosophical Theory and Scientific Practice*, pp. 274–90. Cambridge University Press.

(2010). *Knowing Full Well*. Princeton University Press.

Spencer, S., Steele, C., and Quinn, D. (1999). Stereotype threat and women's math performance. *Journal of Experimental Social Psychology*, 35, 4–28.

Sreenivasan, G. (2002). Errors about errors: virtue theory and trait attribution. *Mind*, 111, 47–68.

Stangor, C., Carr, C., and Kiang, L. (1998). Activating stereotypes undermines task performance expectations. *Journal of Personality and Social Psychology*, 75, 1191–97.

Stanley, J. (2005) *Knowledge and Practical Interests*. Oxford University Press.

Steele, C. M. and Aronson, J. (1995). Stereotype threat and the intellectual test performance of African-Americans. *Journal of Personality and Social Psychology*, 69, 797–811.

Steglich-Petersen, A. (2006). No norm needed: on the aim of belief. *Philosophical Quarterly*, 56, 499–516.

(2009). Weighing the aim of belief. *Philosophical Studies*, 145(3), 395–405.

(2011). How to be a teleologist about epistemic reasons. In A. Reisner and A. Steglich-Petersen (eds.) *Reasons for Belief*, pp. 13–33. Cambridge University Press.

Stone, J. (2002). Battling doubt by avoiding practice: the effect of stereotype threat on self-handicapping in white athletes. *Personality and Social Psychology Bulletin*, 28, 1667–78.

Stone, J., Lynch, C., Sjomeling, M., and Darley, J. (1999). Stereotype threat effects on black and white athletic performance. *Journal of Personality and Social Psychology*, 77, 1213–27.

Stöttinger, E. and Perner, J. (2006). Dissociating size representation for action and for conscious judgment: grasping visual illusions without apparent obstacles. *Consciousness and Cognition*, 15(2), 269–84.

Strack, F., Martin, L. L., and Stepper, S. (1988). Inhibiting and facilitating conditions of the human smile. *Journal of Personality and Social Psychology*, 54, 768–76.

Strandberg, C. (2011). A dual aspect account of moral language. *Philosophy and Phenomenological Research*, 84(1), 87–122.

Sturgeon, N. (1985). Moral explanations. In D. Copp and D. Zimmerman (eds.) *Morality, Reason and Truth*, pp. 49–78. Totowa, NJ: Rowman and Allenfeld.

Templer, D. (2008). Correlational and factor analytic support for Rushton's differential K life history theory. *Personality and Individual Differences*, 45, 440–44.

Templer, D. and Arikawa, H. (2006). Temperature, skin color, per capita income, and IQ: an international perspective. *Intelligence*, 34, 121–39.

Treanor, N. (In press). The measure of knowledge. *Noûs* 47(3), pp. 577–601.

Turri, J. (2011). Manifest failure: the Gettier problem solved. *Philosophers' Imprint*, 11(8), 1–11.

Tversky, A. and Kahneman, D. (1973). Availability: a heuristic for judging frequency and probability. *Cognitive Psychology*, 5, 207–32.

(2002). Extensional *versus* intuitive reasoning: the conjunction fallacy in probability judgment. In T. Gilovich, D. Griffin, and D. Kahneman (eds.) *Heuristics and Biases: The Psychology of Intuitive Judgment*, pp. 19–48. Cambridge University Press.

Velleman, D. (2000). On the aim of belief. In J. Velleman (ed.) *The Possibility of Practical Reason*, pp. 244–81. Oxford University Press.

Vogel, J. (2000). Reliabilism leveled. *Journal of Philosophy*, 97, 602–23.

Walton, G. and Cohen, G. (2003). Stereotype lift. *Journal of Experimental Social Psychology*, 39, 456–67.

Wason, P. (1966). Reasoning. In B. M. Foss (ed.) *New Horizons in Psychology*, pp. 135–51. Harmondsworth, UK: Penguin Books.

Wedgwood, R. (2002). The aim of belief. *Philosophical Perspectives*, 16, 265–97.

Whitcomb, D. (2010). Curiosity was framed. *Philosophy and Phenomenological Research*, 81(3), 664–87.

White, R. (2007). Epistemic subjectivism. *Episteme*, 4(1), 115–29.

Whyte, J. T. (1990). Success semantics. *Analysis*, 50, 149–57.

Widiger, T. (1993). The *DSM-III-R* categorical personality disorder diagnoses: a critique and an alternative. *Psychological Inquiry*, 4, 75–90.

Wiggins, J. and Trapnell, P. (1997). Personality structure: the return of the Big Five. In R. Hogan, J. Johnson, and S. Briggs (eds.) *Handbook of Personality Psychology*, pp. 737–65. San Diego: Academic Press.

Williams, B. (1995). Internal reasons and the obscurity of blame. In *Making Sense of Humanity*, pp. 35–45. Cambridge University Press.

(2002). *Truth and Truthfulness: An Essay in Genealogy*. Princeton University Press.

Wolterstorff, N. (2010). Ought to believe: two concepts. In T. Cuneo (ed.) *Practices of Belief*, pp. 62–85. Cambridge University Press.

Wooldridge, D. (1963). *Machinery of the Brain*. New York: McGraw-Hill.

Wright, C. (2004). On epistemic entitlement: warrant for nothing (and foundations for free?). *Aristotelian Society Supplementary Volumes*, 78, 167–212.

Wright, L. (1973). Functions. *Philosophical Review*, 82, 139–68.

(2012). Revisiting teleological explanations: reflections three decades on. In P. Huneman (ed.) *Functions: Selection and Mechanisms*, pp. 233–43. Synthese Library 363. Dordrecht, the Netherlands: Springer.

Yeung, N. and von Hippel, C. (2008). Stereotype threat increases the likelihood that female drivers in a simulator run over jaywalkers. *Accident Analysis and Prevention*, 40, 667–74.

Zagzebski, L. T. (1996). *Virtues of the Mind: An Inquiry into the Nature of Virtue and the Ethical Foundations of Knowledge*. Cambridge University Press.

(1999). What is knowledge? In J. Greco and E. Sosa (eds.) *The Blackwell Guide to Epistemology*, pp. 92–116. Oxford: Blackwell.

(2001). Must knowers be agents? In A. Fairweather and L. Zagzebski (eds.) *Virtue Epistemology: Essays on Epistemic Virtue and Responsibility*, pp. 142–57. Oxford University Press.

(2004). Epistemic value and the primacy of what we care about. *Philosophical Papers*, 33(3), 353–77.

(2012). *Epistemic Authority: A Theory of Trust, Authority, and Autonomy in Belief*. Oxford University Press.

Zajonc, R. B. (1980). Feeling and thinking: preferences need no inferences. *American Psychologist*, 35(2), 151–75.

(1984). On the primacy of affect. *American Psychologist*, 39(2), 117–23.

(2000). Feeling and thinking: closing the debate over the independence of affect. In J. P. Forgas (ed.) *Feeling and Thinking*, pp. 31–58. Cambridge University Press.

Zimbardo, P. G. (1992). *Quiet Rage: The Stanford Prison Experiment* (DVD). Stanford Instructional Television Network.

Index

Lightning Source UK Ltd.
Milton Keynes UK
UKOW05f1045070517
300649UK00026B/899/P